Girl Trouble

Girl Trouble

•

Female Delinquency in English Canada

Joan Sangster

Between the Lines
Toronto

Girl Trouble

First published in Canada in 2002 by
Between the Lines
720 Bathurst Street, Suite 404
Toronto, Ontario
M5S 2R4

National Library of Canada Cataloguing in Publication Data

Sangster, Joan, 1952-
    Girl trouble : female delinquency in English Canada
Includes bibliographical references and index.
ISBN 1-896357-58-X

1. Female juvenile delinquents – Canada.   2. Juvenile justice, Administration of –
Canada.   I. Title.
HV9108.S23 2002   364.36'082'0971   C2002-900109-9

Cover design by Jennifer Tiberio
Text design and page preparation by Steve Izma
Printed in Canada by union labour

Between the Lines gratefully acknowledges assistance for its publishing activities from the Canada Council for the Arts, the Ontario Arts Council, and the Government of Canada through the Book Publishing Industry Development Program.

Contents

Acknowledgements vii

One   Introduction 1

Two   Defining Delinquency 13

Three   "An Ounce of Prevention" 41

Four   Judging Girls in Court 69

Five   Treating the Intractable 103

Six   Race, Gender, and Delinquency 144

Seven   Conclusion 171

Notes   181

Index   208

Acknowledgements

My greatest debt is to the girls whose stories appear in this book. Although the girls are protected by anonymity, my hope is that their very real, sometimes painful conflicts with the law – their trials and tribulations from courtroom to training school – will keep our sights focused on an analysis of "delinquency" that looks towards social transformation rather than mere punishment and control.

The staff members at Between the Lines were a true pleasure to work with. Their support for this book helped me to push it to completion: thanks especially to Paul Eprile, Joanna Fine, and Jennifer Tiberio, and to Robert Clarke for his fine editing. I am also grateful to Toronto Youthlink, the Hamilton Big Sisters Associations, the staff at the Ontario Archives, the Toronto City Archives, and the National Archives of Canada for their aid in uncovering sources, and to students and colleagues at Trent University whose interest in and support for the project sustained my determination to finish it.

Heather Murray provided important research aid in Ottawa, and Ruth Ritchie helped me prepare charts and graphs for the manuscript. Tamara Myers generously provided me with unpublished chapters of her own book on the juvenile court in Montreal, while the women who attended a workshop on women and criminal justice, held at Trent University in 1999, helped to develop and stimulate my thinking on this topic.

Dorothy Chunn and Amanda Glasbeek have been especially important as intellectual comrades, and the ongoing support of Veronica Strong-Boag and Judith Fingard is deeply appreciated. Friends and family also provided essential emotional support, tolerating my writing preoccupations and sustaining both my sense of humour and sense of proportion in life. My sister, Carol Baerg, my partner, Bryan Palmer, and our own teenagers, Kate, Beth, Laura, and Rob, are never far from my thoughts.

Last but not least, I'm grateful to the women I work with at Elizabeth Fry: we muddle through the contradictions of providing band-aid support for women in conflict with the law while trying not to lose sight of a more utopian desire to change the workings of the law entirely. The goal of "abolishing prisons" sometimes seems so remote that we can easily lose sight of its importance. I hope that the story of these young women in conflict with the law will not let us forget.

One

Introduction

"A Generation of Outlaws" and "Killer Girls": the right-wing magazine *Alberta Report* routinely uses headlines like these to describe contemporary youth crime; readers are told that a massive upsurge in law-breaking, particularly violent assaults, is taking place across the country. While this approach is extreme, the mainstream news media employ similar, though more sedate, strategies: discussions of Canada's Young Offenders Act (YOA) often open with alarming statements of "fact" concerning escalating youth crime and violence. Even one recent scholarly study of delinquency bombards readers with tale after tale of random, terrifying attacks on unsuspecting citizens; after a cursory reading, I too felt afraid to venture out of my door.[1] Discussions of youth disobedience and violence have become so much a part of "common sense," argues Bernard Schissel, that we are now in the midst of a moral panic about delinquency, in which "child-blaming" has become a national pastime. Moreover, this construction of adolescents as "folk devils" whose wrongdoing is generated by unpredictable evil focuses its condemnatory sights on the dispossessed, on single mothers, on the racially marginalized.[2]

Public perceptions of youth crime are extremely important, not the least because they place popular pressure on our political system and thereby contribute to new educational policies, policing strategies, and even changes in the law. But many criminologists and service providers in the juvenile justice system reject the notion that youth crime is increasing dramatically, and they disclaim the notion that the YOA is soft on teens, who supposedly laugh in the face of law and order as they walk out of court with no lesson learned. Studies point out that since the advent of the YOA in 1984, closed custody sentences have increased and in some regions informal (non-custodial) processes such as diversion are precariously insecure; moreover, the numerical increases in violent offences may be partly the product of increased surveillance, policing, and charging due to public fears of crime. Some studies, though, indicate that the public is less than enamoured with punitive retribution;

1

offered a range of informed options, most people are more likely to opt for prevention, not prisons.[3]

While there appears, for instance, to be an increase in charges against girls for violent offences, the cases generally involve minor personal injury and do not bring serious charges; and the increase may also reflect new "zero tolerance" definitions of violence, such as cracking down on bullying and verbal, as well as physical, assaults in schoolyards and public places.[4] Despite a few sensational cases of female violence – analysed ad nauseam in the press, precisely because they appear to contradict gender norms – girls' delinquency remains, by and large, a minority of the total legal cases, and tends to be concentrated on small property, drug, and "non-compliance" offences (for example, not following a court order concerning probation).

A few horrific and tragic cases of violence perpetrated by girls have been used, especially by anti-feminist writers, to suggest that female equality will inevitably produce women who are just as violent as men. Feminism apparently encourages us to emulate men, and then provides us with feminist myths and excuses, such as battered woman syndrome, to explain away our wrongdoing. Patricia Pearson's claims that feminist criminology has helped evil women refashion themselves into helpless victims, all the while claiming preferential treatment, and her wild statements – "Teenagers like intimidating people. . . . They like the power, it makes them feel good" – are symptomatic of this writing.[5] Unfortunately, such simplistic and sensational sentiments command considerable attention in the media's tabloid treatment of girls' involvement in crime, and in the process other issues, such as racism, are masked and obscured. For instance, after the murder by schoolmates of fourteen-year-old Reena Virk in Victoria, B.C., in November 1997, the media coverage of the case was obsessed with the issue of "girl on girl" violence but ignored evidence that racism played an important part in the killing.[6]

But is all this new? To what extent were the concerns about the law's inherent weakness, the causes of delinquency, the prescribed cures for youth crime – ranging from the kindness of therapy to drilling and discipline – novel over the course of the twentieth century? Moreover, do we take the criminalization of girls any more seriously now than we did fifty years ago? In the days of the Juvenile Delinquents Act (JDA), which preceded the current YOA, public concern, research, and policy were decidedly focused on boys. Yet some feminist criminologists argue that girls, even though they represent as much as 20 per cent of youth now charged, still remain a mystery to law- and policy-makers. On the one hand, girls and women are simply neglected in many studies, with boys' and men's crimes portrayed as the generic norm (and certainly not as the product of their own gendered contexts).[7] On the other hand, assumptions of gender-neutrality in the new YOA mask the ways in which discriminatory practices and punishment still confront girls in conflict with the law, especially when they step out of the bounds of accepted feminine norms.[8]

This feminist interpretation of the YOA is countered by criminologists who argue that the higher numbers of girls in custody or mandated into "treatment" under the new law reflect a "protective," and not a patriarchal or discriminatory impulse, for the YOA is now gender-neutral, having jettisoned the status offences, such as promiscuity, that so often landed girls in trouble under the JDA. If girls are selling their bodies at fourteen, if they are addicted to drugs and unable to escape the harsh life of the street, the criminologists continue, some sort of forced treatment in custody may be their only hope – though they do admit that services to aid addiction and abuse may not be forthcoming, or even successful. This issue of "protection" underscored a controversy in 2000 concerning Alberta's "child prostitution" laws, which had been struck down as unconstitutional by the courts but were still being promoted by the police and some child welfare advocates. Opponents of the law argue that no matter how well intended, forced protection might actually alienate the girls and make them more vulnerable to pimps; as well as being unconstitutional, the law might be just plain useless in offering girls alternatives to street prostitution.[9]

To historians, the word "protection" also sends off alarm bells. Protection was precisely what girls supposedly received under the JDA. Protection meant the increased moral surveillance of working-class and poor girls; protection meant incarcerating "promiscuous" girls who had not broken the law, but were deemed in need of moral re-education. Protection did sometimes offer some abused girls a second chance, away from their families and communities. But protection could also slide into judgemental surveillance, which slid into stigmatization, marginalization, and incarceration. Protection was always differentially applied according to class, and it could become racialized paternalism directed at Native girls. We therefore need to ask hard questions about current protective practices in light of yesterday's experiences.

This book is an attempt to bring to light those past experiences by focusing on three questions. What underlying material structures, social conditions, and ideological norms shaped the very definition of delinquency under the Juvenile Delinquents Act, and how was that definition gendered? What were the prescribed legal and social cures for girls' wrongdoing, and how successful were they? Last, but not least, how did girls and their families understand and react to their designation as delinquent, and to their experiences in court, probation, and training school? My focus is on delinquency within a broad sweep of our history, from the initial years of our Juvenile Delinquents Act, passed in 1908, to the first major, sustained critiques of its usefulness in the 1960s. Although gender is a major theme, I concentrate primarily on the retrieval of girls' experiences, which have often been hidden from history by the overwhelming concern, in the past and present, with boys' potential criminality. English Canadian and U.S. debates about delinquency provide the broad outlines for this study, but my illustrations and case studies derive from the records of Ontario training schools, courts, and reform groups.

Drawing on the tradition of critical legal studies, this study understands the law in its broadest context: as a product of social life, an arena of political struggle, a means of constituting class, colonial, and gender relations, a tool of control, and a means of resistance. Never a singular text or code, the law also encompasses the practices, personnel, rituals, and social apparatus surrounding its implementation and its popular reception. Moreover, delinquency laws need to be examined in light of the overlapping processes of "private and public policing,"[10] in which the family, the dominant culture, and medical and welfare surveillance, as well as the state, are all involved in prescribing the proper behaviour for young women, as well as the appropriate discipline if they transgress society's norms. The regulation of girls has never been the sole provenance of legal institutions; historically, the juvenile justice system was often a last resort, used to regulate girls' behaviour after other strategies had failed.

My emphasis is on a feminist and materialist exploration of delinquency, in which crime and criminality are located within both the political economy and the moral culture of the times. To understand girls' conflicts with the law, we must analyse the daily, lived economic, and social circumstances of their lives, the dominant discourses concerning "normal" as opposed to "deviant" behaviour, and the mutually reinforcing relationship between these realms of the material and the discursive. As Maureen Cain argues with reference to current criminology, our search for a "transgressive feminist" criminology, with social justice as a desired end, must first take into account the broader "herstories" of women's lives, rather than only focusing on the narrower issue of their offence: "We must start from the outside, with the social construction of gender, women's experiences of work, domesticity, family, community, and from there, move towards an understanding of crimes, the courts and penal practices."[11]

While recognizing that girls' experiences have been shaped by patriarchal norms, and that they have been subject to violence and oppression, we should also avoid constructing a story of the completely victimized, criminalized female, lacking any agency and incapable of violence. The danger of the "woman as victim" story, as Elizabeth Comack points out, is its easy replication of the limiting dualisms of the criminal justice system (victim/offender, criminal/law-abiding).[12] Nor does it enable us to develop explanations – unlike the simplistic ones of Patricia Pearson – for some girls' wilful rejection of social conformity or some girls' violence. A delicate balance is needed as we weigh the themes of regulation and resistance, structure and agency. In the period under study, counterposing the very real power of the law were the attempts of girls and their families to use, evade, or negotiate the legal solutions proffered by the justice system. To be sure, concrete class, race, and patriarchal structures shaped girls' lives and options, sometimes in debilitating ways, but how these structures intruded into girls' inner selves as ideals, emotions, and experience, and how girls wrestled with them, varied dramatically.

I begin the story of girls' conflicts with the law with the very definition of the concept "juvenile delinquent" and then turn to the well-intended efforts of reformers to aid the "pre-delinquent" girl from slipping into a life of crime. Assuming they failed, I then turn to girls' encounters with juvenile courts and to the final solution for the most intractable: training school. By examining how the law and professional experts delineated delinquency, we can secure insight into the changing (or sometimes constant) understandings of its meaning, and presumed origins. Some criminologists argue forcefully that the term delinquency should itself be seen as a social construct. Delinquents were children in conflict with the law, but they could also simply be *"in conflict with society."*[13] Under the JDA, delinquents were not simply defined as children who broke a law; they might also be children presumed to be neglected or abused, perhaps *likely* to break the law or become corrupted by their immoral families. They might simply be engaging in actions considered inappropriately adult for their age.

Delinquency, in other words, was a subjective and flexible concept, measured in ideological terms. It involved the moral censure of children and families who were out of line with dominant norms – those standards articulated as normal and superior by the respectable, secure, and affluent. The law embodied attempts to reshape youth in order to create good citizens for the future – citizens whose family, sexual, and work lives would help build a moral and law-abiding nation. The child, as "the most precious asset of the State," one juvenile court judge noted, "must be impressed with the mystery and majesty of the law."[14] Although the more recent YOA was purposely designed to be less subjective in its definition, and more attuned to children's legal rights, some criminologists argue that it too is ideological in its implementation. It inevitably targets certain children and their families for more punitive attention than others.

Official definitions of delinquency, as they changed over time, were inextricably linked to class. They were profoundly gendered, and increasingly racialized. Even when tales of middle-class delinquency, such as affluent suburban children engaging in sex and drugs, became more prevalent in the 1950s, no one really assumed that the youth of wealthy enclaves like Rosedale in Toronto were the truly dangerous potential criminals. From the mass media to social-work writing to reform narratives, it was clear that the working class and the poor, the uneducated, and racialized minorities were considered more likely to be gang members, thieves, and prostitutes. Regardless of their background, girls were presented with a common image and dire warnings of delinquent endangerment, usually involving a fall from sexual grace. Yet, implicitly, it was assumed that purity, virtue, and a caring, passive femininity would be more easily evaded or discarded by those who came from socially marginal families, lacking good role models. As Native girls became the increasing focus of concern by the 1950s, for instance, their reserve, cultural, and racial backgrounds became part of the social "pathology" used to explain their descent into drinking, sex, and criminality.

The dominant understandings of the causes of delinquency in part shaped the cures prescribed by the juvenile justice system. Yet the most comprehensive indictments of the causes of youth crime – poverty, lack of housing, and the failures of the educational system – defied easy solutions. Even if some progressive social workers included economic security and employment for youth in their prescriptions for change, they were ultimately limited to more band-aid solutions in their actual practice: counselling youth, advising families on good parenting, temporarily removing children from violent homes, or offering them the education befitting their gender and class position in a reform institution.

An examination of the reform efforts of volunteers to halt the pre-delinquent in her tracks, as well as of state-monitored probation, reveals the goals, successes, and limitations of the immense reform, medical, and social work apparatus surrounding the JDA. It is a truism now accepted of the JDA era that "treatment" or what is called a "welfare" approach to delinquency reigned supreme during those years. Indeed, in the current, excessively punitive political atmosphere, one judge has referred, almost wistfully, to the "golden era of JDA paternalism."[15] But we should avoid exaggerating the benefits of the earlier era, because its treatment of juveniles also had a decidedly punitive edge; moreover, paternalism was a double-edged sword that was used to censure and control, as well as care for, children.

For disobedient teens the final threat, the final solution, was industrial school, later renamed training school – yesterday's version of the closed custody now offered by the YOA. Only a small percentage of teens found their way into training school, as other diversionary measures, such as probation, tended first to come into play. Indeed, the best cure for delinquency was age. If teens in the past were at all like today's teenagers responding to self-report studies on their crimes, then we can presume that many committed minor offences but only a few were caught and charged. Of these few, some rode out the probation system, altered or hid their behaviour, and moved into adulthood, where things like drinking or sex were not illegal and the theft of bicycles held out less attraction.

Still, we should not dismiss the experiences of the minority who were sent to training school. For one thing, the prescribed remedies offered in training schools reveal much about how delinquency was defined, and about its assumed causes and cures. The girls sent to industrial and training schools were those considered most at risk, in need of a complete character makeover; their misdeeds became the measuring stick against which "good" girls were encouraged to position themselves.

In the first half of the twentieth century very few Native girls were sent to training school; by the 1960s, they were being incarcerated in alarming numbers disproportionate to their small percentage of the overall population. Their sentences were part of a larger effort to continue the project, begun in the previous century, of assimilating First Nations peoples to the supposedly superior norms of middle-class, white, Anglo society. After World War II, the stated intention of policy-makers was to extend the benefits of the welfare state – including delinquency prevention – to Native families by removing girls from the reserve to correctional institutions. Like their working-class comrades in training school, First Nations girls were presumed to need character reformation and the inculcation of work skills appropriate for the labouring class. Yet the cultural divide and racism that Native girls encountered in such institutions marked out their experiences as distinctly alienating, sometimes tragically so.

The training school experience, while it varied for different girls, could be profoundly alienating. Girls knew full well that the regime they faced did not simply involve their voluntary embrace of treatment. Rather, it was correctional and intended to punish as well as reform. Girls' responses to institutionalization, stretching from acquiescence to violence, remind us again that they were also actors within the juvenile justice system, even if their voices are more difficult to locate and interpret, even if their responses sometimes appear self-defeating or self-punishing. Unfortunately, the abuses that some girls endured in such institutions remained hidden for many years. Only recently the Ontario government has "apologized" to a group of women for the "physical and sexual abuse" they suffered while incarcerated in Grandview, the former Ontario Training School for Girls. Yet that apology appeared as a few lines hidden away in the back pages of *The Globe and Mail*, and it had already been pre-empted in that same newspaper by a full-page frontal attack, by anti-feminist writer Donna Laframboise, on the veracity of former Grandview inmates' claims of mistreatment. Portraying the women as liars and criminals, Laframboise even declared that the former guard who pleaded guilty to sexual assault was probably innocent as well.[16] Surely we can only conclude that the voices of those deemed less important simply because they *were* inmates of the school remained discounted in 1999, just as they were decades earlier.

Certainly, some of the attempts to define and prevent juvenile delinquency can be chalked up to "good intentions." We should not criticize the endeavours of middle-class anti-delinquency reformers in the past, chides historian D. Owen Carrigan, because, after all, they meant well. Undoubtedly, good intentions operated on the part of some parents who took their "promiscuous" daughters to court to stop their sexual actions, as well as on the part of Big Sisters volunteers and probation officers, or even of judges sending girls to training school. But evaluating the inner conscience of these predecessors is far too simple, and uncertain, a task. The more difficult question is: what were the ideological suppositions that shaped those good intentions, and did they serve to undermine, reinforce, or question prevailing class, race, and gender relations? Did those good intentions offer real alternatives to girls, or simply more surveillance?

Over the entire period from 1908 into the 1960s, panics about delinquency rose and fell, but the fear of youthful deviation, and the expressed need for the legal and social regulation of youth, never did entirely dissipate. Social reproduction was always a crucial issue for those concerned about creating decent citizens for the future, and a nation in *their* image. Indeed, youthful law-breaking and social anxiety about such crimes existed long before the twentieth century. Native societies had their own methods of social control for the young, often stressing mediation, restitution, or ostracism rather than incarceration. In both English and French settler societies, youth crime assumed characteristics that remained common until long after Confederation: boys' minor offences, such as theft and nuisance charges, were most visible, often in urban contexts. While girls were known to pilfer just like boys (though not in the same numbers), they might also be prosecuted for prostitution, abortion, or infanticide.[17]

What was disturbing to some, however, was that mere children were often detained in the squalor and violence of adult prisons, a punishment some late-nineteenth-century reformers increasingly found reprehensible, not the least because prison appeared to turn naughty children into hardened adult criminals. By the late nineteenth century, intensifying urbanization and industrialization, along with population increases and immigration, compounded anxieties about youth crime; unsupervised boys were especially worrisome as they roamed city streets, perhaps working as newsboys or bootblacks, but also being exposed to crime and adult vices such as gambling and drinking. Victorian middle-class reformers found an institutional cure for these boys and indeed, temporarily, for Native youth as well: industrial schools. These institutions, established to educate, discipline, and train delinquent, neglected, and abused children, were portrayed as "home-like" refuges, yet this child rescue was premised firmly on a class-based project of instilling discipline, moral values, and the work ethic into poor and working-class children. By the turn of the century, many industrial schools for girls had also been established by alliances of well-placed philanthropists and provincial governments. Some of these began within the confines of an adult reformatory, then later became separate buildings and programs; although they offered young girls a different regime of care and education from adult offenders, they often prescribed the same future dismal work future – domestic service.[18]

This Progressive period of institution-building, and of intense debate and concern about juvenile crime, produced the provincial and federal legislation that laid the groundwork for the 1908 JDA.[19] Reformers' hopes that the JDA would usher in a new era of juvenile adjustment, however, were not met in the immediate years following its enactment.

Juvenile courts were gradually set up in some major cities, and a strong child welfare movement, including prominent advocates such as Judge Helen Gregory McGill, thrived after World War I, lobbying for improvements to the JDA and enhanced services for children in court. However, anxieties about youth crime persisted, reinforced by increasing arrests and convictions, and in the "roaring twenties" by an intense public debate about youthful licentiousness and abandon. The prospect that youth were "dancing themselves to perdition,"[20] and the disrespect for adult authority that critics feared would lead to other crimes, were portrayed as classless and generalized. Yet discussions of delinquency in the social work literature, even in religious tracts, betrayed an underlying concern that non-Anglo and working-class families in crisis were more likely to produce delinquent teens.

The Depression of the 1930s did nothing to dispel that notion, because many commentators, from the police to social workers, argued that economic dislocation, unemployment, and the loss of family leadership and cohesion would lead working-class and impoverished youth to despair and lawlessness. But anxieties were not always explained by economic crises or crime statistics. Youth arrests did not rise precipitously throughout the whole Depression and actually fell in many cities near the end of the decade. When arrests soared at the outset of World War II, the increase was perhaps linked to demography and policing as much as to actual law-breaking. Wartime prosperity did not assuage anxieties about delinquency. "Jitters over juveniles" escalated,[21] fed by media reports of delinquency, by the partial closure of some training schools to provide space for military training, and by experts fretting over the disruption of the family in war – absent fathers, shift work, the lure of money and materialism, and, of course, neglectful working mothers. Indeed, there were distinct echoes from World War I, when the absence of the stern hand of older brothers and fathers supposedly led to youthful lawlessness – a theory of "patriarchy imperilled" still endorsed by some criminologists.[22]

Public anxiety about delinquency persisted after World War II, fed by ideological campaigns to shore up/re-create the male breadwinner/female homemaker family and stabilize family life in the face of Cold War anxieties.[23] Calls were made for new reforms and infrastructures of support, from organized recreation to parenting courses, and, by the 1960s, for group homes for troubled youth unable to live with their families. Over this entire period, public fears might shift – in the 1920s, drugs were a new concern, in the post-World War II era, gangs were the focus of consternation – but delinquency never completely disappeared as a social issue. The post-World War II anxiety about delinquency, for instance, linked to containment of the nuclear, heterosexual family and fears of youth sexual misbehaviour, was not completely unlike concerns articulated in the Depression, even if these were now intensified and refracted through the lens of the Cold War phenomenon. Nor was delinquency _only_ a social construction, for certain social, economic, and political contexts might well temporarily escalate youthful rebellion or wrongdoing. As Eric Schneider suggests, one problem with attributing delinquency to recurring moral panics is that this approach ignores structural conditions that may well lead to increased alienation or law-breaking, and it "also robs working-class adolescents of their one token of agency: their ability to cause trouble."[24]

Delinquency was redefined and reinterpreted over time, but even if its meanings altered and shifted, many of the stresses, inequities, and pressures sustaining it as a social problem remained constant over the course of the JDA. No amount of well-intentioned counselling or parenting courses, no scattered removals of children from problematic families, no end of social work studies, could completely alter this pattern. Many of the constants shaping delinquency – racism, dispossession, violence, material deprivation, social and educational marginalization – remain with us today, and though it is true that not all of the girls who come into conflict with the law are from deprived backgrounds, there is no doubt that the juvenile justice system disproportionately regulates and targets these children, just as it did in the past.

As Paul Havemann and others have argued, over the last twenty years we have also witnessed a shift in the legal discourses concerning delinquency: the dominant rationale for the JDA – that is, welfare, treatment, and child-saving – has been replaced by a new, punitive emphasis in law and public opinion on parent-blaming and child-blaming.[25] The idea that society and the state have a responsibility to rescue youth _through the law_ has been replaced by provincial legislation decreeing that parents should be punished _with the law_: the Ontario law introduced in 2000 to make parents pay for their children's crimes puts the onus on parents to explain why their failures and "bad parenting" were _not_ the cause of these crimes.[26]

Of course, the opposition between the two eras is not quite that stark. The record of the treatment of girls under the JDA reveals that parent-blaming and child-blaming often lurked just beneath the surface. Girls' experience of everything from forced gynecological exams to incarceration when they were victims of incest also suggests that we should be less than sanguine about constructing a golden age of paternal, kindly care linked to the JDA. Still, the shift from a more positivist, modernist, optimistic view that delinquents might be reformed through diagnosis and care (however wrong-headed past cures might seem now) to the contemporary view that delinquents may be unsalvageable or inherently evil, is quite clear. Despite the differences between the era of the JDA and the era of the YOA, then, all indications are that we have failed to come to terms with delinquency. Even more worrisome is the current climate of pessimism and punishment, which might dispel our hopes of transforming the lives of youth in conflict with the law.

Two

Defining Delinquency

The argument that delinquency is a social construct, a form of labelling, rather than a firm, scientific, or morally absolute measurement of good or evil, right or wrong, moral or immoral, is nothing new. By the post-World War II period many leading criminologists, including American Paul Tappan, were emphasizing that delinquency was "a culturally defined product." The labelling theorists of the early 1960s, following Howard Becker, stressed the way in which crime was a definition or label, constructed by those groups with social power and influence.[1] In the early 1970s a popular book exploring the myths of delinquency rephrased this equation as a rhetorical question: who are the real delinquents, Canadian Elliot Leyton asked, as opposed to those children we label as such? After sympathetically probing the lives of troubled teens written off as hopeless and maladjusted, Leyton suggested that society itself was delinquent for allowing poverty, violence, and alienation, particularly in the underclass, to persist, warping the lives of the young.[2] By the 1970s, critiques of the construction of delinquency had taken on a more trenchant structural form as writing by feminist and Marxist social critics condemned the unequal relations of class and gender underpinning the criminal justice system. More recent theoretical trends, utilizing post-structuralist theory, take these ideas in new directions, exploring the complex intersection of power and knowledge, how some youth behaviour is "normalized" and other behaviour is pathologized as deviant and unacceptable.

Although there are important differences in this long tradition of thinking about the construction of delinquency, one fundamental insight is repeatedly offered: definitions of youth misbehaviour and the creation of a criminal category – the delinquent – were and are established within a web of power relations, reflecting the prevailing social definitions of what are perceived to be civilized, appropriate, moral standards of behaviour. These definitions may alter over time, but they are fundamentally shaped by the political and economic exercise and experience of power based on race, class, and gender; the law is one means of justifying, legitimizing, explaining, and sustaining the dominant social norms, and sexual and familial relations.

Delinquency was defined, not only in law, but also by the various experts and professionals who explained its symptoms and causes, helping in the process to create the juvenile justice system. Those definitions were also gendered: these discourses, or systems of knowledge, produced meanings that clearly distinguished boys' and girls' abnormality, their bad behaviour, their social needs. While the definition of delinquency did not remain static over these decades, certain themes reappeared consistently in legal and expert pronouncements on delinquency – themes that highlight how the issue of delinquency was demarcated as a social problem of youth, class alienation, and gender deviation.

The Legal Regime

The Juvenile Delinquents Act of 1908 is often seen as a watershed in Canadian legal history. While there is a measure of truth to this, the Act built on existing, piecemeal legislation and social thinking, which from the late nineteenth century on emphasized the possibility of saving children who were exposed to evil environments but were potentially useful, law-abiding citizens. In 1891 a major Ontario inquiry into correctional institutions declared, "The causes of child crime are want of proper parental control, lack of good home training and the baneful influence of bad homes, largely due to the culpable neglect and indifference of parents and evil effects of drunkenness." Shorn of this Victorian language, the same sentiments could be heard echoing through pronouncements on delinquency for decades to come.

In a federal system in which child welfare was a provincial matter, the first proponents of the JDA had to tread carefully; though the bill fell within the federal Criminal Code, it involved aspects of child welfare and correction germane to the provincial realm. It was introduced to Parliament by a senator whose son, W.I. Scott, a prominent lawyer and head of the Ottawa Children's Aid Society (CAS), was a vocal child-saving advocate, and later a leader in the Canadian Welfare Council. This Canadian JDA, shaped in part by similar U.S. experiments in Progressive-period legal reform,[3] was hailed as a more humane, forward-thinking approach to juvenile crime, both then and in some subsequent historical accounts. Two concepts, integrated from British law and already apparent in the late nineteenth century, were a central part of the legal thinking behind the Act: *parens patriae* (the state might need to step in as a surrogate parent in the best interests of the child); and *doli incapax* (young children were incapable of deceit or evil, thus limiting their individual responsibility and accountability for wrongdoing).[4] Rather than punishing young offenders *for* crime, the state should try to rescue children *from* crime.

Various legal precedents – such as allowing separate, closed hearings for juveniles – had already been set, but the JDA was still a comprehensive, ambitious attempt to create a more holistic, reformative system of juvenile justice. The Act promised to remove juveniles from corruption by older, violent criminals in degrading jails, stressing, first, the classification and care of the child according to his or her needs and, second, the treatment, aid, and rehabilitation of children outside correctional institutions. The original (1908) and revised acts refrained from designating delinquency as a state or condition (as in some U.S. laws) but came as close as they could by specifying the "offence" within an extremely broad framework. Delinquents were those between ages seven and sixteen (in some provinces other than Ontario, the age was stretched to eighteen)[5] who had contravened any federal, provincial, or municipal law, or ordinance, who were *liable* by reason of any act to be committed to an industrial school or reformatory, or who were guilty of "sexual immorality or any similar form of vice."[6] Any of these conditions could be labelled an offence that put children in a state of delinquency, though the individual child was to be dealt with "not as an offender but as one in a condition of delinquency and therefore requiring help and guidance and supervision." The law also said that juveniles were to be tried summarily (by a judge alone), shielded from public scrutiny, and protected from testifying against themselves if they did not understand an oath – unless other "material" evidence was at hand. Young children (under twelve) were not to be sent to an industrial school until efforts were made to deal with the problem in the domestic home, and no child was to be incarcerated in a penitentiary.[7]

The federal law established a "local option": cities and counties could have the Act proclaimed for their jurisdiction and could set up their own juvenile courts. Since these courts were normally financed locally, only large centres such as Vancouver, Toronto, and Ottawa had put them in place by the early 1920s. By 1936 eighteen cities across Canada had opted in, and the number increased dramatically in the post-World War II period. However, invoking the JDA locally did not necessarily mean separate judicial buildings, administration, or judges. The local magistrate or judge could simply "change his hat" and double as juvenile court judge, with the same applying to adult court probation officers. Such was the situation, for instance, until the 1950s in

Hamilton, which processed a high number of juvenile cases.[8] Juvenile justice was always differentially experienced by region and city size. Policing was more intense in urban areas. Children in rural areas, appearing before smaller courts, did not have access to the social service, probation, and psychiatric facilities associated with large courts like those in Toronto, Montreal, or Vancouver.

In all aspects of delinquency, the federal criminal justice system was closely intertwined with provincial laws: once sentenced to an industrial (later training) school, for instance, a child in Ontario came under provincial jurisdiction. Moreover, some children who came into conflict with the law were apprehended under the provincial acts regulating industrial and training schools. Like the federal JDA, these provincial statutes often exhibited great latitude in the definition of delinquency and in the provision of many non-legal options for dealing with delinquents. One of the key sections of Ontario's Training School Act (1939) allowed children to be sent to training school if they were deemed "incorrigible and unmanageable," a status that covered anything from violent acts to truancy to simple disobedience. Parents could bring the child to court, and so too could police and local Children's Aid Societies. Indeed, the child could be incarcerated on the intervention of the minister (advised by his Training School Advisory Board) without even appearing before a court. This supposedly protected children from a traumatic court appearance, but it also allowed local Children's Aid Societies to sidestep the legal process, and in a few cases it also allowed individuals to apply political or personal pressure on the minister to admit a child.

Flexibility in sentencing was key to this legal regime: the court could suspend its decision, adjourn the hearing indefinitely, commit the child to the care of a probation officer or a volunteer group like the Big Sisters or Big Brothers Associations, impose a fine, allow the child to remain in the home with outside supervision, place her in a foster home, commit her to the care of the CAS, or send her to training school. Flexibility did not, however, mean lax surveillance. Once deemed a delinquent or sentenced under the Training School Act, the child was potentially under the supervision of the court – through parents, social workers, probation officers – until the age of twenty-one (after 1949, the Ontario age was lowered to eighteen).

This surveillance was related to a crucial aspect of juvenile courts: their ideological embrace of informal or socialized justice. Socialized justice encompassed three key ideas: individualized treatment of the deviant, reliance on non-legal experts (such as doctors or social workers), and the corollary use of administrative rather than legal solutions.[9] After World War I, one group of reformers urged the state to embrace the principles of socialized justice by establishing separate family and juvenile courts (sometimes called domestic relations tribunals). They were opposed by defenders of legal formalism who resisted the expanded power of judges with no legal training; and they were also sidelined by disinterested provincial governments. But by the end of the 1930s, the tide turned: a key Supreme Court decision concerning jurisdiction of family courts ushered in an era in which family and juvenile courts, based on socialized justice, were an established, and much lauded, part of the Canadian criminal justice system.

Socialized justice for juveniles was facilitated by the immense latitude in sentencing that judges had within the JDA and by the growing symbiosis and information-sharing of the welfare, social services, educational, and legal systems. It was buttressed also by the reigning social service and medical discourses of the time, which assumed children needed "treatment before conviction."[10] This train of thought saw delinquency as a social problem needing preventive and ameliorative attention, with the helping professions taking an integral role in the child's reformation. Still, notions of criminal wrongdoing and punishment of the child were not completely absent. The 1937 federal royal commission on the penal system and a 1954 Ontario inquiry into delinquency, for instance, both relayed public complaints that juveniles were treated "too leniently" and required tougher correctional lessons, even corporal punishment.[11] However, from the inception of the JDA to the 1960s, a strong state and professional rhetorical emphasis on solving delinquency through socialized justice rather than incarceration remained in place. The large Toronto Family Court most dramatically shows the very real outcome of this thinking. Between 1912 and 1952 the number of probation officers there increased from four to fourteen, the number of cases officially handled by the court declined, and those unofficially handed though socialized justice increased by 900 per cent.[12] How positive this change was is a point of academic disagreement. Some scholars laud the use of probation, and others argue that the overall consequence of socialized justice was the increased surveillance and moral regulation of the poor and marginalized.

Those reformers advocating the extension of juvenile courts across the nation would have recoiled at the word surveillance; they believed that their efforts offered protection and treatment. What appealed to these early legislators and child-savers were principles that remained basic to the JDA throughout its long life. First, family responsibility and authority for children were not fundamentally challenged, even if the state was extending its control over parental responsibility and morals. Delinquent children were to be aided first within the family if possible, with the judge acting as a surrogate form of authority dispensing firm paternal (or in some cases maternal) advice and orders to problem families. Family and juvenile courts, noted one Ontario judge, had a common goal: their "primary aim was to preserve strong, wholesome family life."[13] Parents, however, had to assume some blame for the production of delinquents; under the Act they were criminally liable for fines and imprisonment for "contributing to juvenile delinquency" if they "abetted" delinquency in any way. Recent calls for legislation to "make parents pay" for their children's crimes are directly in line with this tradition, a throwback to the first decade of the century. The emphasis on parental blame was never abandoned under the JDA, even if the juvenile justice system stressed other environmental causes and cures for youth crime. These contributing clauses in the JDA were taken seriously; between 1920 and 1950 in the Toronto court, for example, more parents were taken to task for contributing to delinquency through immorality than for assaulting their spouses.

Second, advocates believed that the Act addressed the causes, rather than simply the outcomes, of crime, offering real alternatives to incarceration. They saw it as preventive, as pinpointing "criminals in the bud" and positively altering their future. By protecting the child, society would also be protected, with moral citizens produced. Why, then, have some historians been so critical of this legislation? Scholars in law, history, and sociology have debated whether the JDA was an expression of "ruling-class" attempts to manage and regulate the unruly, potentially criminal working class and poor rather than to substantially change their social circumstances. Some liberal criminologists correctly point out that a wide array of upper- and middle-class reformers, not simply a small economic elite, promoted the JDA, and that they often had to battle to secure support and resources to implement the treatment necessary to implement socialized justice. Still, the corollary conclusion – that the JDA was not a "conspiracy to keep the unwashed masses in check," because reformers were often "public service motivated women . . . not dupes of capitalism"[14] – misses the mark in its simplistic equation of historical materialism and conspiracy theories. The passage of the JDA may have been the result of a broad coalition of propertied and middle-class professionals, philanthropists, and politicians, and it may have promoted rehabilitative ideals, but it was also posed and used as a solution to social problems that were fundamentally class-defined. State "benevolence" applied through the JDA was directed primarily towards the more "dangerous classes," whose ignorance, poverty, unemployment, and immorality were perceived to stimulate delinquency. Moreover, whether we call its offerings judgemental surveillance or kindly treatment, the Act still could not, and did not, address the root problems stimulating delinquency.

Complex and contradictory forces were thus apparent in the legal regime relating to delinquency. For one thing, despite the emergence of a new system of juvenile courts, final deliberations in many Canadian locations may well have proceeded along the lines of the older Magistrate's Court. For another, while separate welfare legislation to protect neglected children was distinct from the JDA, the aims of "crime prevention and child welfare"[15] often overlapped in practice as the JDA's mandate included children perceived to be "at risk" or, as the Act put it, those "in need of guidance and supervision." As well, although the system was supposed to avoid incarceration and punishment in favour of treatment and rehabilitation, the law also allowed for arbitrary, long-lasting powers over juveniles. Ultimately, this feature meant that juveniles could be taken to court or incarcerated for behaviour not even deemed a crime in the adult world. Girls, for example, could be incarcerated for promiscuity while an adult prostitute, even if guilty of breaking the law, could simply receive a suspended sentence.[16] As commentators noted in their mounting critiques of the Act in the late 1950s and early 1960s, a child was often tried simply on the basis of "personality and social background," not because of an actual breach of the criminal code.

Enter the Experts

Legal definitions are important, but they are interpreted and applied within a historical and social context, and from the advent of the JDA in 1908 determinations of delinquency were tied to knowledge generated by many experts other than judges. Indeed, commentators often characterize the middle decades of the twentieth century as a time when the modern expert, trained in medical, social science, or social work paradigms, became absolutely central to the criminal justice system – so much so that it was the expert who came to define what was criminal, delinquent, immoral, or insane.

The dominant discourses defining juvenile delinquency through criminology, psychology, and the social work and psychiatric professions in those decades are a book unto themselves. They did alter over time, and they were not of one piece. Still, a number of key themes appear repeatedly in professional writing and were echoed in government reports and the mainstream press. On a most general level, throughout the entire period from 1908 to the 1960s, two themes run through explanations of what delinquency was, and why it existed. One theme stressed innate, inherent individual pathologies and limitations; another accented the social and environmental problems creating delinquency. Neither was used entirely alone, and they sometimes overlapped in the experts' minds, with the focus often on one blameworthy institution: the family.

Authors have often drawn on the theories of French philosopher Michel Foucault to indicate how systems of knowledge or "disciplines" – such as psychiatry or criminology – are themselves a form of power relations, offering up versions of human nature that are influential because of their stature as scientific, true, and irrefutable.[17] Delinquency was not just defined by, but was indeed created through, the dominant discourses of these powerful disciplines. According to this analysis, a strategy of inclusion/exclusion, or "normalization," demarcates normal and abnormal behaviour through a series of techniques: comparing, differentiating, homogenizing, excluding, and creating hierarchies. But while this analysis of the process through which delinquency is constructed is enlightening, contrary to some Foucauldian writing these disciplines did not supplant legal institutions and the state; rather, they worked hand in hand to define and prescribe a cure for delinquency. Indeed, in the last resort, judges commanded the most important claim to truth and justice, and in their sentencing they might even disregard experts' opinions. Perhaps the best way of conceiving of this process is to adopt Allan Hunt's suggestion that we examine the law and the disciplines as they interacted and combined over history, not presupposing one or the other as dominant. Coupled together, often reinforcing each other, they became a potent means of regulating modern youth.[18]

Who were these experts? Aside from the police, who were on the front line of regulation, many children in conflict with the law encountered Children's Aid Society workers, and in larger courts, probation officers, who were increasingly trained in the social sciences or in social work. CAS workers, especially in rural areas and small cities, could be drawn from the ranks of local "respectables" with philanthropic connections until professional training increasingly became the norm in the post-World War II period. CAS and probation officers, or case workers, were often in charge of assessing the child's history, from birth to schooling, including family and emotional life, using interviews with the child and family to detect problems. Over time, two other groups of professionals became important. The system utilized psychologists to assess intelligence, "normal" child development, and behaviour, while psychiatrists probed the deeper, psychic rationale for children's deviance.

Psychologists and psychiatrists, along with social scientists such as criminologists, were the most influential authorities writing on delinquency. Psychologists, as Mona Gleason argues, used the niche carved out for their expertise in the interwar period to secure increasing influence in Canadian society during and after World War II. Their pronouncements about normal child and family life were the defining words of the age, offered up to worried parents on the radio and in the mass media as well as in professional journals. Gleason also argues persuasively that psychological advice was based less on science than on ideology. The advice helped to set up "unattainable ideals" for most parents, ideals that "normalized patriarchal, white and middle-class values."[19]

At the apex of expert influence stood psychiatrists, whose professional training as specialist doctors, along with their particular claim to understand the inner mind, secured them considerable prestige. Even in the 1970s, law and psychiatry were still the "double force of authority" in juvenile courts, and probation officers grumbled to one investigator that psychiatrists were too often revered uncritically, even though they spent less time with the children than did other, more "lowly" court workers. However, until a broader critique of psychiatry emerged by the late 1960s, the criticism that psychiatry had too much "permeated public thinking on delinquency" was rarely heard.[20]

Although psychiatry and psychology increasingly influenced criminologists and social workers too – all these disciplines overlapped – some differences occurred in various expert assessments of youth behaviour. In the 1930s, for example, a psychiatrist writing in a medical journal on "Boys and Girls, the Family and Delinquencies" maintained that anti-social children were often the products of inadequate parenting and distorted family relations rather than "external" factors. In the midst of the Depression, he reassured his readers that the economic background of the child, whether they ate "hash" or steak, mattered little, for the affluent "father at the golf club," ignoring his children, could just as easily produce a delinquent.[21] Given the emphasis of psychiatry on individual pathology, examination, and treatment, this writer had a clear professional interest in promoting this argument. After all, if questions of class, the economy, or hash and steak did matter, his expertise would be less useful. The gist of his argument, stressing individual pathologies, whether they be intellectual, mental, or psychic, appeared repeatedly over time in various medical models.

In contrast, social workers writing in *Canadian Welfare*, the major professional social work journal in Canada, also discussed individual pathologies, but they simultaneously surveyed broader stimulants to delinquency: a child's exposure to peer (gang) pressure, learning problems at school, parental drinking, and poverty, for instance. During the Depression, case workers from the Toronto Juvenile Court noted that the majority of their delinquents came from poorer homes on relief, and a study of Toronto juvenile car thieves in *Canadian Welfare* stressed that 21 per cent of the culprits came from impoverished and broken homes. At the height of intense social work faith in the possibilities of treatment and reform, at the end of World War II, one Toronto Welfare Council study declared (presaging Simone de Beauvoir) that "delinquents are made, not born." As such, they could be unmade, through a combination of "child psychology" to rectify the youth's "lack of personal security and confidence" within the family, and social work aid to provide educational supports and community services.[22]

The police and court workers also cited youth and adult unemployment, hopelessness, and idleness as causes of crime. "These people are not bad at heart," wrote one police chief in an unusually generous gesture, "but the unfortunate [Depression] conditions . . . encourage Juvenile Delinquency."[23] During the subsequent war years the police could just as easily turn to an opposite explanation: boys' wages, they claimed, were too high, thus encouraging dissipation and delinquency. Indeed, police assessments, even if they embraced some of the rhetoric of environmental child-saving, were also notable for their embrace of law, order, and discipline alongside their calls for self-control and individual morality. Toronto's "iron heel" Chief Constable Denis Draper railed in 1944 that a "lack of parental control" in the home – which was the "fountain of all morality for the nation" – caused delinquency. The corruption of "liquor, beverage rooms, motion pictures, crime magazines" and the lack of "Church going and Bible studies" were the "causes" most offensive to him. His pronouncements would ring true today for the conservative political current that demands a mix of religion and the rod for young offenders.

Over time some differences showed up in these expert discourses. One of the most noticeable was the rise and decline of eugenics, which preceded the rise and consolidation of psychology and psychiatry. From World War I until the late 1930s a strong mental hygiene movement existed, led by eugenicist advocates such as Dr. C.L. Clarke and Dr. Helen MacMurchy. Their views, relayed in professional writing in journals dedicated to mental hygiene, as well as in government inquiries into such matters as the feeble-minded, venereal disease, and public welfare, stressed the need to identify and classify – and limit through sterilization – the nation's feeble-minded because those unfortunates and their progeny were a significant cause of crime and delinquency. As Jennifer Stephen points out, however, Dr. Clarke's assessments of who was a "moron, imbecile or idiot" were shaped by "moral as much as scientific considerations." For Clarke, feeble-mindedness was often synonym for working-class females whose sexual behaviour flouted all middle-class norms and conventions.[24]

By the 1940s and 1950s, eugenic and purely hereditary theories of genetic abnormality were in decline and the delinquency experts were spending less time searching out the mental defectives and more energy probing mental health and social pathology through Freudian-influenced analysis or psychology. Psychiatry had gained tremendous prestige, and children and teens were its fastest-growing patient group.[25] Psychology was also on the rise, particularly the functionalist approaches of doctors William Blatz and Samuel Laycock, whose highly publicized theories stressed the basic mutability of children's behaviour. According to these behaviourist thinkers, self-control – clearly a preventive for delinquency – could be inculcated through parenting routine and schooling.

What drew many of these experts together was a modernist, positivist, technocratic world view: delinquency was a disease, which could be logically identified, defined, analysed, and treated. The experts developed theories on the symptoms of pre-delinquency, so that delinquency could be treated before it became the full-blown disease of law-breaking. As a prominent juvenile court judge argued: "One might compare a child before the court to a sick person before a Doctor whose duty is to diagnose the cause of illness and treat it. . . . the Court uses the advantages of modern science" to save the child.[26] The metaphors of symptoms, illness, and treatment were used repeatedly by doctors, criminologists, philanthropists, and government agencies involved in corrections, at least in their public discussions. The Ontario provincial Training School Advisory Board (a collection of notables who advised the government) argued that delinquents had simply been "mishandled environmentally" and needed "preventative" and professional care – an advertisement for the training schools they oversaw. As the 1960s dawned, the illness metaphor was still strong: "It is true that some [delinquents] appear to be psychopaths in the bud," the same Board stated, "but by modern treatment, anti-social behaviour can be discovered, as we diagnose an illness. Most [delinquents] deserve pity, not censure."[27]

Criminologists today, influenced by theories ranging from feminism to Foucault, are more likely to be suspicious or ambivalent about claims of expert scientific accuracy concerning the meaning of youth crime. This scepticism may not be completely unwarranted, even if it veers towards the pessimistic. Some would even argue that "narratives" rather than proven truths underlie our understanding of crime.[28] While this is an extreme position, nevertheless the experts did clearly tend to relay their definitions of delinquency through stock stories and vignettes, the conventions of which reveal much about their understandings of youth endangerment and misbehaviour.

Narratives of Delinquency

The definitions of delinquency were the product not simply of an abstract medical measurement like a thermometer, but of ideology, power relations, and the legitimation of certain social behaviours and familial relationships. Underpinning the notion of the normal child was an image of a white, middle-class, patriarchal family as the preferable bedrock of citizenship. An analysis of delinquency in relation to class and ethnicity reveals how much youth criminality was equated with the urban underclass and the working classes, even while some experts were declaring it classless. At certain points in time, the claim of classlessness – that delinquency could strike any family like the chicken pox – became strong, if not shrill, as middle-class parents were warned about the threats to teen morality and respect for authority. In the 1950s, for instance, teens supposedly embraced postwar prosperity by engaging in drugs and drink, even sexual orgies, according to one sensational media exposé.[29] Not unlike a sensational *Globe and Mail* article in April 2000 suggesting that demure, upper-middle-class "college girls" were becoming "call girls," these arguments were based on anecdotal and occasional, rather than predominant, experiences.[30] While middle-class children certainly did violate laws and sometimes came into contact with the juvenile justice system, a more enduring theme in expert and popular writing was the notion that certain classes, family types, and neighbourhoods produced delinquency, so much so that criminality was defined *by* these connections. Moreover, given the material deprivation, social alienation, and overpolicing of poor areas that led to youthful conflicts with the law, this particular construction had a self-fulfilling rationale.

These themes were apparent in the publications of both juvenile courts and youth reform organizations, which promoted the rehabilitative treatment they offered with documentary accounts of their successes. During the 1920s and 1930s, the Toronto probation officer (PO), for instance, published his "actual probation histories." These were narrative renditions of his cases, replete with detailed, colloquial conversations, acute physical descriptions, and intricate plots that unfolded as morality tales for the curious reader. As Karen Tice shows, the "case record," particularly in child welfare, had become a central if not "canonical" part of social work by the 1920s and was utilized as a commodity in the attempt to legitimate and professionalize social work, setting it apart from unflattering images of "unscientific" feminine charity work. There were internal debates about whether "art, objectivity or science" should shape presentation of the case file; some argued that the worker should "share textual space" with the client; others opted for "documentary realism" as articulated through the workers' eyes. Despite this flexibility, the PO reports evocatively captured one recurring theme: the use of these narratives as evidence of "social work accomplishment" and progress in the quest for public approval for probation work.[31]

The probation officer's stories usually focused on boys who came from single-parent families, headed up by either a virtuous struggling widow who could not control the boy or an immoral mother who did not try. As one story noted, "Mother working, deserted . . . living in a poor district . . . no home life." Her boy had "rough speech." The message of underclass status was clear. In this case, Jerry, known to his gang, the Evergays, as the Eel, was an accomplished petty thief. The mother agreed to move to a better section of the city so that Jerry would be removed from his corrupting associates. Yet Jerry succumbed to another cigarette heist, and his final salvation came only when, egged on by his paternal probation officer, he informed on his gang to the police. The denouement of the story explained that the gang was led by a nefarious couple, "modern Fagins," though the real culprit was the woman, who "dominated" her husband – "a not unusual state of affairs," the PO editorialized.[32]

As well as theft, boys' misdeeds included truancy and incorrigibility (such as disobedience and rudeness to parents). One boy, whose widowed mother could barely support the family, was spending his food money on candy and acting up in the home. The PO chastises the boy for his immaturity and failure to assume a more responsible masculine role within the family. A job was found for him on probation, and once he was contributing his earnings to the family economy, he began to grow up properly.[33] Some eight years later the PO described the family of a boy caught stealing. Following the usual dramatic conventions of case-work storytelling, the PO, whose self-image was that of kindly, strict paternal authority (he informed his readers that he sometimes invited the boy to his home), slowly revealed the boy's "real" problem: his non-conforming, underclass parents. His stepfather (step-relations were invariably problematic) was a busker with a trained monkey; the house "looked like a zoo"; and the stepfather was domineering, overstepping his role as the "unnatural" father. All that saved poor Mickey was his removal to "new and decent surroundings," a boys home where regula-tion, discipline, respectability, and a job aided his salvation. Mickey's final comment to the PO was revealing: "You and Mr. Morgan [of the boys home] treated me white."[34]

If Mickey's comment was a revealing equation of fair treatment with the entitlement of whiteness, it also alludes to a subtle theme in some of these tales, especially in the early years of the JDA and the interwar period. Ethnicity and immigrant status were not primary explanations for delinquency, but they were often a subtle subtext in descriptions of delinquent children. Studies and statistics repeatedly revealed that most children in court were native-born Canadians, not recent immigrants, but ethnicity, some professionals still suggested, was linked to low income, bad neighbourhoods, and the appeal of gangs. They believed that parental non-Anglo ethnicity marginalized a child, or possibly caused a rift between the parents' old world culture and modern "Cana-dian" (that is, Anglo) values. Billy, who had stolen some coal near his Toronto home, and later gloves and a pocket knife, was first identified in the PO's story as a "Macedonian" boy living in a "very poor district in a poorly furnished, untidy" home. His mother "barely spoke English," and his father was indifferent to his problems. Completely sidestepping the question of what he stole (obviously items of necessity to an impoverished family), the PO found Billy's salvation in assimilation to the Anglo order: Billy joined a Boys Club and Sunday School, and these new cultural influences, combined with his older brothers' efforts to improve the family abode, so it was "tidy, clean and had furniture," led to his reformation.[35]

Other professional writing, especially in the interwar period, also assumed that "children of foreign born parents" might be susceptible to delinquency. The fear that non-Anglo male youth were more likely to form gangs and engage in violence had been a staple of the popular press since the turn of the century, and it was sometimes repeated as a historical and contemporary fact backed by little critical thought on the part of criminologists.[36]

Girls in immigrant families might also be characterized as victims of value conflict. "Conflicts are inevitable," wrote the Big Sisters Association (BSA) in Toronto, "between the 'old' traditions of the parents and the 'new' Canadian ways" that young people wanted to take advantage of. Although "naturally suspicious of authority," these families do "respond to kindly interest," they added, reassuring the public that they were trying to make these foreign families, including "a few Asiatics," into "assets as citizens rather than a menace to the country."[37] Delinquency prevention therefore overlapped with the ethnocentric Anglo impulse to assimilate children, breaking ties with their parents' "backward" cultures. This is not to deny that some intrafamilial tensions may well have existed in immigrant families; when a group of teenage working-class girls from Toronto made up their own questionnaire for a study carried out during World War II, one of the questions they asked was, "Why are foreign parents more strict than those from Canada?"[38]

It was no accident that middle-class reform groups like Big Sisters often used vignettes of non-Anglo immigrant children in their promotional stories. Describing their good works in 1931, Toronto Big Sisters listed their clients as "Olga, a little Ukrainian girl, who was so lonely since her mother died; Carmen and her sisters, attractive little Italians, whose parents can barely speak English, and who need someone to help them adjust in a new country."[39] More than once the director of the Hamilton Big Sisters told audiences the story of an immigrant daughter who wanted to leave home at a young age because her parents would "not accept Canadian ways." The girl had to give all her earnings to her parents, could not buy her own clothes, and had an early curfew and no dates. Intervention by the Hamilton BSA social worker saved the day. A "compromise" was reached: once allowed some "healthy recreation," the girl did not run away. Of course, the same social worker later admitted that this desire of working teens for independence was very common; working teens often phoned her office wanting to know if they could get out of the house at age sixteen.[40]

Despite a subtext of anxiety about immigrant parents and children, medical and social science literature did not construct non-Anglo ethnicity as a major cause of delinquency. In some cases, judges and probation officers might display ethnocentric prejudices, but disquiet at non-Anglo parentage could also be overcome if the parents appeared to be part of the "respectable" – that is, non-drinking and hard-working – working class.

Initially, race was also not a defining category in expert writing on delinquency in Canada, at least not to the extent that it was in the United States. Certainly, racism might surface in the few cases in which children of colour were involved. People of colour, particularly Asian and Black citizens, had been targets of hostility and discriminatory policing concerning the drug trade from the very inception of narcotics legislation at the beginning of the century.[41] Such racist scapegoating was particularly acute in certain periods, such as the 1920s, when notables like Judge Emily Murphy charged that people of colour were responsible for narcotic importation and the increasing corruption of young women through addiction. Also, Canadians' heavy reliance on U.S. expert studies meant exposure to analyses asserting that Afro-American racial characteristics, such as supposed lower intelligence and sexual promiscuity, stimulated delinquent tendencies. Moreover, race became central to the definitions of Native delinquency in the post-World War II period.

On occasion race could also be used to explain the very opposite: the low level of delinquency for non-white teens. Judge Helen Gregory McGill conducted an extensive survey of "Oriental delinquents" in her Vancouver Juvenile Court in 1936, in order to understand why statistics showed "remarkably low" delinquency rates for these children, even though they lived in the same neighbourhoods that the court had demarcated as "high delinquency." McGill opened her study by repeating the maxim that tensions between parents' "ancient customs" and children's "new world" manners often produced revolt and disobedience. She also acknowledged the prejudices and contempt automatically directed towards Asian immigrants. If these tensions were real, she asked, why did so few Oriental children ever appear in her court?

Using interviews, letters, and questionnaires drawn from missionaries and teachers, as well as from leaders within the Chinese and Japanese community, McGill developed a number of hypotheses. She decided that the emphasis put on family honour and obedience to one's elders, as well as the teaching of religious ideals and inculcation of respect for the law within Japanese and Chinese language schools, were important in preventing crimes. She reasoned that minor problems were adjudicated within these tightly knit communities, which understood Canadian courts to be "alien" and perhaps unsympathetic to them.[42] Her general tone of respect and her explanation stressing family structure, internal social control, education, and religious belief were a far cry from Judge Murphy's racist denunciations of Chinese drug pushers, although *Maclean's* published Murphy's writing, not McGill's, a telling fact in itself.[43]

Intertwined with Murphy's racist narrative was an important theme found in all delinquency narratives concerning girls: the threat of sexual corruption and downfall. In the Toronto Big Sisters Association, narratives of girls endangered were actually acted out in dramatic form by the staff at the annual general meeting; later these morality plays were printed up in the official annual report. In 1933, after staff had performed acts 1 and 2 of the life of "Daisy," the agency director gave an analysis of this "typical" case. Daisy was "sullen, resentful of authority and headed for trouble." She was "handicapped because she came from a broken home" and had an overly strict mother (either too much or too little discipline were parental faults). Daisy had also inherited a tendency to "irresponsibility" from her father, who had deserted the family. She was choosing bad companions, had drifted away from Sunday School, had lost interest in school, and sought out pleasure in "joyriding, dance halls and movies." Her "natural craving for pretty clothes" was unfortunately translated into risqué "extreme dress and make-up" designed to garner boys' attention and signalling sexual availability. Her lifestyle just screamed endangerment to proper passive femininity and sexual purity. Luckily, after BSA intervention, her energy was redirected into wholesome channels: she assumed a "smarter" dress and she found employment as a mother's helper with a middle-class Big Sister who provided her with the role model of a "harmonious home."[44]

Over a decade later, at the end of the 1940s, the Hamilton BSA, which often employed similar narratives to describe its work in annual reports, public lectures, and pamphlets, told the story of two girls whose delinquency also reflected a lack of discipline and untamed femininity, the result of bad mothering. Two young girls, Joan (thirteen) and Eliza (nine), were caught stealing the milk money of people on their street. It was because "they had no money [of their own] to spend." When they were arraigned in court, the real problem soon manifested itself: a rude, "abusive, poorly dressed, dirty mother" who railed that "everyone was against her." She was so uncouth, continued the story, that she was told to leave the courtroom. A widow on mother's allowance, with five children, she expressed some interest in co-operating in order to keep her girls, who were put on probation, under the care of the BSA. First they were taught about grooming: brushing their teeth, washing and combing their hair, washing their underwear. Then they both joined the YWCA, learned how to knit, and the youngest, who was unacceptably "loud and boisterous," learned to be more subdued and polite. Just as the story seemed to be moving towards a hopeful denouement, a temporary setback occurred. The mother was seen "keeping company" with a man, even drinking beer with him. (Her rejoinder to the BSA that she "enjoyed the occasional glass of beer and saw no harm in this" was not taken as a positive sign of female independence.) Although it seemed the girls might again be lost to irresponsible parenting, the story took a final positive twist when the mother remarried. Her new husband was "steadily employed" and "took an interest in the girls," thus creating a "happy united family" for them. The reconstituted nuclear (and male-breadwinner) family, along with correctives for "bad parenting" and the transformation of girls who had been wild, unmannered, and unfeminine, provided a happy ending.

In both boy and girl narratives of delinquency, therefore, predominant themes – broken homes, single mothers, poor neighbourhoods, neglectful parents, bad housing, and low incomes – came up again and again. The narratives might allude to parental abuse and addiction, though often portraying these elements as the result of poor self-control, wilful indifference, and adult indulgence. The overall supposition that delinquency was bred in the slums remained strong. Since many offences under the JDA were status offences – that is, involving a child *in danger* of becoming criminal – this equation was an integral part of the very definition of youth crime and its informal regulation by the police. In the 1960s, when U.S. studies mapping delinquency by geographical neighbourhood were still popular, one Canadian study followed suit, looking at arrest and occurrence records by neighbourhood in a large industrial city. Not surprisingly, it concluded that the prime area producing delinquency was also characterized by "incomes below average, low education, poor housing." The study also pointed to one reason why occurrences were focused on this neighbourhood: the police *targeted it* as a potential source of crime. Moreover, social science and social work critiques of the "dysfunctional" neighbourhood or community producing delinquency did not emanate from or produce a radical critique of capitalist economic social relations. Instead, this writing veered towards what would later be termed a "culture of poverty" theory, which ultimately blamed distorted family, personal, and social relationships for the problems of the inner city. Not unlike current social science discourses decrying "welfare dependency,"[45] this writing suggested that one could reform ingrained behaviour or bad attitudes rather than transform impoverishment and oppressive social relations.

Most government reports also situated delinquents within lower-class contexts, though a second crucial ingredient of delinquency was inadequate or neglectful parenting. Why do we have young offenders in their later teens, who have already been failed by the juvenile courts? asked the 1938 royal commission on the penal system. Many were "reckless, adventurous or temperamentally unstable . . . taking up with bad companions, victims of the economic system, from economically straitened homes." Unemployed, without direction, these streetwise youth also lacked another crucial ingredient of law-abiding youth: "proper parental training."[46] The sanctity of the nuclear family, with caring mother, concerned authoritative father, and monogamous, moral parents, was seen as a crucial deterrent to youth corruption. In 1931 one Toronto PO reassured the public that the Depression was ushering in a new era of decency, as the "sex experimentation, unfaithfulness to wedding vows," and other indecencies of the Roaring Twenties had ended. Delinquency, he sighed, would now surely decline. He was wrong, of course, for future POs and judges continued to cite sexual and other immorality as a cause of delinquency. In the 1930s one of the issues that galvanized social workers involved in delinquency issues was the Orde legal decision, in which a maverick judge had the temerity to declare that simply living in the midst of adultery did not endanger a child's morals, thus making them liable to prosecution under the JDA (and other acts). Other judges, social workers, and the Canadian Welfare Council disagreed and pressed repeatedly for federal legislation to make adultery, and thus also common-law unions, de facto "immoral."

By the end of the 1950s and into the 1960s, at least a small change of heart had occurred. Not all courts saw common-law marriages as uniformly immoral or problematic. Even still, one study in the late 1960s found that "unmarried parents" and "family instability" were factors prompting harsher dispositions by judges for juveniles.[47] The issue of girls' sexual promiscuity had also not disappeared. Indeed, although delinquency was often spoken of as if it were gender-neutral, it was not. Delinquency was decidedly gendered when it came to both the definitions of wrongdoing and the antidotes prescribed for boys and girls.

Gendering Delinquency

A consistent concern with boys over this entire period was their propensity for petty theft and attraction to gangs. Boys were violating laws of private property, which indicated their lack of respect for authority and the social order. Fears of boy gangs were expressed in the early part of the century, took on more intensified form during the Depression, and became especially prominent in the 1940s and 1950s. Gangs were seen as breeding grounds for delinquency because they encouraged truancy, theft, violence, and in-your-face antagonism to the adult world. Boys' delinquency was often defined by its peer-related contours, and gangs were considered an integral part of marginalized, urban "boy culture." Indeed, one Toronto Big Brothers worker suggested in the Depression that a boy "without a gang was like a dog without a bone ... [gangs] teach a boy how to be a man."[48] By the post-World War II period, criminologists were exploring the anomie or the social strains that produced male delinquency. In the 1950s, for example, working-class male gangs – a frequent source of public fascination – were portrayed as a form of "status discontent," a logical reaction of boys to being shut out from the opportunities of middle-class society.[49] Even to this day, argues Anne Campbell, accounts of male delinquency stress the peer group, while accounts of female delinquents see the girls as "isolated and inept, pitiful figures trying to assuage their loneliness through brief, promiscuous liaisons with boys." Campbell's own research on girls in gangs challenged this dominant perception of girls as camp followers and "mindless nymphomaniacs."[50]

These differences point to an enduring theme in the expert literature on delinquency: inattention to gender and to females. The theorists and researchers often employed delinquency as a gender-neutral term, but in reality their discussions were predominantly shaped by questions of boys' wrongdoing and its impact on society. If girls were discussed at all, they might be pressed uncomfortably into these masculine moulds or dismissed as unimportant because their levels of offending and arrest were much smaller.[51] From 1920 to 1960 the social work journal *Canadian Welfare* published few articles dealing with female delinquents, but a considerable number exploring boys' delinquencies. Despite two full chapters on youth in the 1938 royal commission report, girls received barely a mention; in their extensive fact-finding junket to England the commissioners visited countless Borstals for boys, but not the girls' institution.[52] As late as the 1970s, Gloria Geller notes, a "classic" image of the delinquent still dominated within the Toronto Family Court: "He was a lower class male, from a broken home, headed by a mother ... lives in a slum, acts out aggressively, and is often an immigrant in rebellion against his parents."[53]

Although the family was often a blameworthy cause of delinquency for both boys and girls, family maladjustment took on gendered forms. Both delinquent boys and girls supposedly lacked discipline and caring, upstanding parents. But boys needed a firm, guiding hand to develop into honest workers and *social* citizens, while girls needed discipline, protection, and self-control to develop into *moral* citizens. During World War I, Big Brothers advertised their good works in a pamphlet declaring that some delinquent "lads" who were simply suffering from "energy plus" needed the "advice, friendship and encouragement" of a father figure: "Too many citizens of tomorrow are going wrong for the lack of friendly guidance of the father who is in France." It was the patriotic duty of respectable "gentlemen" to take these lads under their wing, to help them choose the path to "good citizenship" rather than that of "a criminal career."[54] Advertising the merits of socialized justice, one social work article approvingly relayed a juvenile judge's paternal lecture to a "fair haired, blue eyed" (read: redeemable) boy, whose training school sentence would transform him into a model "social individual" by helping him to develop "habits of industry and fair play."[55] In the 1950s the Training School Advisory Board was still echoing similar aims, claiming that training school produced boys who were "good citizens of democratic society, with respect for authority and law . . . clean, polite, aspiring to reach their educational limit."[56]

While girls too had to develop habits of work and industry, one judge, in his sentencing address to a girl sent to training school in the 1940s, couched the matter very differently: "This world needs good women now more than ever before and there is nothing in the world that grows into good women except good girls. . . . You can't go picking up strangers. You don't know what he might do to you."[57] The superintendent of a girls' training school agreed. Her girls needed "mental, moral, physical and vocational training," but they had to be "jolted out of their cynical ways, shown that to be considerate is not soft, to lie is not smart, while immorality leads to heartache and tragedy."[58]

Canadians relied heavily on influential U.S. studies of girl delinquents. Many of these studies started from the premise that girls' delinquency involved rejection of their gender roles relating to sexuality, domesticity, and motherhood; and often they presumed that girls' delinquencies reflected individual, psychological, or psychiatric maladjustment. W.I. Thomas's *Unadjusted Girl*, published in 1923, and influential for at least a decade, argued that female delinquency resulted when a girl was not taught the most important "moral code" about femininity and her "value" as a future wife and mother.[59] By the 1930s and 1940s, U.S. studies by Sheldon and Eleanor Glueck – a veritable machine of academic production on crime – were popular. The Gluecks' major investigation of young reform school women, using interviews and the girls' case files, defined female criminality in strongly sexual terms and concluded that many of these youthful criminals were the products of broken homes. This finding was hardly surprising, since many girls had been placed in the reformatory for running away from home.[60] The term "broken home" in delinquency literature repeated itself like a broken record, and it could assume different meanings according to who was using it. Some commentators saw the term's linkages to the emotional strain and economic impoverishment associated with single parenthood, widowhood, desertion, and divorce; others saw it as a synonym for parental inadequacy and the moral failure to construct the "normal" nuclear family.

As well as being the product of a broken home, girls' delinquency was defined by a wide variety of behaviours, from truancy to stealing to prostitution. But the most constant theme was girls' non-conforming sexuality. Girls' normality/abnormality was measured by transgressive sexual acts, ranging from mere "treating" (offering sex in exchange for dates, gifts) to illegitimate pregnancies to prostitution. Promiscuity absolutely absorbed the experts, sometimes vicariously so. During World War II, one author wrote, instability, transiency, and a "devil-may-care" attitude among the young were leading to female "sex hunger for adventure and sociability." While the writer admitted this alarming lust was largely a social and not a legal problem, the role of the juvenile court was precisely to nip girls' social transgressions in the bud.[61] Promiscuity was essentially a female, not a male problem. Although male sexuality was monitored for its "normalcy" (for example, adolescent pedophilia and exhibitionism were the subjects of surveillance), sexual encounters with girls were not a cause for intense alarm. In one social work report, for instance, boys' sexual escapades were chalked up to mere "immaturity and inadequate sex training." Girls' "sexual offences" were the product of more "mature [serious] delinquency" and "social maladjustment."[62]

One typical study, emanating from the influential Institute for Juvenile Research in Chicago, examined the psychological factors in female delinquency, using "scientific" measurements from questionnaires and interviews. Like recent self-report studies, this one drew on girls' experiences, expressed in their own words. Yet the girls' accounts were sometimes at odds with those of the investigator. The girls admitted to frequent stealing, but noted that this was not the central issue for the investigating authorities, who were more interested in their sex lives. Indeed, rather than defining delinquency through theft, the study leaned in the direction of sex. Delinquency, the author concluded, was not an "isolated incident, but a package of problems often reaching back to early childhood." First, "A broken home was often a contributing factor, with the family at a "low economic level." Even more important was a particular pattern: "early sex stimulation before adolescence," absence of familial discipline, and failure to offer "normal socially accepted personal habits and satisfactions [other than sex]," as well peer pressure encouraging overt sexual promiscuity.[63] All of these conditions led to the girls' downfall.

In the post-World War II period, and well into the 1960s, criminological experts offered remarkably similar assessments. In fact, as a "grab bag" simplistic Freudianism took popular root, character and family dysfunction became even more deeply embedded in the definition of female delinquency.[64] The experts defined normality according to an acceptance of heterosexual and familial maturity (sex within marriage/motherhood/passive femininity), representing exactly the patriarchal, middle-class standards used by psychologists to define the well-adjusted family. They described girls' rejection of these norms as fallout from an arrested ego, super-ego, or warped Electra complex. Girls' rebellions were thus defined by their thwarted emotional life and there seemed no end to the variety of psychic distortions that girls could fall victim to. In one collection by noted criminologists in the 1960s, authors argued variously that girls' delinquency was accentuated by "basic feminine needs to serve . . . be loved . . . and fear of rejection" or that the girls "failed in pre-adolescence to liberate themselves from their pre-Oedipal mother." Such deep-seated neurosis also made girls "harder to treat," for they were likely to be "seductive, impulsive, fickle, insincere, vengeful and capricious." Even girls' stealing was cast within this paradigm. While boys' vandalism and stealing suggested their "discharge of aggression" and search for "mastery of the world," girls' stealing was a "kleptomania" born of their mothers' emotional coldness.[65] One of the popular *bêtes noires* of psychology in the 1950s was the overbearing mother figure. Usually her crime was emasculating her sons, but given the tradition of mother-blaming in delinquency writing, this dominant mother not surprisingly also came to represent a cause of female delinquency. The increase in girl runaways, wrote one expert, was due to "maternal dominance" in the home, although other authors claimed that the teenage girl might be "warding off the unconscious threat of an incestuous relationship with her father."[66]

The interpretation of sexual abuse and its links to delinquency within these discourses were especially important. As Gleason notes, psychologists' advice repeatedly claimed that the absence of a father figure might thwart the development of normal adolescent sexual maturity.[67] Discussion of sexual abuse by parents, however, was almost completely absent in social work and psychological circles. If incest was discussed, it was often portrayed as more illusion than reality, or if experts accepted that

it happened, it represented human slippage into the realm of unconscious desire. It was not, as later feminists would argue, a violent expression of patriarchal power, causing concrete psychic trauma.[68] Incest as
fantasy, perhaps desired by the daughter, for example, characterizes Sidney Halleck's classic psychiatric text. "A common pattern," he wrote, is
"inadequate love from the mother, with the daughter turning to the
father" and the close relation "taking on a latent sexual quality." To
"avoid incest," she turns promiscuously to other boys.[69] Another theory
claimed a very normal "unconscious incest desire" might occur if the
frigid mother rejected her husband, or if the daughter was prematurely
pushed into a mothering role.[70]

In the main these experts were simply more likely to perceive girls,
like women, as potential psychiatric cases. If males were considered
within psychiatric models, they were analysed as respondents to the
external world, whereas women were "internal" creatures, less likely to
employ their own agency; more likely acted upon by others.[71] Indeed, a
study of the Toronto court found that girls were proportionally more
likely to be referred for psychiatric assessments than boys.[72] Even some
sympathetic female criminologists writing in the 1960s agreed that
delinquent girls saw themselves as "objects, not subjects" and that girls
internalized the society's image of their behaviour as pathological, in
contrast to boys' endorsement of their anti-social acts as normal. These
attitudes were neatly summed up in a major Canadian social work study
in the early 1960s: "Girls are more [emotionally] disturbed than male
offenders . . . female delinquency is rare in being atypical, and thus the
mental pathology that compels them to break law makes them hard to
treat. . . . Most girls were sexually promiscuous, most [due to] . . . emotionally depriving backgrounds . . . they have a lack of insight . . . some
masochism and impairment of self image."[73]

The literature on girls' sexuality, particularly after the 1920s, did not
endorse absolute abstinence from every vestige of romantic contact;
some experts endorsed a measure of physical contact during dating.[74]
But there was always a dangerous, uncontrolled, compulsive sexuality
that stood in opposition to acceptable healthy contact. Nymphomania, a
female disease of body and mind constructed by various medical discourses, lurked as the danger, first associated in the eugenic era with the
feeble-minded hypersexual and, later, in the Freudian era, attributed to
girls' "anxiety, a hunger for power, hostility, incestuous desires, latent
homosexuality, narcissism, rebellion, self-hatred, a sexually repressed
childhood, among other [causes]."[75]

These analyses of female delinquency, especially the Freudian-inspired ones of the post-World War II period, appeared on the surface to apply to girls from all backgrounds. Yet they still tied sexualized delinquency to class. Experts often saw the origins of delinquency in either environmental or neurotic factors, and it was presumed that the two were more likely to combine fatally in the working and underclasses. Noted psychiatrist Sidney Halleck's characterization of delinquent female teens as "hysterical and histrionic" and his claim that they rebelled with "exaggerated femininity and controlling passivity" appeared superficially to categorize by gender. Yet Halleck also admitted, "In practice the labelling of female delinquency is determined by class." Citing his own experience of treating middle-class college as well as "Training School" girls, he admitted they often committed similar crimes but college girls were seen as emotionally unstable and rebellious, needing therapy, and the training school girls as the product of inadequate families and needed discipline.[76] Moreover, middle-class girls, already the beneficiaries of "rewards for good behaviour," were more adept at knowing when to cut their losses and appear obedient.[77]

Similar assumptions about sex and class made their way into popular writing on delinquency in the mainstream press. A persistent theme in Canadian mass circulation magazines was journalists' reliance on, and respect for, the views of experts. Whatever their particular slant, many magazine pieces agreed that one solution to delinquency was more professionals and improved social, educational, and therapeutic services for children – a further endorsement of the experts. Some journalists resorted to generalized denunciations of youth character as "arrogant ... thinking the country owes them a job with high pay and little work," but in the main, writers stressed the need for social analysis of delinquency's causes, and "reform, not mere punishment." That this last quote came from the conservative *Financial Post* indicates the generalized acceptance of the expert view of delinquency as a treatable social illness.[78]

Journalistic renderings of delinquency were often alarmist in tone, warning with each decade that a new era of juvenile crime was nigh. There was some welcome debunking of these claims, and there were also some fierce debates, especially over the role of the media itself – movies, crime comics – in destroying morality and encouraging violence.[79] Yet, in general, a consensus existed on the origins and definitions of delinquency, which was usually equated primarily with teenage boys. "Slum conditions" and overcrowded houses with "bickering families" were the phrases repeatedly used by journalists to create a mental image of delinquency. Journalists often communicated the experts'

analytical stress on internal familial pathologies, especially bad mothering, and various external dangers, such as gangs, poverty, or material
temptations, causing delinquency.

During World War II, a female journalist warned her readers that
absent soldier fathers and working mothers left girls out on the streets
or in "hamburger joints" looking for "a pick up," a sure danger signal.
Delinquency, she wrote, was partly a youthful rebellion against the
monotony of working-class labour and home responsibilities. But it was
also stimulated by the rapid escalation of parental "immorality, desertion, cruelty," which were now "standard," she scolded, making a
sweeping indictment of Canadian parenting. Her analysis could have
been taken directly from wartime speeches by social workers at the
Canadian Welfare Council.[80] The press used mothers who abandoned
their children to carouse with new beaus to represent the worst symbols
of parental disregard, yet even honest working mothers came in for criticism for ignoring their children.[81]

Certainly, some journalists tried to relay the experts' multicausal
analyses in their popular writing. Delinquency, said one *Saturday Night*
article, was an integral part of larger social problems caused by the inter-
play of "psychological stresses, economic inequalities, lack of recreation." Yet the writer's conclusion could have been extracted from the
1891 Ontario inquiry into correctional institutions: "99% of all juvenile
crime could be traced to the home."[82] A consensus also existed on what
delinquency consisted of for boys and girls. A range of activity, from
theft to disorderliness to violence, was equated with youth criminality,
and not surprisingly journalists were preoccupied with these quintessentially "male" misdeeds. Again, if girls were discussed, sex was usually
somewhere in the picture. An article on delinquency in the Maritime
provinces written in the 1950s, for instance, equated girls' delinquency
with sexual abandon, illegitimate pregnancies, and "parental indifference to teen morality."[83] Girl gangs were occasionally a public concern,
but females were more often seen as sexually available molls, not as
ringleaders. One article describing a typical female delinquent in the
inner streets of Winnipeg summed up many of the popular prejudices
ranging from mother-blaming to fast girls. "Kay," the journalist wrote of
her subject, is "a gang groupie with a drunken mother."[84]

As the 1960s dawned, the press was exploring new ideas on delinquency prevention, but again the focus was primarily on boys. In 1964 a
Maclean's journalist sang the praises of a "Harvard man" who was dedi-
cating his life to work among the delinquent "have-nots" of Toronto's
rough Queen Street area. A new version of the settlement-house worker,

this college grad's attempts to "salvage" these troubled boys took him into the "pool rooms and sleazy restaurants" of their gang haunts and out on endless car trips with the boys in order to earn their trust. Girls were tangential to this mission, mentioned only as potential sex partners or eventual wives of the boys. Underneath the picture of Harvard Jim and his rough followers was a sidebar article on the worrisome "have-delinquents" – those middle-class lawbreakers who from time to time worried parents and authorities. This journalist, however, conceded quickly that the court more often "smiles down on" these "haves," refusing to send them to reform school. "It's a bitter thing to realize," he quotes a court worker as saying, "but there is still one law for the poor and another for the rich."[85]

The Roots of "Girl Trouble"

In my generalizations about these decades of history, then, recurring themes emerge in the definitions of delinquency over time. Both boys and girls in conflict with the law were often assumed to come predominantly from working-class or underclass backgrounds, with a constellation of factors – broken homes, parental immorality, violence, bad neighbourhood – encouraging their rejection of authority. A dual dynamic of environmental factors and individual or neurotic pathologies were the dominating themes in delinquency studies, though the final blame was often laid at the doorstep of the inadequate, immoral, or neglectful family. Pessimism, however, was not the order of the day. The various experts often articulated a positivist, optimistic view that delinquency might be cured through social engineering and individual reformation. As expressed through the writing and casework of more affluent middle-class professionals, however, these positive prognoses did not identify the need to alter fundamentally flawed economic and social structures as much as they offered their guidance in overcoming personal, familial, and cultural limitations.[86]

Family and individual pathology might be identified in both boys and girls, but the former was determining for girls, less so for boys. Definitions of girls' deviance put more emphasis on their violation of expected sexual and familial roles, with girls' sexual rebellion indicating more internalized, self-destructive behaviour. The notion that "the predominant expression of [female] delinquency in our society is promiscuous sexual activity"[87] thus remained a recurring theme for decades. The powerful knowledge created by these professions, circulated through the courts, training schools, educational institutions, and government, and publicized in the media, designated promiscuity as the key "sign" of girls' deviation and future criminality. For boys, the equivalent sign was theft and gang membership. Girls, as Geller concludes about the 1960s and 1970s, were labelled immoral; boys were "frustrated and aggressive."[88] In one sense this made girls a more urgent problem, because virginity could not be recouped in the same way that boys could return a stolen item. "Even the unenlightened," wrote a training school superintendent in the 1950s, "know that girls are committed to training school for 'boy trouble' whereas boys are usually committed for theft, a more acceptable offence."[89] The characterization of the delinquent girl as the "lonely nymphomaniac" thus has deep roots in this era, and arguably remains with us today.

Also in the past, as today, the dominant images of feminine sexuality were not simply the provenance of expert discourse; they were also embedded in language and constituted in everyday experience, influencing the way in which families and peers defined and judged other girls. As a contemporary researcher of British working-class teens argues, the "policing of sexual reputation" starts in adolescence; through everything from images to gossip, insults to violence, girls are made painfully aware of the penalties of being designated a "slag" (the promiscuous) versus the protective payoff of conforming to the image of marriageable respectability.[90] Families participated in policing their daughters' reputations through the courts precisely because this patriarchal image of female sexuality operated so powerfully at both a social and individual level.

Internationally, feminist studies in the 1970s and 1980s broke new ground by unmasking the sexualization of female delinquency in these earlier discourses and revealing the resulting biases in court dispositions.[91] One more recent critic has countered that these second-wave feminist criminologists "essentialized" females in their analysis, reducing them to their sexuality and ignoring other factors such as "race and the welfare system" in their analysis.[92] However, we need not make a choice between race, class, and gender. It is undeniable that the experts defined girls' criminality by sexual non-conformity, but these definitions were also inextricably linked to class differences and racial prejudice. Although justified as scientific and rational, these definitions were also profoundly ideological and moral. And they may have been very well intended, for many professionals believed that a girl could be ruined by promiscuity, sexually transmitted diseases, and street life – still all familiar concerns today. The problem the experts encountered, though, was that efforts to protect girls from delinquency could neither transform the material and social conditions of teenage alienation nor alter the apparent determination of some girls to reject the advice of their elders.

Three

"An Ounce of Prevention": Managing Girls' Misdemeanours

What do children really need? Love, friends, play, someone who understands their fears and dreams, their troubles, the magic of birthday candles and the warmth of hot cereal. . . . Guidance and understanding has helped teen age girls take their place in the community as worthwhile citizens – after all, these girls are the mothers of tomorrow.[1]

With these words, spoken sometime in the 1940s, the executive director of the Hamilton Big Sisters offered a compassionate view of how young girls, situated precariously on the precipice of female adulthood, and possibly tempted into delinquency, might be directed by thoughtful mentors towards a law-abiding, productive future. She invoked the rhetoric of citizenship, though not surprisingly it had a gendered quality: girls were to be the *moral mothers* of tomorrow. Although the juvenile courts often maintained that they were on the front lines of delinquency prevention, a host of other voluntary, reform, and religious groups also participated in efforts aimed at either discouraging delinquency or rehabilitating girls and young women who had experienced initial brushes with the law, police, or truant officer.

Exploring delinquency prevention provides a vantage point or median between the expert definitions of delinquency and girls' actual encounters with the law. It allows us not only to further analyse the social construction of delinquency, but also to see how class and gender anxieties were lived out in concrete encounters between young women, often from disadvantaged backgrounds, and more affluent, educated reformers attempting to save them from a life of crime. These encounters were not an entirely new venture, for a previous generation of middle-class reformers had introduced similar rehabilitation projects, sometimes invoking the same class tensions; indeed, some former suffragists were the founders of Big Sisters Associations. But in the period after World War I and the triumph of suffrage, middle-class women, newly integrated into the body politic and more immersed in professional social work, became more deeply involved with girls in conflict with the law. In the process they developed more complex, sometimes problematic attachments to the state and the criminal justice system. Almost always respectful of juvenile courts and judges, they rarely criticized the modus operandi of the criminal justice system. The work of delinquency prevention, then, remained trapped within the definitions of the experts and beholden to the ideological suppositions of the juvenile courts and Juvenile Delinquents Act, despite the best intentions of many reformers and professional social workers and their professed sympathies for females in conflict with the law.

Probation was one link that formally joined the efforts of reformers and the courts. In the early years of the juvenile courts, many probationers were monitored and counselled by organizations like Big Sisters, which relied on volunteers, as well as paid social workers, to oversee young girls. Moreover, in Ontario, Big Sisters were sometimes called in to help seventeen- and eighteen-year-olds, who were in the difficult situation of being outside the provincial definition of the JDA and liable to be sentenced to adult reformatories even though they were still teenagers. Even after professionals lodged within the courts had taken over probation – often by the 1950s and 1960s – groups like Big Sisters continued to provide services to disadvantaged or troubled teens. Until at least the 1950s, this work was officially labelled "delinquency prevention," though in later years both the language and substance of BSA work changed as the organization redirected its efforts to causes such as group homes and children's mental health.

Theories of the Child

Through the twentieth century the various definitions of delinquency were connected to broader, evolving discussions on the nature of childhood. These ideas, embodied in institutions and social practices, had an impact on the strategies designed to prevent delinquency. Over the first part of the century, childhood increasingly became a site *needing* expert guidance, intervention, and classification. As Cynthia Commachio shows, child welfare moved from a "voluntary, female-oriented reform sphere" to become "the object of more male-dominated professional and state-sponsored campaigns."[2] Although a male-dominated medical profession was extremely influential in defining child health, a new cadre of educated women was filling the ranks of social work practice relating to children. These women usually shared similar class backgrounds with the voluntary reformers involved in organizations like Big

Sisters, but they also believed quite fervently in utilizing their own trained, professional methods of dealing with social problems.[3]

These medical and social work professionals undertook various campaigns to improve family life; often, the public, interventionist, and state-monitored programs that resulted were intended to show women how to become more informed, efficient mothers.[4] With the growth of a mental-hygiene movement geared towards children's mental and emotional health – by the 1950s renamed as "child psychology" – the programs also increasingly classified and treated children according to intelligence, disability, and psychological needs. Over these decades medicine and the social sciences increasingly monitored childhood as a "psycho-biological problem," first through eugenics, later through psychology and psychiatry.[5] Childhood emotional and mental maladjustments of various kinds proliferated under the gaze of these professionals, though the practitioners would have characterized their work as scientific identification and treatment.

Adolescence also became the focus for more expert concern. Although many histories assume that professional theories on the difficult, rebellious adolescent (summed up in a whole new psychological category, "adolescent behaviour disorder") mushroomed with the post-World War II baby boom, such theories had been incubating for decades. During the 1920s child-guidance clinics sprang up all over the United States. The clinics hired hundreds of social workers, psychiatrists, and psychologists, who not only worked with delinquents but also counselled "normal" teens on how to stay that way and avoid psychological maladjustment. North American writing on the trials and tribulations of adolescence multiplied. When authors tackled issues of sex, many of them began to condone heterosexual dating, dancing, and socializing, even allowing a measure of intimacy – an endorsement that may have grown in part out of increasing fears of sexual intimacy between young women. Some of the "new woman" professionals of the post-suffrage era touted the importance of girls' autonomy, even warning against overbearing parental repression – though this liberal message was not applied so tolerantly to the working-class, immigrant girls who found themselves before the courts. By the 1940s fashionable texts such as Caroline Zachary's *Emotion and Conduct in Adolescence* celebrated girls' interest in beauty, appearance, and the opposite sex, because properly nurtured that interest would evolve into stable, monogamous, heterosexual marriages. Heterosexual romance, dating, and kissing were thus "good." Premarital intercourse and sexually assertive girls remained "bad," the line at which normal ended and delinquency began.[6]

These theories of healthy childhood and adolescence, along with the notion that delinquents were made, not born, and usually within dysfunctional families, became important ingredients of voluntary and state efforts to prevent delinquency. As the Big Sisters Association never tired of reminding the public, "An ounce of prevention is worth a pound of cure." Nora Lea, a social worker and Canadian Welfare Council leader, lectured a public audience: "We need to attack the problem [of delinquency] where it begins. A story is told of an insane asylum where patients are put in a room with the tap on, and water running. They are told to mop up the water, and those who first turn off the tap, are judged sane. Would our taxpayers pass this test?"[7]

Failing Lea's mop test, society would continue to produce delinquents. The results, Big Sisters warned, offering the example of a former "Little Sister" now in the reformatory, were tragic: "Some things broken or mutilated can simply not be fixed."[8]

An Ounce of Prevention: "Maternal Justice" in Action

The work of one urban reform organization, the Hamilton Big Sisters Association (HBSA), highlights the attempts to prevent girls' conflicts with the law. From the organization's inception in 1919 to the late 1950s, its program included delinquency prevention. Indeed, its analysis, goals, and strategies, and those as well of the Toronto Big Sisters Association (TBSA), reveal how definitions of delinquency were put into practice by reformers who combined charity, reform, and advocacy in their attempts to create moral female citizens.[9]

Drawing on U.S. models, the Toronto Big Sisters was founded in 1912 on the urging of a juvenile court judge and a middle-class women's reform organization, the Local Council of Women. As well as having some suffragist connections, many early supporters were wives of Toronto's business and philanthropic elite. Their example inspired the founding of the Hamilton Big Sisters Association seven years later, also by a group of upper and middle-class women with well-placed spouses and fathers. The thinking of these groups reflected the mainstream, middle-class women's reform movement of the period: the women stressed the importance of providing protective, preventive, and uplifting assistance to less fortunate girls, optimistically avowing that good citizenship could be inculcated and internalized, especially in the young.

The Big Sisters founders were inspired by a sense of social responsibility, emanating in part from their privileged class position but also based on their moral, maternal sensibilities as *women*. As the Hamilton

Big Sisters explained in 1924: "We have the great privilege to have responsibility from which we cannot escape. Women set the social standards in the world, on the enlightenment and high ideals of women, the moral standards of the nation depend. . . . We are trying to change an influence for evil into one for good, helping a girl to see she counts for much in the big scheme of things."[10] Their desire to help girls rise above unfortunate circumstances originated from an idealized image of the innocence of childhood, as well as from an environmentalist, behaviourist conception of female youth as malleable and salvageable. Undoubtedly, saving young, presumably compliant girls from delinquency was more appealing than working with "hardened" women criminals, a task that interested few reformers of the time. Big Sisters thus sustained and enhanced an earlier tradition of "maternal justice" – that is, the idea that women could provide more humane, caring support, and thus rehabilitative hope, to girls and women in trouble with the law.[11] Though stronger in the United States, this reform tradition had also encouraged Canadian feminists' support for the first juvenile courts, which they thought would deliver firm familial guidance rather than unproductive punishment for children.

Like many reform organizations, Big Sisters began with considerable contact between its volunteers and clients, but over time the Association ceded much of this work to trained social workers who, in turn, drew on the knowledge of the "psyche" professionals – psychiatrists, psychologists, doctors – as well as on the advice of teachers and principals. Alongside professionalization, there existed for many years a volunteer program in which better-off women, the Big Sisters, mentored their assigned Little Sisters. Although complete professionalization had become the norm in some Big Sisters Associations by the post-World War II period, a matching program of trained volunteers aiding Little Sisters persisted in other BSAS – as indeed it did in Hamilton. In some senses Big Sisters combined the earlier traditions of middle-class women's activism identified by historians as "traditional or sentimental" maternalism – the provision of philanthropic aid to society's disadvantaged children – with a more "pragmatic, progressive maternalism" – promoting the ideas of professional women trained as social workers, women who were often advocates of social change.[12]

A pamphlet prepared for a number of Big Sisters Associations in the 1920s summed up the preventive possibilities of volunteers acting as social mothers by mentoring disadvantaged girls. It stressed a child-centred approach, designed to build a girl's values and self-esteem, and also urged family-oriented casework, reflecting a belief that moderating the

DEFEND OUR CHILDREN!

Humanizing the Courts (Source: *Women's Century*, July 1919)

girl's immediate living environment, and providing her with a good example, might prevent her contact with crime:

> Don't patronize; call on a girl at her home; get acquainted with the mother and father (show you can help); see what can be done to

improve home conditions (which are usually the problem); get her into school or work (arouse her ambition); find out where she spends her evenings (provide better options); do not give money except in extreme cases; be interested in her interests (give her good books, take her to a clean play or concert); invite her to your home and make her feel welcome (this may be a new revelation of 'home' to her); if you are away from town, keep in touch; keep your promises; remember her birthday; be patient and sympathetic; report on her progress to the BSA.[13]

While a dominant theme in all BSA literature was a belief in the scientific advice offered by psyche and social work professionals, the work also initially had a moral, religious impetus. Although the HBSA described itself as non-denominational, some Big Sisters were middle-class Protestant churchgoers who drew on their contacts in local churches to build their membership. Following in the footsteps of earlier social gospellers who tried to apply Christian ideals to social reform, they pointed to the need for girls to imbibe "moral lessons, religion, respect for the law and parents." In the interwar period the importance of religion was also indicated by religious separatism: Catholic and Protestant women declined to unite their services. They worked separately, though co-operatively, dividing up the girls to be looked after according to religious heritage. Some BSAs also sought out Jewish women who could act as mentors for Jewish girls, and the Toronto group even declared it had "colored" Big Sisters who worked with "colored" girls, a form of polite segregation that was altered by the 1940s. However, even if some BSA supporters lamented the lack of religious devotion in youth and lauded church attendance, the Big Sisters never insisted on churchgoing as a prerequisite for their help, or considered it the only means of saving girls from delinquency – and certainly not so in the post-World War II period. Moral lessons, they believed, could be imbibed through other means.

The moral lessons imparted by "maternal" care and kindness can, of course, also be depicted as a form of regulation. Although portrayed as innate, natural, or "common sense" sensibilities, the maternalism of prison reformers, according to Kelly Hannah-Moffat, is better characterized using Foucault's notion of "pastoral power." The "pastoral" care, kindly advice, and attention to emotional needs offered by Big Sisters to the Little Sisters was a form of individualized "salvation" creating a "shepherd-like" relationship, though the practice simultaneously offered the Big Sisters salvation for their virtuous devotion to the lost and wayward girls. The ideology of motherhood "entailed the right to care for others," but the care offered, influenced in part by expert opinion, was also a subtle form of power or discipline.[14] In a study of the "maternal rule" of female probation workers in the Montreal Juvenile Court, Tamara Myers captures the complex nature of this maternalism. Though intended to provide feminine understanding and protection to delinquent girls, the maternal advice that probation officers offered was profoundly shaped and limited by the "social distance of class and age" between the client and the girl being helped. Indeed, one of the ironies of the maternalist logic was that it led to judgmental blame being assigned to the inadequate mothers who created girl delinquents, set in contrast to the superior mothering of the more educated, affluent reformers like the Big Sisters.[15]

In the 1920s, when Hamilton Big Sisters first started visiting the juvenile court to act as counsellors for girls appearing there, the volunteer members did admit to being overwhelmed by the procedures and responsibilities involved. As officers of the court, they also had to confront some girls who deeply resented their charity or tried to manipulate their do-good naiveté, claiming, for instance, that the Big Sisters did not understand their probation terms – though they, of course, did. Nor were all probation cases successful. Yet this contact at least usefully pressed the affluent Big Sisters into compelling contact with the material impoverishment and emotional traumas faced by young working-class girls, a contact increasingly lost with professionalization. Thus, the very early years saw the Hamilton organization involved in a wide range of teenage difficulties, from unwed motherhood to runaways to those needing money for shoes and dental work. Aided after 1923 by one social worker (later more staff), these women found themselves visiting the court, searching for baby clothes and domestic positions for an unwed mother, taking children to hospitals, and locating a boarding house for a runaway abused by her father. Another eight-year-old, who they described, oddly, as an "amorphrodite," was sent to the institution for the feeble-minded, while a teen was offered emotional support through the court case in which her father was suing a man for her seduction.[16]

By the 1930s the HBSA work focused almost entirely on aid to deprived girls and on curing teenage behavioural problems. Unwed mothers, declared one staff member, "should not be our concern," nor "should relief issues or finding jobs for the many girls who wanted employment."[17] Even though juvenile court visits and probation work remained part of its mandate (until the court assumed all probation work in 1959) the HBSA repeatedly and publicly stressed that those functions were a small part of its mandate, representing as little as 8 per cent, though sometimes as much as 15 per cent, of its cases. The stigma attached to those already in contact with the courts was considerable. "We don't want anyone to think that because a girl is a little sister, she has been in Police Court," they fussed. We may have "started with girls in Court but our work is extended to all kinds of unfortunates."[18] The HBSA also noted that employers were hesitant to hire its Little Sisters, probably because of the lingering negative association, and even parents asking for help sometimes echoed an abhorrence of court contact. One "wilful and impatient" seventeen-year-old who ran away in 1920 to Buffalo, and could not keep a job when she was brought back, ended up in a boarding house with a landlord who the HBSA deemed was of questionable character. The family, however, did not want the "shame" and publicity of a court case needed to send her to the reformatory. When she disappeared once again, the HBSA could only hope that she would "listen to reason" when they found her.[19]

By the 1930s and 1940s the organization was trying to concentrate on delinquency prevention, though it also admitted that this effort might mean seeing "girls in the early stages of delinquency before a Court appearance." An informal agreement worked out with Eaton's and Woolworth's, for example, meant that some girl shoplifters were referred directly to Big Sisters rather than the courts in the hope that counselling would prevent a second theft. In any year in which the referrals from court were low, the HBSA trumpeted this as a sign of its own success in preventing girls' conflicts with the law. By World War II and after, the Association was increasingly positioning itself as a counselling agency for troubled teens, which on the surface would appear to be a somewhat "classless" mandate. As much as half of all referrals, the organization said in 1941, came from parents, which it took to be a sign of its good reputation, for "wise parents bring a child showing problems to us."[20] Good parents were thus defined by both professionals and volunteers as those who understood the value of expert advice, for the "earlier we reach [girls] we can straighten out their truancy, late hours, poor companions, and general behaviour problems."[21]

Despite the emphasis on the generalized, classless traumas of adolescence, much HBSA work focused on less economically advantaged girls and their families. In the early years, for instance, the agency supplied Christmas baskets (a traditional charity) to families, and newspaper headlines praised the affluent women's work with "The Unfortunates." Like the Toronto BSA, Hamilton's group had various "circles" of women within it, with their own nicknames and specific mandates, often geared towards charitable fundraising. Some circles focused on traditional bridge games and bazaars (like the Hamilton one named after Juvenile Court Judge Henry Burbidge). Others sewed camp clothes for the girls, set up a lending library, or raised money for scholarships or to send poorer girls to camp. A circle of "Junior Big Sisters," sometimes college or high-school girls, occasionally former Little Sisters, set up recreational clubs for the girls or held chaperoned dances in the Blue Triangle Club in the east-end (working-class) YWCA.

The distance between the Big and Little Sisters was most clear in the interwar years, when young girls sometimes worked as domestics in the volunteers' homes (as well as being "treated" to a visit there on special occasions). But the distance never did entirely disappear. It was visually apparent in the newspaper photos of the 1930s to 1950s, when splendidly hatted women held sumptuous, elegant garden parties (later fashion shows) to support their work for far more modestly dressed little girls pictured at camp and in Big Sister clubs. Moreover, a substantial number of BSA referrals came from other social agencies, such as the welfare office, mother's allowance board, mental hygiene clinic, and principals and truant officers in the school system. In the early 1930s at least 50 per cent of Toronto's Little Sisters came from families on relief, and into the 1940s at least one-third of the Hamilton girls were sent to the BSA by welfare and social agencies, as well as by teachers and principals whose concerns were not inattentive to problems of economic disadvantage as exemplified by a girl's demeanour, clothing, and health.

Delinquency prevention work thus joined traditional philanthropy with reform work aimed at changing the lives of girls. While philanthropy did not presume a need to change the social system, Big Sisters did venture into social advocacy: it called for more economic, social, and housing aid for the disadvantaged, and it indicated that the educational opportunities it was providing should instead be automatically provided to girls by the state. This shifting mixture of charity and reform, philanthropy and advocacy, was accomplished by the distinctive mixture of HBSA funding and personnel that consisted of volunteers, aided by professionals, supported by both donations and state aid.

In its public and promotional literature, the HBSA often separated out distinct aspects of its work, unintentionally replicating a good girl/bad girl dichotomy. Its organization, explained one HBSA staff member in the 1930s, consisted of three things: aiding "bright, ambitious girls with scholarships"; dealing with the pre-delinquent, whose behavioural problems were often the product of broken homes, poor social conditions, drunkenness, and immorality; and, last, "dealing with delinquents from the Courts."[22] The agency did not see the first group of girls as maladjusted, just deprived. In Hamilton (unlike Toronto) a separate "crippled children's committee" existed from 1923 on, raising money for braces, shoes, operations, and other forms of care for disabled girls, and Big Sisters volunteers used their cars to drive these girls to Toronto for treatment. Although the pre-delinquent girls' names were eventually removed from the minutes (indicating knowledge that they would be stigmatized by their designation under BSA care), "crippled girls" – seen as disabled, but virtuous – continued to be cited by name, and their letters of grateful thanks were often quoted as evidence of BSA good works.

Likewise, scholarship work – undertaken in Toronto and other BSAs as well – was a way of supporting virtuous, intelligent girls who could not afford the books and clothes for high school, or the fees and carfare for business college. As the scholarship reports from Hamilton and Toronto indicate, this aid was deeply valued by parents and daughters who often came from working-class, mother-led families for whom high-school education was far too costly. Thanks were often profuse, and some women who moved into white-collar jobs sent cheques back to the BSAs to support other young girls coming after them.

But the scholarship work was not totally alien from delinquency prevention, even in the minds of the BSA women. With these new opportunities, they believed, girls were more likely to be economically independent or able to aid their families. Employed and respectable, they would be less likely to succumb to the temptations of loose living and the streets. Moreover, a subtle surveillance over scholarship girls kept them on the straight and narrow; girls who were unfeminine, rude, lazy, and ungrateful were cut off their scholarships. During the 1920s the Toronto BSA listed most scholarship recipients as success stories, but a certain "Irene" proved the exception. The TBSA's initial assessment of Irene was positive. Despite a "hard life with her mother with whom she did not get along," she was "nicely mannered and quite refined." She had a solid, feminine ambition to be a nurse. Irene, granted a scholarship while she boarded with an aunt, soon turned the tables and became "saucy, demanded good clothes, stayed out late, and did not do well at school, failing two subjects." Despite her plea for continued support so that she could try Business College, the Association cut her off.[23]

According to the HBSA, delinquency prevention meant linking concerns ranging from charity to broader social reform. After all, the "breeding ground for delinquency," its members often explained, was "bad housing, overcrowded living and economic insecurity."[24] Even if the organization sometimes distinguished between those needing

material aid (everything from clothes to cavity-filling) and those with behavioural problems, the two aspects could well be intertwined, as the
organization itself admitted. As the HBSA's listing of its problem cases
one year during the 1940s indicated:

> Lois, 13, truant, referred by Juvenile Court. Most discontented, a
> pretty girl who simply wants ballet lessons. Economic situation
> poor. . . . Lillian, ran away to New York City. Parents separated, father
> no interest in her. Mother works long hours in a factory. . . . Just
> wants to have an office job and nice figure. . . . Rita, her sister called
> saying she swears. She wants the BSA to make her behave. Does stay
> out late, but the real problem is that she can't keep a job.[25]

Because the HBSA emphasized that neglectful or inadequate families
were a major cause of delinquency, the material and psychological
aspects of cases were also connected in their analysis of how to aid girls.
In one case in the 1950s, for instance, Mary Jane, just under sixteen,
was caught stealing a blouse from her employer. The eldest of seven
children in a "working man's family," she could not both buy the things
she wanted and provide financial aid for her family on her meagre
wages. Both wage work and helping out at home were "too big a load
for her young shoulders," said the HBSA. To prevent more law-breaking
they found her a "more interesting job," sent some of her younger siblings to camp to relieve her mother's domestic burden, and counselled
the parents on their need to offer Mary Jane more emotional support.
Part of the reason for her stealing, they surmised, was that she was not
"cherished enough" at home.[26]

Another more crudely materialist interpretation, of course, is that
Mary Jane and her father just didn't make enough money. Ultimately,
the Sisters would never have simply embraced this prognosis, as it would
have been anathema both to their class position and to the dominant
ideology of child-saving that they embraced. Even in the midst of the
massive economic dislocation of the Great Depression, individual character, as much as poverty, was perceived to be in need of repair. Despite
the HBSA's own laments about the economic strains suffered by local
families in the Depression, its members argued that such "extreme
poverty brought with it either resignation or communistic view, both
damaging to future citizens." Poverty invariably "lowers standards and
our girls more than ever are in need of character building assistance."[27]
Yet when employment picked up during World War II, with Hamilton
becoming prosperous, they now countered that the "good financial situation is not a magic wand to cure teen problems." Presaging what would

become a refrain in the 1950s, they claimed that shift work and a lack of parental supervision, higher wages for irresponsible children, and the consumerist desire of children to spend like their parents were all dangerous incentives to delinquency. Again, character-building was in order.[28]

Certainly, some of the cases that the HBSA dealt with, such as sexual or physical abuse, clearly defied simple economic solutions. And to its credit the organization recognized that in cases in which families were partially employed or underemployed, or in which single mothers struggled to make ends meet, the girls' problems might be material as much as emotional. Indeed, the HBSA repeatedly called for the extra "gay bits" for a girl's life, something that would go "beyond the basic necessities," noting that nice clothes could completely alter an impoverished teen's outlook on life, her desire to go to school, and have a social life, not to mention that job searches were easier when "you didn't look like a ragamuffin."[29]

It is revealing too that many girls and their families came to the Big Sisters looking for concrete financial aid. In the 1940s one report baldly stated that most girls came to the office looking for "employment and swimming."[30] Big Sisters did try to find jobs for its own clients, while it offered free swimming lessons through a connection to the YWCA. Parents too might use the HBSA to deal with temporary family crises. A board member in the late 1950s told a long story (as part of a criticism of a staff member) about a woman who kept sending her two daughters back to the organization simply for the allowance it offered and any second-hand clothing her girls might obtain. Indeed, she often demanded better clothing than the agency was offering. The board member criticized the mother's supposedly demanding, mercenary motives, indicating that the parent clearly wanted to avoid the counselling that accompanied the cash (and was, perhaps, not grateful enough for the philanthropy). Bribing children into therapy, warned the critical board member, was bad social worker practice.[31] Perhaps so, but some families clearly saw their problems as material and eschewed psychological explanations and counselling. In the BSA's early years, admits the Toronto BSA's historian, some families resented the patronage or unconsciously condescending manner of the volunteers, and the girls themselves did not always benefit from a quick Christmas invite to the stately homes of the leading Sisters, which only underlined their own cramped living quarters and difficult lives.[32]

Drawing on this two-sided strategy of combining individual casework with social reform, the HBSA often focused on two major solutions to troubled teenage-hood: stabilizing the family and introducing com-munity-based recreation. The heart of preventive work concentrated on redressing the social and psychological problems of the girl and her fam-ily; indeed, the family was often the bad environment contributing to potential delinquency. Sometimes, noted the Hamilton executive direc-tor, the family is at fault, sometimes the girl, but "often it is the family." The citing of "defective home conditions" was the preamble to many Big Sister and Big Brother expositions on the need for their work. The primary definitions of such frictions included parental quarrelling, poverty, broken homes (including desertion, divorce, widowhood), "no home life" (presumably meaning no emotional or intellectual attention for the child), low moral standards, poverty, and too much discipline or inadequate discipline (parents had to walk a fine line here).

Although the agency often reassured the public that its first line of defence was to keep the family intact, its practitioners also quietly admitted that some girls simply needed their independence, even before the legal age of majority. From the 1920s on, the HBSA tried to have a rented safe room – a precursor to today's shelters for battered women – in reserve for teens forced to flee their homes. Sometimes the girl stayed for a night, or a week, and once for a whole summer; most were escap-ing alcoholic or violent parents. In an early Big Sisters pamphlet issued in the United States, though used in Canada, the author also bravely noted incest and violence as causes of girls' unhappiness and attempts to escape the home. Indeed, just after it was founded, the Toronto BSA tried to protest the lax treatment that judges sometimes offered men who "violated" their daughters, a crime that the women clearly found odi-ous.[33] A later annual report from the same organization during World War II repeated widespread anxieties that fathers' absences at the front would lead to broken family syndrome, or laxity in discipline, but it added that some homes beset by male violence were "much happier since the fathers' enlistment." Citing one such example, the Big Sister concluded cryptically, "Here's hoping he may [continue to] do his duty for his country."[34] Although the agency documents did not often cite physical and sexual abuse, such violence was clearly one of the problems that occasioned girls' contact with the agency.

As well as counselling the girl, the HBSA often tried to supervise the parents, though it advertised its efforts as "mediation" to allay family frictions over curfews, money issues, work, or school commitments. In such mediation, the agency workers and volunteers did not, in every instance, focus their sights on the parents' failure to understand adoles-cent needs. The fault might also lie with the girl: her choice of bad companions, her emotional instability, suggestibility, and, of course, wilfulness. A stubborn desire for hedonistic good times was always a major concern, particularly if girls lived in poorer areas, such as Hamilton's North End, which supposedly bred crime and gangs. At the end of World War II, the Toronto BSA executive director also lamented the "non-conformist" girls and boys who "hang about street corners, cheap grills and beverage rooms in order to satisfy their need for excitement." (She was also an ardent critic of parents who drank.)[35] In an amusing confession, some of the affluent Big Sister volunteers told how they went slumming one night to secretly investigate these questionable teenage hangouts, to witness the very birthplace of delinquency. They confessed that they found only snuggling teens, kissing and sipping soft drinks, hardly a vision of crime and sin.[36]

Along with immoral leisure, other signs – truancy, defiant attitudes, and improper dress and demeanour – indicated that a girl required counselling. The BSA's ongoing probation work, as well as its monitoring of pre-delinquent girls, encompassed the subtle encouragement, and sometimes more coercive promotion, of what it deemed normal gender roles. After all, the narratives of reformed Little Sisters included pictures of their altered cleanliness, neatness, and quiet, subdued, modest femininity and dress – signs they had been saved from delinquency. In one early BSA publication from the United States, the author used the example of a girl at risk who was delinquent and emotionally unstable: she was "very masculine, mentally and physically." It could be sexual "introversion" (indicating lesbianism) or "extroversion" (an aggressively sexual girl), but either way it spelled signs of danger.[37]

The sexual double standard and the class-based image of subdued femininity at the heart of these norms were rarely questioned. In the early 1920s the HBSA noted that its work was not the same as that of Big Brothers because of the sexual double standard and the emphasis on girls' virtue: "We are different from Big Brothers, because you cannot exploit a girl without the danger of a stigma. . . . The boy or man who is reclaimed is a hero, not so the girl."[38] In a case two decades later, in which a teen was keeping late hours with bad companions, the HBSA tried to intervene as an outside counsellor, fearing that her conductmight irrevocably ruin her life: "Someone outside the family might explain to her how inadvisable it is to keep later hours, to point out the dangers of ill-chosen company: a good reputation is a precious thing, and once lost, takes quite a while to regain. . . . Maybe she is bored, and finds glamour and excitement in late nights. We can help before it gets too late."[39]

The HBSA narratives of its very worst case records – offered for public consumption to legitimize and advertise its good work – often pointed fingers at families in which immorality was evidenced: "The father was a drunk, the mother deserted and is living common law with 2 illegitimate children. The girl was spending nights in a car with no steady job, not caring about anyone. Who is to blame, her or her parents?"[40] Rhetorical parent-blaming, however, was not the only negative side of reformers' failure to question these norms. Girls too might be implicitly blamed, even for violence directed against them. In one public presentation the HBSA executive director told the story of a girl who was downtown late one night partaking of commercial leisure and was subsequently raped by three youths who drew her into an alleyway. As a morality tale, this one focused on the girl's unacceptable leisure and her parents' failure to police her properly: she was out "unaccompanied at night." The incident had aroused guilt in her "respectable" parents, the executive director explained, in a clear equation of respectability with the preservation of pre-marital chastity.[41]

Assuming that some families were unacceptable, the HBSA also wanted to set up a properly chaperoned home for very young working girls (which had been the reform strategy of the YWCA for some years), and in 1961 the agency turned its main focus on creating a residential home for girls who could work or go to school on their own. Of course, these were not "anti-family" measures; indeed, the residential home had house parents and was described in familial terms. A measure of moral surveillance was always part of the alternative housing strategy. The removal of girls from families combined a humanitarian concern for the individual girl with the belief that the state, or its surrogate child welfare officials in the Children's Aid Society or Big Sisters Association, could and certainly should step in to provide morally superior parenting – precisely the idea behind juvenile courts.

Removing the child and providing separate accommodation, however, could not solve one of the most pressing problems that girls faced: low wages and limited employment opportunities. Many of the Little Sisters were early earners, working by age fifteen or sixteen to support families or themselves. Until the 1940s the BSA often fell back on recommending domestic work to girls who, in opposition, wanted to avoid servant life for the freedom of store and factory work. By the 1950s the executive director was lamenting the tendency of girls to cut short their education to look for immediate economic independence, or even for the "over the rainbow" hopes of matrimonial bliss. For young girls from economically strained backgrounds, both paths seemed to make sense as an immediate quick fix.

New moral values along with scientific casework were thus the basic mantras of those working with pre-delinquent girls, and it was the faith in the psyche professions that led to HBSA's lobbying for an observation or detention home in which children could be placed for intensive medical and psychological examination. That goal was realized in 1937, and HBSA volunteers added support for this institution to their efforts. Big Sisters Associations, along with other women's groups in Ontario, also lobbied successfully for the construction of a new provincial Training School for Girls in Galt, Ontario. The school opened in 1933 and supposedly provided psychological treatment and vocational education as well as discipline. One could certainly criticize these upper-class and middle-class reformers for so blithely sending working-class girls to institutions where their own children would never have been sent. Part of the initial impulse, though, came from their immense faith in professional treatment; few probably foresaw the extent to which Observation Home would become, more accurately, a detention home, and the Galt experiment would become a stigmatizing prison for many girls.

Prisons or Playgrounds? Recreation as a Cure for Delinquency

The Hamilton and Toronto BSAs also targeted another social problem leading to girls' delinquency: a lack of wholesome recreation. They shared this cause with many other experts, reformers, and politicians, and it was seemingly tied up with a view that teens had extra amounts of nervous and emotional energy that, unless expended in healthy leisure, would explode into unhealthy sexual pleasures or criminal activity. Since the founding of organizations like the YWCA in the late nineteenth century, recreation was seen as a means of maintaining girls' virtue and constructing ideal adult citizens. Experts on adolescence, such as the U.S. educator George Stanley Hall, writing in the 1890s, or the later Canadian child behaviour expert, Dr. William Blatz, writing in the interwar period, had long seen leisure as a strategy for transforming unruly teens into "normal" adults. While the intent of such managed recreation varied over the decades, at some points stressing the sublimation of youthful sexuality through physical activity, at others stressing the positive construction of inner character, the recreation strategy itself remained a constant.[42] Through recreation a girl was to become feminine, virtuous, religious, skilled in domestic attributes, physically fit, and keen to embrace honest labour. By definition, this was not a delinquent girl.

The recreation agenda of Big Sisters, like that of the YWCA, was geared towards girls' physical development through sports, as well as the inculcation of appropriate gender and work roles. Big Sisters directed a major part of its volunteer labour towards raising money so that Little Sisters could have swimming lessons, or use the Y, and so that it could set up age-specific clubs, with handicraft activities for younger girls and appearance- and clothes-related projects for older girls. In the 1950s attendance at a YWCA homemakers club was prescribed as the solution for one difficult Little Sister who was having problems getting along with her parents. This "cure" taught her appropriate domestic skills, overcame her isolation in an unhappy family, and engaged her in a wholesome and useful pastime. Very occasionally the agency also sought individual solutions for talented girls: one Hamilton Big Sister, for example, sought out a volunteer to offer free music lessons to a promising violinist. Usually, though, recreation was more group-oriented. An example was the summer camp where girls were sent to engage in healthy sports and recreation and learn co-operative and leadership skills, while also assimilating a less aggressive and rambunctious femininity.

Providing recreation was seen as citizenship-building work, and it followed logically from the Big Sisters' emphasis on mentoring: by experiencing the example of wholesome recreation, girls would integrate the positive values they learned into their future sexual, family, and work lives. In advertising the value of this approach, the Hamilton BSA told the story of one rather wild girl. Mary, deserted by her mother and ignored by an alcoholic father, was by age ten living on her own in boarding homes, with no understanding of "how to spend money, no acceptance of adult authority." The agency found her a job and, most important, had her join clubs in a community centre. "I didn't know you could be so happy, just being good," Mary reportedly enthused after her conversion to healthy recreation.[43]

Some Big Sisters also directed their efforts towards having state authorities monitor various forms of commercial leisure that, in their perception, put girls at risk. In the 1920s both the Toronto and Hamilton organizations protested the conditions in commercial dance halls, which they saw as encouraging underage drinking and heterosexual intimacies that would lead girls down the path of delinquency. In effect, this protest was simply a continuation of the pre-World War I campaigns for social decency. During the next two decades they turned their focus of concern on other forms of popular culture. In the 1930s mass-market crime comics became the scapegoat of many anti-delinquency crusaders, who were convinced that the raw images of sex and violence in these publications encouraged like-minded behaviour in youth – though disaffected teenage boys were again probably the primary social concern, given the comics' reliance on images of big-breasted cleavage and phallic, oversized guns.[44]

Ironically, when juvenile delinquency rates fell in the late 1940s the anti-comic campaign scored some legal legitimacy with 1949 federal legislation allowing customs to ban such material at the border. By that time movies were also being blamed for youth wrongdoing. While the "libertine" sexual messages in movies had been a concern of moralists and censors since the 1920s, the late 1940s and 1950s witnessed new denunciations of pop culture coming from delinquency prevention advocates. A 1946 *Saturday Night* article declared that youth needed "constructive channels" for their energies, rather than the contemporary "corrupting influences of cheap detective stories, crime magazines, horror comic books and sexually eccentric movies."[45] The writer warned that youth (presumably boys), forced to find their own amusement, were turning to "pool rooms and beverage rooms." The superintendent of the Toronto Board of Education, reflecting the Board's intensified concerns about delinquency in the 1940s, similarly seethed over the bad example set by movies and magazines, among other evils: "When one considers the liquor consumed in Toronto homes, the crime and sex pictures in the movies, the thrillers heard on radio, the prominence given to crime in the press, and some of the magazines available to children, one wonders why there is not more juvenile delinquency."[46]

While calls for the censorship of movies and comics did not go unchallenged, the motherhood appeal for wholesome recreation as an antidote to delinquency was seldom questioned. During and after World War II, when the rhetoric of citizenship was at an all-time high, stimulated by the state's promise of reconstruction for a democratic welfare state, a national consensus, at least among social work experts, was emerging on the recreation issue. Big Sisters now found themselves part of larger coalitions dedicated to preventing "Prisons with Playgrounds." A public affairs show on CBC Radio focusing on volunteers working with pre-delinquents in Winnipeg's working-class North End offered listeners precisely this rhetorical choice of "Prisons or Playgrounds?" Calling for active citizen participation, good role models, and adequate recreation for youth, the volunteers interviewed were concerned primarily with teenage boys, though the standard cures of education and recreation they cited were often simply extended, without any reflection, to girls as well.[47]

Indeed, CBC Radio took up the question of delinquency a number of times in the 1940s on its popular "Citizens' Forum" radio show, which encouraged ordinary citizens to organize local study and action groups around its broadcasts. These broadcasts both underlined the gendered understanding of delinquency and the renewed emphasis put on recreation, positivist social science, and education as cures for youthful wrongdoing after the war. In part, the public and media were looking for a quick fix to put an end to the activities of male gangs, which appeared to be increasing in strength. One show, "Meet the Gang," interviewed a Big Brothers worker who had assumed a disguise and spent his summer infiltrating boy gangs in the big city. A major reason for boys' anti-social behaviour, according to undercover agent Clifford Pugh, was that parents – in this case he only noted bad mothers – let them run the streets and did not provide them with companionship or alternative recreation. "Our citizens' role is to clean up the slums and give these boys the activities they crave," he told the national radio audience.[48] In a similar vein, the Canadian Welfare Council published *Your Town*, a popular primer on how to stop delinquency in its local tracks. Marketed in bookstores under the banner "Are You Interested in Gangs?" *Your Town* advocated parental education (which some parents and social workers wanted to be mandatory) and professionally organized "clubs and athletics," which would distract youth by providing recreational alternatives to delinquent behaviour.[49]

In another attempt by CBC's "Citizens' Forum" to wrestle with the delinquency dilemma, talking heads from the Parent-Teacher Association (PTA), the juvenile court, and the teaching and social professions offered up similar solutions. The PTA lady wanted ignorant and unknowing parents educated, by pressure if necessary; the social work professor, reflecting the growing expert emphasis on child creativity rather than mere discipline, wanted delinquents to acquire "democratic" rather than "autocratic" values; and the educational expert wanted more specialized teachers hired. Confidently ignoring the program's earlier commentary about a wide range of economic stresses and deprivation that hurt children, the moderator summed up the experts by saying, "The speakers have all said that juvenile delinquency is a psychological problem, not an economic one."

Since the fault lines of delinquency fell along familial and psychological lines, the solution appeared to be "rec and role": recreation and role models. Recreation was also linked to a new stress put on community development as local politicians and social workers urged urban areas to (in today's parlance) take ownership of their crime problems. In Toronto, for instance, Big Sisters was involved in a Mayoralty Task Force on Delinquency, which reported in 1949-50. Although the report portrayed delinquency prevention as a gender-neutral campaign, most of the attention focused on teenage boys – despite the admission of Toronto police that the gang issue had "been exaggerated."[50] Recreation solutions followed suit: if boys were "working off their energy at baseball, hockey, [they] are not likely to break street lights."[51] Aside from this obvious gender bias, the suggestions for delinquency prevention were not particularly new. Citing four sources of salvation – the home, church, school, and community – the task force reiterated long-standing calls for slum clearance, recreation, counselling, probation services, mental hygiene in the schools, and parental education. Although the task force gave a cursory nod towards religion, church services could not be mandated in the same way that educational or legal ones were, making the churches a weak link in the reform program.[52]

Indeed, a rare study of recreation that *was* geared towards girls clearly articulated the failure of the churches to create attractive recreation for young girls and teens. This 1943 study, which attempted to decipher Toronto teens' opinions and views, not only revealed how delinquency prevention through recreation was tied to gender anxieties, but also reflected class differences that separated reformers from their working-class clientele. Drawing on information from girls under the care of the Big Sisters Association, as well as on school, club, and workplace interviews, the study tackled the age-old dilemma of reformers since the turn of the century: why did working-class girls eschew organized clubs with a religious or reform flavour, such as Girl Guides, Canadian Girls in Training (CGIT), or Catholic youth groups, in favour of street life, commercial entertainment, and the proverbial temptation, dance halls?

Most girls answered that they preferred the movies, roller skating, "walking around" the streets in informal "gangs," and, of course, dancing, especially in places that had minimal or no chaperoning and, possibly, older servicemen. If they were to "club" together, they wanted to talk about date etiquette, boys, even sex. The problem with organized groups was precisely their moral and educational agendas. Asked why they did not like the Girl Guides, one group replied that they "got tired of running around in silly games. . . . [We] just sat around and watched each other. What fun is there in sitting around and tying knots?" When asked about her time in CGIT, another girl shot back, "Too much religion."[53]

The lack of teenage girls' interest in organized recreation designed to save them from delinquency was in part related to their class background. As one school principal admitted, as many as 25 per cent of the young girls, or one-third of high-school girls, were working part-time. Other teens had heavy responsibilities caring for siblings at home, because their mothers worked for wages. The study also carried out interviews with girls barely sixteen and already in factory jobs. They were on shift work and laboured beside older, more worldly women. These teens looked for flexible, unstructured leisure activities that they could fit around their work schedules. Moreover, their own labour – offering them one foot in adulthood – let them stake a claim to partake in more adult pleasures, not childhood games.

In contrast, middle-class reformers' notions of organizing leisure assumed a longer period of protected, financially supported childhood, a scenario that did not speak to the work and family experiences of these working-class girls. Organized recreation was also clearly focused on preserving and creating a femininity that was healthily heterosexual, but never overly sexual. But the girls involved in the study also made up their own questionnaire, in which they showed that they were interested in pushing these boundaries – at least in discussion – beyond chaperoned dancing to sex. In their list of questions, Little Sisters attached to the Toronto BSA included queries such as: "What is a French safe?" "Is jitterbugging vulgar?" "Is it unmannerly to smoke in the street?" "Is it wrong to be deeply in love at sixteen?" "How much of your pay should your parents get?"[54] These questions were a far cry from the interviewer's questions concerning games at Girl Guides.

By the mid-1960s, new initiatives embracing old remedies – recreation and work – were afoot to address the issue of alienated youth and prevent delinquency. Citing both school drop-out rates and the traditionally sexualized markers of delinquency, namely venereal disease and illegitimate pregnancies, one leading social worker warned that youth needed to be rescued from "crime addiction" by means of new objectives and positive activities. Failure to do so would result in events like a teenage Victoria Day riot in Hamilton, in which boys threw rocks at police while their girlfriend molls egged them on, urging them to "trample the flatfeet."[55] Often, those concerned still assumed that male alienation was the most pressing problem, although the halfway houses and job-information and drop-in centres advocated would have served teenage girls as well. Canadians were undoubtedly influenced by U.S. inner-city youth work, which had some limited success in using the carrot of social programs to distract youth from gang violence.[56] As the 1960s dawned, youth workers and teachers were also using another means of preventing delinquency: films.

Delinquents on Celluloid: Using Film to Curb Delinquency

If recreation was one means of preventing delinquency, another was to use movies, the very medium that reformers fretted would corrupt children. Hollywood movies like *Rebel without a Cause* and *Blackboard Jungle* (both 1955), featuring rebellious delinquent youth, were deemed so incendiary that the Toronto school board protested their public performance to the Ontario Censor Board.[57] On the other hand, the National Film Board's "On the Spot" newsreel series could be used as a counterweight in theatres, providing positive images of youth and the law, and as filmstrips and 8-mm movies were introduced into the school system across the country, the mainstream corrupting cinema could be countered with educational, documentary films deromanticizing rebelliousness and praising lawfulness. This preventive strategy of educational cinema used both Canadian and U.S.-made movies to make the case for recreation and role models to combat delinquency.

Most of the work focused on teenage boys. The NFB's newsreel series, for instance, produced a film called *Police Club for Boys* (1954), which trumpeted the great success of the Montreal police in curbing male delinquency by setting up athletics clubs – and later a music program – for boys. The film features many of the standard images of male delinquency, such as boys fighting in the playground, breaking windows, and loitering (underage) in smoky poolrooms. It also constructs another popular image: the friendly, helpful, and paternal but stern police youth worker who rescues boys from a life of crime. While the script asserts that viewers might find troubled teens even in "respectable, comfortable" homes, the visuals of vacant lots, high-rises, and small houses suggest that most of these families are not well-to-do, and the film portrays parents in dramatic re-enactments as vaguely incompetent, unable to control their children, or sometimes overreacting with too much anger. Luckily, boys can find an outlet for their anti-social energies in the police-sponsored clubs that provide free, supervised sports. What could be more quintessentially Canadian than the scenes of boys playing hockey on an outdoor rink, with a reassuring interviewer, Fred Davis, telling us that 160 teams were needed to fulfil the insatiable demand for this successful anti-delinquency effort. Swimming, baseball, and boxing, he adds, were also being taught. "These young boxers," he reassures the audience, "used to fight in the street" but "now they are learning team spirit . . . they are fighting for the fun of it!" – a distinction lost on this feminist viewer of the film.[58]

Similarly, the educational film *Youth and the Law* (1961) portrays kindly police youth bureau workers whose understanding of youthful longings allowed them to separate out the misguided but salvageable boy from the irretrievably bad apple. While the film focuses on images of boys and car theft, joy riding, and fighting, the dramatic re-enactment of one policeman's "normal" daily cruise through the spaces of youth culture occasionally brings girls into the picture, though most often as moll appendages. One boy is shown being discreetly interviewed in the principal's office about a "girl delinquent" after his phone number was found in her incriminating little black book. In another scene a boy is goaded into stealing a car by older teens in order to prove his manhood; the misfit girl in the gang (demarcated by her failure to dress in style) is persuaded to go along as his date, supposedly to prove she too is "cool."[59]

A Canadian educational film, *Comes a Time,* focuses entirely on boys' delinquency, using vandalism as the moral example that shows the salvation of one potential delinquent and the simultaneous descent into crime of another. This was a standard device in these films; the contrasting examples underscored the efficacy of the dominant JDA "treatment" regime, while also indicating the lingering anxiety that a few youth were simply not "treatable." *Comes a Time* also modified the standard moral tropes: the friendly police officer becomes the gruff but understanding paternal janitor overseeing the boys' restitution for their vandalism. Females make fleeting appearances only as flirtatious, coy student bystanders or as more threatening (maternal) authority figures in the form of a no-nonsense, strict, bespectacled female principal.[60]

If in these films young, pre-delinquent boys are often saved by older male authority figures (something I'm tempted to read in crudely Freudian terms as a symbolic restoration of paternal authority in a time of frenzied fears of emasculation), in films about troubled girls the need for greater understanding of parenting centres on the mother figure. Films on girls were far fewer, but they concentrated more on the domestic, familial, and emotional contours of girls' lives. *Who Is Sylvia?* (1957), an NFB production, establishes the mood and problematic from the opening frames, with sad, longing music as well as a concerned, paternal voice-over. Sylvia, situated uncomfortably between "childhood and womanhood," is not a potential car thief, but rather an emotionally troubled girl who is "timid, intense, self-conscious, shrill, shy, always hypersensitive." The problems she faces are those of uncertain emotional feelings and intense peer pressure to be accepted rather than ostracized as a maligned "oddball." Her parents' anxieties centre on her late nights and problematic choice of friends – as summed up by her father's anxiety that she will be the kind of girl who is an "easy mark."

After a domestic crisis in which her mother walks in unexpectedly on her entourage of jiving teens and a necking couple (a relatively harmless scene by comparison to other films), Sylvia retreats to her room, longing in her dream for a less censorious and more understanding mother who will talk to her about boys, dating, and clothes.[61]

Many of these films deliver a common message about the pathetic inability of many parents – despite their good intentions – to deliver good parenting. This is also a theme in *Borderline*, a 1956 NFB film featuring Nora, a rebellious, wilful fifteen-year-old who is defiant of parental authority, especially concerning dating, and who is ultimately sent to an institution for emotionally disturbed children. Nora's problems, though more severe than Sylvia's, also centre on her psychological and emotional maladjustment, so much so that she had supposedly become engaged in self-destructive behaviour (only referred to in horrified tones suggesting sexual misdemeanours), which led to her institutionalization. Significantly, Nora's "crisis" or borderline moment, shown in the film, was her insistence on dating an older man of twenty-three, a relationship that did not work out, and that her mother also feared was inappropriate. But her mother's style of discipline, oscillating between strictness and giving in when Nora cries, does not offer Nora the moral guidelines she needs. Throw in a weak father figure, uninterested in taking an authoritative paternal role in the contentious household, and you have a recipe for teenage disaster. If there is hope for Nora's salvation, it is the knowledgeable, kindly but firm father figure of the institutional psychiatrist, who offers Nora's mother corrective advice on parenting and helps Nora herself with "psychoanalytic therapy." Whether Nora will become emotionally adjusted or not is left unanswered at the end of the film, but there is no doubt that she requires better parenting, especially firm, understanding discipline and guidance, as she negotiates the difficult pathway to womanhood. The film's emphasis on the talking cure of psychoanalytic therapy, its critique of the inadequate family, its implied plea for compatible but distinct gender roles, especially firm fatherhood, and its clear instruction that girls' delinquency will manifest itself in sexual rebellion – and downfall – make the film a perfect primer of 1950s anti-delinquency efforts.[62]

The Dance of Power

Feminist historians have long been interested in the dance of power between middle-class reformers and working-class women, between social workers and their clients, between prison reformers and prisoners.

Challenging an uncritical celebration of these reformers, new feminist writing after the 1970s suggested that reformers of the suffrage era, and after, were often motivated by their own class interests and sense of their "female moral authority."[63] The reformers' intent was to remake working-class girls and women in their own middle-class image, pressing them into a moral and domestic mould that had little relation to, or understanding of, the economic inequality, social marginalization, life experiences, and different cultures of the poor and working class. Increasingly, this picture was complicated by recognition of the overlapping, plural aims of regulation, as ethnocentric, racist, and eugenicist impulses to assimilate those of non-white ancestry, or control those deemed "feeble-minded," were added to the equation.

More recent Foucauldian interpretations put a new spin on this analysis, by suggesting that moral regulation was a more subtle process of governing the inner soul, an attempt by the regulators to create a moral, inner conscience in each and every citizen, including themselves. Unsympathetic to Marxist-feminist analyses that stress the structures of class and gender power, this writing has nonetheless usefully highlighted the process by which expert knowledge *becomes* power, by which certain norms, values, and ideals become legitimized and sanctioned as acceptable moral practices in society. Moreover, both approaches ultimately reveal that regulation was not always successful, that clients have their own ideas, values, and agendas, and that they sometimes used, opposed, or manipulated state or reform organizations in order to pursue their own goals. Irene, the aforementioned scholarship student, was, after all, quite happy to have Big Sisters buy her books. She just drew the line at their advice on clothes and curfews. Little Sisters and their families participated in this cross-class alliance, however limited and precarious, in order to deal with the inequalities and crises besetting their lives, and also, in part, because they shared certain tenets of the gender and familial ideology espoused by the reformers.

Admittedly, organizations like Big Sisters, as well as later coalitions of state and voluntary agencies to promote the recreation panacea, both adopted band-aid solutions to the alienation of teens and the problem of crime; their prognoses for change tackled individual and familial flaws and shortcomings rather than more fundamental structural inequalities. Big Sisters were intent on adjusting a girl to her social environment, fitting her into dominant gender norms: girls were generally trained for blue- and white-collar labour, and pressed to accept the value of sexual virtue, passive feminine behaviour, and modest appearance, values that would presumably keep them out of trouble. As well as embracing discipline and responsibility, girls would, it was hoped, adopt a feminine persona that would prepare them for anticipated work and domesticity: they were to be the moral mothers of the future. Because reformers respected the analysis of the experts and the authority of the courts, they rarely developed a more radical analysis, stepping outside of these dominant class and gender scripts.

Another side of the story complicates this interpretation. The "maternal justice" practised by Big Sisters also signified a desire to protect younger women from domestic abuse and violence; moreover, they became advocates for girls whose options were curtailed by economic deprivation and lack of basic educational opportunities. And some of their early uncritical optimism concerning institutions like training schools was tempered over time as they saw the defects in the operation of the juvenile justice system.[64] Some clearly understood – just as social work commentators did – that girls experienced the protection they offered as judgemental control, and that delinquency could not be easily cured with knitting and basketball teams as long as violence and poverty remained endemic to society. As a result, they oscillated from a superficial optimism that they could prevent delinquency to occasional admissions that band-aids might not do the trick. However inadequate their knitting, bazaars, mentoring, and summer camps seemed to be as responses to delinquency, they were not completely unlike some current feminist endeavours, which support band-aids like shelters for battered women or career counselling for women on probation. For those of us – often more privileged women – who engage in endless board meetings discussing how to use bingo earnings to implement some meagre but necessary remedial program for women in conflict with the law, this should remain a sobering thought.

Interestingly, Big Sisters volunteers and staff often admitted that their successes came when they offered girls both material aid (*without* a stigmatizing means test) and friendship; one could hardly expect a girl to cheerfully embrace lessons about discipline or virtue when they were worried about buying school books or finding a job, or longing for new clothes. If this was bribery, as one board member suggested, perhaps bribery worked. As Pat Carlen notes in her discussion of contemporary young women on the margins of the law, unless they see some payoff in adopting the dominant class and gender deal, why bother conforming at all?[65]

That there were tensions between some of the affluent Big Sisters and their more needy Little Sisters goes without saying. There were also other tensions between those women who worked as professional social workers and those who were amateur volunteers, as well as between parents and daughters over whether and how these outsiders would interfere in the family. Moreover, a profound tension always existed between the idealized family that Big Sisters and others promoted, hoping it would be a basis for citizenship, and their concurrent fears that families were inadequate, neglectful, and violent. In part, this tension was managed by their class-based view, lurking beneath the surface, that broken non-functional families were primarily a blight of the working class and poor.

The girls they tried to help were also saddled with this ideological Catch-22. The new Hamilton Big Sisters residence constructed in the 1960s, for example, supposedly carried no stigma for the girls who lived there – at least Big Sisters said so. But was this true? Not only was it constructed like a family, but as long as the nuclear family continued to be idealized, those who were forced to live outside of it also had to struggle with inevitable stigma that theirs was a lesser upbringing. None of these problems were the sole provenance of these social workers and reformers. The same dilemmas were also encountered by judges and court personnel who dealt with teenage girls in juvenile court, after the Big Sisters had failed.

Four

Judging Girls in Court

Boy: caught stealing fishing rods, bikes, then smashing them up.

Boy: threatening another boy with a bibi gun.

Boy: stealing a wallet from a barber shop, skipping school and disobeying parents.

Girl: found with cigarettes and contraceptives in her purse.

Girl: has one illegitimate child, now running the streets until 4:00 am.

Girl: out late at nights and overnight with friends, enjoys keeping company of boys too much.[1]

These entries from Ontario's York County family court records list typical cases brought before a large urban family and juvenile court in the 1940s. The match between the expert discourses on juvenile delinquency and the actual apprehension of children is clear: boys broke the law, and girls violated gender and sexual conventions. Although juvenile justice was never that clear-cut and simple, this stark characterization held an element of truth. Who came into conflict with the law was never a simple lottery of chance: the inequalities of race and class, the vagaries of family dynamics, the assumptions shaping policing, and the very operation of juvenile courts themselves shaped the process. Certain behaviours and attitudes or class and family backgrounds predisposed girls and boys to court supervision. Those who were economically and socially marginalized were especially suspect in the eyes of the authorities; moreover, there were often concrete material reasons as to why these parents and children fell under the gaze of the law, and why some children had less of a chance than others of escaping a punitive training school sentence.

While historical records make it difficult to gauge how girls and their families responded to legal regulation, the surviving records do provide enough clues to lead to some initial conclusions on this score. Examining court records affords us an opportunity to probe more deeply the nature of juvenile and family courts: did they operate much like earlier nineteenth-century police courts, though now accentuating the moral surveillance of working-class girls and families through extensive probation? Can we describe the process of girls' probation and care by the courts as a form of "normalization" – that is, the processes by which ideas, social practices, and institutions produce individuals who adopt social norms, not simply because they are told to, but because this "normality" seems the only possible, even desirable, character to assume? Finally, if these norms were defined at the time as protective, positive, and necessary, why have subsequent historians cast a critical eye on them?

Juvenile Courts in Law and Practice

Although the new federal JDA drew on existing provincial laws and innovations, its implementation in 1908 symbolized more than a mere codification of existing legal practices. The Act defined a whole new offence of delinquency and gave comprehensive suggestions to the courts on how to detain and treat young offenders. Across North America, the first two decades of the twentieth century proved to be crucial for the creation of new juvenile justice structures, as U.S. and Canadian child reformers, legal experts, and governments attempted to build up comprehensive systems of definition, surveillance, and treatment, the bases of which would remain intact for decades to come. It was also remarkable, as Tamara Myers points out in her study of Quebec, how much consensus could be garnered for juvenile courts across age-old dividing lines of religion and culture.[2] Although Catholic and Protestant child-savers were sometimes locked in battle over the question of how best to place foster children from different religious backgrounds in homes – as both traditions sought to sustain or expand their flocks – some common agreement did exist on the legal management of delinquency.

After two decades of experience with the JDA, and consultation with child welfare workers, the federal government added a group of amendments in 1929. Still, these amendments provided only minor changes – for example, clarifying the power of judges and including discussion of parole – while leaving intact the overwhelming emphasis on "procedural paternalism"[3] in the Act. If anything, amendments over this initial period augmented the courts' paternal powers over both parents and children. As appeals began to test out the Act, lawyers discovered "soft spots," which Parliament was quick to rectify. The "contributing" sections of the JDA, for instance, were bolstered in 1921 and 1924 to make sure that a child did not even have to be designated a delinquent in order to have parents convicted of contributing to delinquency; parents could be pursued for not "removing conditions" that were "likely to render" their child delinquent. Likewise, during World War I the federal government introduced a related statute (CC 220a, later 215) criminalizing parents who, through their own sexual immorality, vice, or habitual drunkenness, "rendered the home unfit for a child." The statute was made stricter in the interwar period.[4]

A 1924 amendment added another means of defining a delinquent: as someone who was guilty of "sexual immorality or any similar form of vice." This move was the product of pressure by judges Hawley S. Mott of Toronto and Ethel MacLachlan of Regina, in alliance with the Canadian Association of Child Protection Officers. Mott complained to the federal minister of justice that he could use contributing laws to punish young men who were sexually involved with minor girls, but the girls in question might escape any legal condemnation. MacLachlan agreed that judges needed more powers to deal with girls' sexual immorality and "occasional prostitution," which she feared was on the increase. The result, says Bruno Theorêt, was an amendment posed in gender-neutral language, but which everyone knew was directed at girls. Indeed, given the sexual double standard of the day, this fact was lauded as a protective measure and supported by organizations like Big Sisters. The vague, broad wording of the amendment did not trouble Canada's parliamentarians, who accepted it, after some minor tinkering, with scarcely a second thought.[5]

The amendment was just one example of judges finding that the day-to-day administration of the JDA proved to be less ideal than they had imagined. Juvenile courts also relied on local governments to fund them; this created barriers not only to their initial establishment, but also to their full operation. Court-ordered probation, as Vancouver judge Helen Gregory McGill noted, was the "essence" of the new JDA. Probation officers were to do case studies of the family and the child "in her own environment" and make recommendations to the judge on the "causes of the child's anti-social behaviour" and how the child would best be "readjusted to society." But as McGill herself found in Vancouver in the 1920s, local interests had to fight for money to hire probation officers, sometimes taking on a local government uninterested in such new social work "fads."[6] Even though large urban courts were increasingly able to build up their staff of social investigators and probation officers, as well as drawing on medical and psychological consultants, the spread of the JDA across the country was extremely uneven. As late as 1956, a Canadian Welfare Council report lamented that the JDA had still not been proclaimed throughout all of Canada, offering equal coverage to all youth.[7] Across a vast province like Ontario, the resources available to juvenile and family courts varied dramatically, with serious consequences for young offenders. Large urban courts increasingly acquired a paraphernalia of social workers and psychological experts. Smaller courts might issue sentences simply on the advice of police or a local CAS official, and until professionalization took firmer root in the post-World War II period, Children's Aid staff were not always trained social workers. Children thus received "justice by geography," with fewer probation and foster care options in smaller cities and rural and Northern areas; this was one factor in the incarceration of Native girls from reserves.

Large urban centres had the highest rates of delinquency, which is hardly a surprise given their population densities, concentrations of poverty, and the very proactive policing of urban public spaces. Courts like those in Hamilton or Toronto also spawned observation or detention homes to hold children before trial, prevent them from running away, and act as "safe spaces" for children going through medical and other tests before sentencing. While in these homes children were both detained (as they could not leave) and observed, and misbehaviour there could spell a more drastic sentence. Their bad language, acting out, or disobedience would make their way onto the report that landed on the POs' and judges' desks. What really mattered was not simply whether such facilities existed, but how they were used. When the commissioners for the federal report on juvenile delinquency investigated detention homes across Canada in the early 1960s, they were distressed at the arbitrary use of detention, including by the police, as a means of "softening up" recalcitrant girls. In one city Catholic nuns and a priest admitted that police used their detention home to threaten girls suspected of immorality, and as a means of securing girls' co-operation in questioning. After what a priest referred to as "brutal questioning" by the police, one girl in the home finally "admitted to being sexually immoral" six months earlier.[8]

Larger courts also provided a new avenue for women's employment and social activism. Not only were some women – like the Big Sisters – volunteers in the courts, but a small but growing cadre of women worked as social investigators and probation officers, or in closely related child welfare agencies such as the CAS. Indeed, working with children was seen as an ideal way of joining women's natural affinity for child care with their social work training, though male probation officers still dominated the rosters of many large courts. Some women also became juvenile court judges. Helen Gregory McGill and Ethel MacLachlan were early examples in the West, while Helen Kinnear and others were appointed to Ontario family courts in later years.[9] Because juvenile and family court judges did not have to be trained lawyers, and because their jurisdiction was the family (and was less prestigious than other forms of law), that arena was seen to be appropriate for women. McGill believed that her maternal touch broke down barriers in the juvenile court, encouraging offenders to speak openly and honestly, but we do not have clear evidence that women judges were substantially different in their rulings. Indeed, MacLachlan's support for the 1924 amendment, along with Margaret Patterson's decisions in the Women's Court in Toronto, suggests that middle-class female judges could be just as strictly censorious as middle-class male judges. As Amanda Glasbeek argues, the familial rhetoric of "maternalism" justifying middle-class women's increased presence in the courts masked and legitimated their class authority and moral policing of "wayward" working-class girls.[10]

Juvenile courts did, ultimately, depend on an element of autocracy, if not fear, in their administration of justice. As one Toronto judge astutely noted, the court could not simply act as the child's friend; it also had to awe the child "with the mystery and majesty of the law."[11] Even if kind advice and psychological treatment were the mottos of court work, children had to fear the consequences, or why else would they bother to change? Evidence certainly exists indicating that juvenile courts, despite their desire to create a family-like atmosphere, also traded on the more intimidating culture of the criminal justice system. The velvet glove, symbolizing compassion and coercion, paternalism and pressure, remained an integral part of the new and supposedly kinder juvenile courts of the twentieth century.

One of the complaints of child welfare workers in a 1942 report was that juvenile courts were located in the same buildings as police courts, so that "the atmosphere of the police court remains."[12] In a study of the Metro Toronto juvenile and family court done in the 1960s, a researcher found that the robed judge still sat above others on a raised dias, that children found the language and proceedings difficult to comprehend, and that many parents could not even hear the evidence. The high number of guilty pleas, he concluded, was in part due to police screening of which cases went forward, but it was also because parents, even if they knew they could have counsel, often did not get it. As a result they tended to accept a quick guilty plea, especially after being told their child would receive "help" for his or her problems. Ashamed, nervous, and intimidated by the court, and worried about missing work, parents sometimes waited for hours on benches, losing badly needed wages, before they even got into the hearings. Neither they nor the child cross-examined witnesses or challenged hearsay evidence.[13] Moreover, the court's claim to be providing a "non-adversarial," benevolent justice simply led to "poor fact finding" and a disregard for concrete evidence, with deliberations resting instead "on perceptions, tensions and animosities." Paternalism, in other words, masked very real and arbitrary power, keeping in place a "hypocrisy" that even the "delinquent" sometimes recognized as unjust, which was hardly a good start to his "rehabilitation."[14]

Judges symbolized the supreme authority in the juvenile justice system, and their pronouncements constituted important ideological messages, legitimating the dominant social norms and sanctifying a version of proper gender and family roles that reflected their own middle-class and often Anglo backgrounds. Their styles of delivering justice differed, and their methods of pressing girls to change varied according to whether they saw them as compliant, regretful, aggressive, or unyielding. They expressed anger not only with girls who were defiant, saucy, or unapologetic, but also with parents who were insufficiently deferential and concerned. They also simply warned, lectured, or cajoled girls into changing. "You are headed for a life of misery" if you stay on the street, one judge warned a teen. "Men will use you then kick you out when they are through." He told her she would have "the worst life in the world" to look forward to.[15] Some judges tried to bolster a girl's sense of confidence, telling her she could be a model citizen if only she changed her ways. After one despondent and unhappy foster child was brought to court for spending a night with a man in a hotel, the judge tried to persuade her that her happiness depended on inculcation of her own self-respect. "Don't cheapen yourself. . . . There is nothing wrong with sex but there is a proper place for it in our lives and you have not found the proper place. You are attractive and will look back on this and worry about these escapades when you meet the right man."[16]

Judges rationalized their decisions by invoking their own superior knowledge, even though lesser court and child welfare workers often believed that they had more hands-on direct knowledge of the girls' problems and probationary progress. Court and child welfare workers were on the front lines of "normalization," working to persuade the girl to "gain the insight to change her own attitudes" and pressing the family to "work with social agencies," accepting their advice.[17] Social investigators for the courts (as well as CAS officials) found themselves working as private detectives, trailing girls to their favourite haunts, searching for runaways through city streets. Although these front-line workers experienced periods of high optimism about curing delinquency with social investigation and psychological counselling, their optimism was also sorely tested by the meagre resources accorded to child welfare and, most important, by their daily encounters with girls unwilling or unable to conform to an ideal that took a middle-class Girl Guide as the embodiment of adolescence.

Conflicts with the Law

How did girls actually end up in court? The formal charges that they faced indicate the streaming of girls and boys in the juvenile justice system. Boys far outnumbered girls in the system; they were often ten times more likely to be before the courts. Police more often initiated complaints against boys, while parents initiated a higher percentage of complaints against girls. Girls were rarely charged with what were termed "major delinquencies," such as common assault or break and enter; in that category, theft was the most common category of charge levelled against all youth. In the category of "minor delinquencies," girls were often brought to court for offences such as truancy and incorrigibility, and the latter was an elastic term that for girls often involved sexual nonconformity or endangerment. Although boys too were charged with being disorderly or incorrigible, such charges comprised a smaller percentage of their total delinquencies in comparison to girls. (See Tables 4.1 and 4.2.)

Table 4.1
Minor Delinquencies by Offences, 1925-45, in Ontario
(M = Male, F = Female)

	1925		1930		1935		1940		1945	
	M	F	M	F	M	F	M	F	M	F
Bylaw infractions	378	/	130	6	119	1	141	6	161	14
Disorderly conduct	420	3	150	2	69	0	29	1	89	8
Incorrigibility	22	22	50	30	63	35	75	66	143	136
Trespassing	245	12	177	/	118	3	85	1	137	1
Truancy	167	29	257	32	124	28	138	35	223	95
Breaking probation	36	3	29	5	72	3	24	2	30	9
Vagrancy	66	13	12	7	13	2	12	7	18	5
Other	235	5	54	12	39	5	74	7	59	3
Total	1569	87	859	94	617	77	578	125	860	271

Source: Dominion Bureau of Statistics (DBS), *Annual Reports on Juvenile Delinquency.*

Girls were thus more likely to be charged with status offences (offences of "being," character, morality), and boys with property

Table 4.2

Major Delinquencies by Offences, 1925-45, in Ontario

(M = Male, F = Female)

	1925		1930		1935		1940		1945	
	M	F	M	F	M	F	M	F	M	F
Theft	1045	72	1420	58	1149	85	1135	41	828	65
Auto/bicycle/$ theft	244	5	340	218	322	6	291	22	275	16
Break & enter	394	3	415	2	491	7	629	5	756	20
Common assault	52	7	47	14	35	7	43	5	49	4
Immorality	30	16	14	19	5	11	12	15	13	9
Property damage	251	8	279	8	441	6	326	4	316	10
Other	218	3	267	0	109	7	184	8	248	19
Total	2234	114	2782	319	2552	129	2620	100	2485	143

Source: DBS, *Annual Reports on Juvenile Delinquency.*

Table 4.3

Major and Minor Delinquencies by Offences, 1950-65, in Ontario

(M = Male, F = Female)

	1950		1955		1960		1965	
	M	F	M	F	M	F	M	F
Common assault	25	1	24	2	101	10	200	4
Break & enter	739	16	698	12	1227	33	1806	63
Theft	674	53	899	79	1919	198	2656	412
Auto theft	377	9	327	2	386	25	610	14
Property damage	383	11	359	14	631	26	729	35
Bylaw infractions	102	7	72	1	175	3	158	7
Incorrigibility	216	174	203	172	229	287	341	395
Truancy	76	43	38	30	110	61	142	85
Vagrancy	n/a	n/a	27	20	44	68	2	2
Immorality	28	12	29	16	25	23	12	52
Other	573	31	518	63	970	147	1865	474
Total	3193	357	3194	411	5817	881	8521	1543

Source: DBS, *Annual Reports on Juvenile Delinquency.*

offences such as damaging property, theft, and theft of various vehicles, whether bicycles or cars. (See Table 4.3.) For example, in the large Toronto juvenile and family court, in the interwar years 50 per cent of boys were charged with property offences, and 40 per cent of girls were charged with status or moral offences. In the 1940s and early 1950s, more than half of the boys, and only 27 per cent of the girls, faced theft charges. Three distinct snapshots from this one court emphasize this pattern: in 1920 most boys were arrested for theft, and most girls for vagrancy; in 1935 theft again dominated boys' offences, with truancy leading the list for girls; in 1950 some 56 per cent of the boys were in court for theft, and 47 per cent of the girls were there for incorrigibility.[18] Aside from "breaking probation," one of the most common charges encountered by both boys and girls in Ontario over these years was truancy – reflecting concerns that youth would not benefit from the socializing role of schools and would not receive the skills they needed in the labour force.[19] Girls' truancy, however, also suggested that they were on the streets, courting sexual or other immorality. (See Figure 4.1.) Contrary to the narratives of reformers, federal statistics also underscored that the majority of children in conflict with the law came from working-class families and were native-born Canadians. Even those with parents born outside Canada were a minority.[20]

Figure 4.1
Property and Truancy Offences: Girls vs. Boys

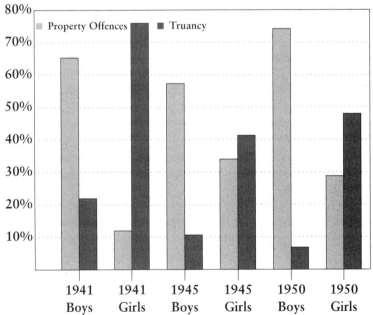

Source: Toronto Family Court, *Report.*

The dispositions of girls facing formal charges also reveal how juvenile justice worked itself out. Only a minority of children ended up in training school; in almost every year from the 1920s to the 1960s, less than 15 per cent of Canadian children charged were thus incarcerated. In Ontario the numbers were similar; though they did oscillate over time, they usually stayed below 15 per cent, with girls more likely to face training school than boys. (See Figure 4.2.) Across Canada, once children were before the court, only a minority of charges were dismissed while the majority of cases were found to be "delinquent." However, the predominant options taken up by judges were a form of adjournment or *sine die*,[21] a suspended sentence, or some form of probation. (See Table 4.4.) Fines were less frequent, and rarer in Depression years in some cities. Dispositions did vary from one city and province to another. In McGill's Vancouver court during the 1920s and 1930s, probation, involving surveillance of the child and family, was the first option, while in the Toronto court, suspended sentence/dismissal was the first option, followed by probation. Similarly, throughout Ontario, the most frequent outcome for children in the interwar years was a warning after their hearing. The courts could also claim that this was a successful strategy, since the majority of children were not repeaters or recidivists: in the Toronto court only 25 per cent of the juveniles were repeaters, while the Ontario and Canadian numbers were usually under 30 per cent. Whether children repeated and did not get caught, however, is a question we can't answer.

Official charges were just that: official, formal, and the tip of the iceberg. In fact, self-report studies and girls' sentencing reports indicate that girls participated in the same kind of misdemeanours as boys did, such as petty theft, even though they were more often taken to court for running away and sexual misbehaviour. Moreover, in large courts many delinquencies were deemed "occurrences," dealt with informally, with no formal charges laid. The girls were warned, or counselled, either alone or with their parents through the probation department. In the Toronto Family Court, for instance, occurrences for adults and children outpaced court appearances by three to two in 1920, and by six to one in 1950. These out-of-court settlements formed the very essence of juvenile justice, although they too revealed gender differences. Boys were slightly more inclined to be warned and dismissed. Girls were more likely to be placed under some kind of formal court supervision and more likely to be removed from their homes. These patterns reflect the assumption that boys could be corrected with discipline within the home, while girls' problems were more deep-seated manifestations of character disorder. Indeed, the process of probation for girls might be more intensive for precisely this reason. One study of Hamilton in the 1930s concluded that boys received on average eight months of supervision, while girls received up to two years, with more visits by authorities to the home.[22]

Figure 4.2
Percentages of Girls vs. Boys Sent to Training School

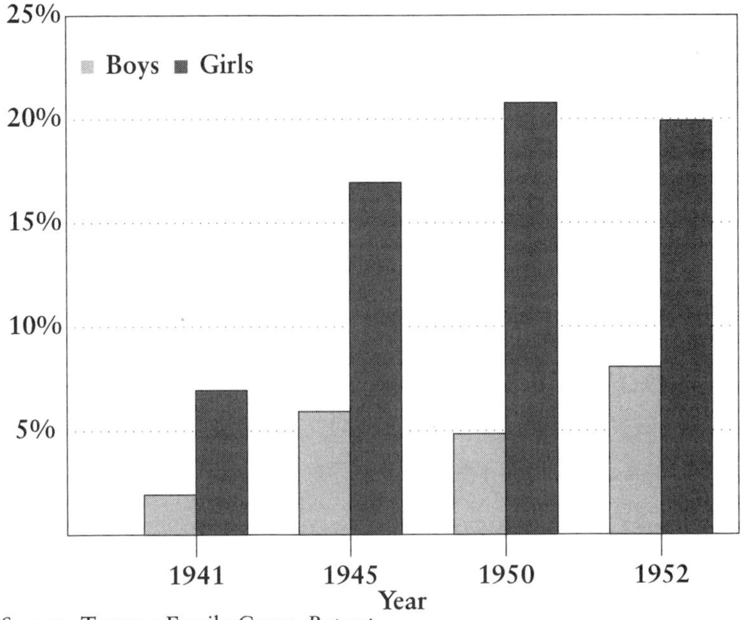

Source: Toronto Family Court, *Report.*

Girls used probation as an opportunity to speak out against parents whom they considered to be cruel, or unreasonably strict. They might secure a sympathetic ear from some probation officers or judges if their list of family troubles included extreme violence or parental "immorality." Indeed, in some situations the court shared the girl's negative appraisal of her home situation, coming to see the parents as the problem. One mother complained to a Toronto family court PO that her daughter disobeyed her, gave away clothes bought for her, used the family's credit without permission, and "wore too much make up." Because social workers already had a preconceived image of "value conflict" in immigrant households, this particular teen, described as "resentful of her immigrant Ukrainian parents' culture," secured some empathy from the PO, who noted critically on her report that the mother was a problem, already "resentful and unhappy" with her own arranged marriage and subsequent life. Nor was the PO above criticizing what the mother wore.[23]

Girls might also condemn parents for their failure to care for them properly or for their choice of step-partner. One small-town teen, Jane, was deeply resentful of her mother, who had been cut off mothers' allowance after having an illegitimate child and was waiting to marry the father – providing the spark that drove the daughter from the household.

The daughter's case, though, also revealed the intricate ways in which material stress was often intertwined with "moral" issues. Jane did well at school, but quit two weeks before her exams, declaring that she could see no "advantage to a general education." She was obsessed with money, said the court sentencing report, because there was "always financial insecurity in the home," especially after the mother was cut off her allowance. Jane, the report continued, now hated her mother as well as the boyfriend who "moved in." During one meeting with the court officer she angrily informed her mother that "she needed her head examined." Jane was finally removed from the home, and in an unusual move (because there was little concern with her "promiscuous" sexuality) was sent to training school. What started as understandable family tensions over new relationships was easily exacerbated by financial stress and by the daughter's truancy in the light of her despair that there would be no future for her other than the poverty that her mother faced.[24] While we should avoid pathologizing blended families as inevitably unstable, as social workers did (and sometimes still do), new step-relations could become catalysts for conflicts in families already under other economic and emotional stresses.

While girls' court experiences did alter over this period, there was a persisting concern with sexual misbehaviour and endangerment, which was common to courts across North America.[25] The legal, medical, and social work experts in the courts did not always concur on the exact definition of sexual promiscuity, but there was some agreement that sex with many partners, inappropriate partners, venereal disease, and sometimes pregnancy were signs of girls' dangerous abandonment of moral codes. Not all girls who became pregnant, of course, ended up in court. By the 1950s especially, other options, such as homes for unwed mothers, had emerged, and there was always some leniency for older teens who got pregnant as a singular mistake on the way to marriage. But even after World War II, pregnant girls were still being described in the social work literature as delinquent, and girls whose pregnancy was perceived to be the consequence of "promiscuous" sex could come under the purview of the court.

Girls' sexual misbehaviour often came to the attention of the courts through parents or guardians who called the police when girls ran away, or when they were found out late or all night. When police officers delivered the girls home, they sometimes urged the parents to press charges and secure aid from the court. "I've tried everything, but she won't listen. I can't manage her" was one mother's lament to a judge in 1940. Her fourteen-year-old daughter had quit school in Grade 7 and was working in a factory. The girl clearly saw this wage labour as her ticket to adult pleasures and hours, including not coming home at night. The judge agreed with the mother that age, not wage work, was the crucial factor to be considered, and that the girl had to abandon her attempts to "live like a 20 year old" or be sent to training school.[26] Other parents might wait until sexual misbehaviour was accentuated by other disobedience before they approached the courts for help in controlling their daughters. One girl skipped school but refused to take a job. She left her eight-year-old sister alone when she was supposed to babysit, and also ran away from home. She was heading off to midnight shows with boys, lamented the mother, who noted with further alarm that "her address book is mainly boys." Picked up by the police in the street with a group of boys, this girl was simply given a warning by the court to behave and obey her parents.[27]

Juvenile delinquency was often deeply interwoven with broader familial conflicts and contests for power, resources, and affection; parents sought out help controlling daughters for an array of reasons, ranging from their fear for their daughter's safety, to anger at her disobedience, to exasperation with her failure to contribute to the family economy. Control over a daughter's non-conformist sexuality was a visible sign of parents' respectability and in their minds was crucial to their daughter's future marriage prospects – or lack of them. The juvenile justice system, in turn, encouraged families to use the state to help them restore respectability, hierarchy, and morality within the family. While highlighting how families, bowing to the dominant gender and sexual norms, reigned in delinquent daughters, this process had a flip side: shaming and differentiating "bad" girls was also the means of producing good girls' conformity.

Once caught up in the system, less affluent parents often lost control of the legal process to professionals in the juvenile justice system. In the saddest cases, they displayed their conflicted emotions and anxieties before the judge, asking to have a daughter controlled but not incarcerated. In 1952, fifteen-year-old Beatrice came before the juvenile court after her mother laid a charge of incorrigibility against her. To support her children the mother sometimes worked away from home at a resort as a cook. She boarded the children out while she was gone. She admitted to being "depressed, in ill health since her husband was charged with assault . . . and deserted." When the court suggested training school as a remedy for the daughter, the mother displayed her conflicted views: "Well she is not really that bad. I can't seem to manage her. She has been associated with the wrong people. . . . I can't go through with it. I don't want to put her away. It is hard to be a mother and father both."[28] It is unlikely that any parent of teenagers, unless the children were unusually perfect and never in trouble, could avoid feeling sympathy for this mother's anguish.

Fears of sexual promiscuity were so strong that even girls originally taken to court for other offences, such as theft, often found the PO or judge asking the parent (or her) whether she was sexually active, and sex would quickly become the central issue for the court. Many girls knew better than to disclose details of their sex lives, but given the interview techniques used – which included listening to the child's side of the story – some girls ended up admitting to sexual encounters. With one admission, court officials might become more suspicious. One thirteen-year-old appearing before the Toronto court had stolen a few household items, but that was not the major reason for her presence; rather, her father had called the police when he found her sleeping with an eighteen-year-old boy. Although Patricia countered that she had been his girlfriend for four months and justified her sexual behaviour as a monogamous relationship, court authorities did not believe she was only having sex with him. "Tell the truth now," they warned, as they tried to coax more sex stories out of her.[29]

Probation rules thus often focused on sexual endangerment or corruption. One fifteen-year-old faced two theft charges, but in court the discussion centred on her bad sexual reputation in high school and on an incident in which she had stayed out all night with her boyfriend. Her probation rules included no nights out, no trips in cars with boys, and going to church in the morning: these clearly reflected fears of sex, not theft.[30] Some girls were brought to court, even sent to training school, to be inoculated against immorality, especially if their home environment was considered immoral. Girls who appeared to be attractive and physically developed "beyond their age" were constantly noted as a source of anxiety because they would attract male attention, or act out sexually beyond their age. A girl seen as "tall and sophisticated," mature beyond her fifteen years, was brought in by the police after an incident in which she and some older teens were intoxicated, trying to "bum some gas for their car." The social worker, drawing on a staple for their investigative work – namely, gossip – noted that she "hears of her promiscuity in the community," so the girl "was headed for disaster." The father agreed. In this case the girl wanted to be sent away from her father as well as her stepmother, whom she had only recently met after being placed in foster homes for years.[31]

A standard means of measuring girls' sexual purity was to administer a physical exam to see if the girl's hymen was intact. Parents might agree to

such exams, but the prospect of this invasive act was undoubtedly intimidating and girls sometimes resisted: one Toronto girl responded by running away from the detention home. After these examinations, doctors
sometimes spoke with amazing certainty about whether a girl was
immoral, a state invariably equated with intercourse. Dr. Edna Guest, a
physician at Mercer Reformatory, declared in the 1940s that one girl she
examined for the juvenile court was not only "immoral" but had also
experienced "rough intercourse" in the last two weeks. That this girl had
originally claimed sexual abuse in the family was not seen as a key issue as
they focused on her suspected subsequent immorality on the streets with
boys.[32]

A girl suspected of immorality was less likely to be removed from the
family home if the probation process was facilitated by parental support –
either a promise to reign her activities in or, occasionally, if they disagreed
with her designation as immoral. One mother, for instance, vehemently
supported her daughter's statement that she was "not sexually active,"
even though the PO convinced himself that "it was likely she was promiscuous" since she was "boy crazy," undisciplined, and precocious. The girl
astutely tried to curry favour in her probation interviews by telling the PO
that her lofty ambition was to be a psychiatrist. The psychologist testing
her looked on her ambition dimly, noting her "poor judgement skills,"
and he predicted a possible "psychopathic personality, though it was hard
to judge on such short notice." (Amazingly, the doctors could arrive at
firm diagnoses after only one interview, leading one to be sceptical about
finding any certainties in these historical documents.) A short-term solution to her running away was a suspended sentence and the supervision of
the Big Sisters.[33]

Sexual immorality was especially feared when girls ran away from
home or stayed out late or overnight with boyfriends or even a group of
teens. The courts often became involved after the authorities linked
together a package of problems: incorrigibility, running away, and sexual
immorality. In one case, for example, some immigrant working-class parents went to court after their fifteen-year-old ran away and later admitted
to sleeping in a park with her boyfriend, who was two years older and
recently sentenced to the Guelph reformatory. She was initially put on
probation, with a strict curfew, and then later sent to a Catholic refuge for
girls to separate her from her "obsession" with an undesirable male.[34]
Cases like these, in which the girl was not apparently coerced into sex,
and might even claim her right to sex, always presented the court with a
difficult dilemma; in one sense, the cases were perceived to be more wor-
rying than those involving coercive sex, in which the girl was a victim

who might be rescued or persuaded of the error of her ways. If the girl was induced to break off her ties with the man whom her parents and the court objected to, she was likely to get probation. One fourteen-year-old, for instance, was looking after her younger siblings during a time when her father was away in the war and her mother was in the hospital. Then the girl ran off with an older man and they "lived as man and wife" for eleven days. Because she agreed to separate herself from the relationship by going to live with an aunt, she was given a suspended sentence. Another girl ran off with a boarder who was twenty-five to her thirteen years. When she was apprehended she agreed not to see him under pain of training school. When she disobeyed and ran off again, she was sent to St. Mary's Training School for Girls on the outskirts of Toronto, though only after she had attempted suicide.[35]

This is not to say that girls who ran away, or became involved with older men, had full control over their sexual options: some were placed in situations in which sexual barter was their only means of survival. Although CAS and court workers were often horrified at girls' mechanical accounting of their practical use of sex in this manner, the girls' own stories reveal a mix of bravado, curiosity, desperation, and confusion. In one instance a girl ran away from her CAS shelter, where she had been placed after a number of foster homes had rejected her. Her run for the next ten days was predicated on her ability to have men pick her up and rent a room for her. The men too were eventually hauled into court (protesting that they didn't know she was minor), and she was assessed for training school. The social worker's report indicated that the girl was boastful when she returned from her trip, counting up her conquests for the authorities. This response may have been a way not just of shocking her keepers but also of reconstructing her tale as one of *her* power, given that her life had already unfolded in ways that had usually left her powerless.

Other girls admitted to being pressured by boys and men into sex, and the youngest girls came to court with so little sexual knowledge that they didn't know what words like "immoral" and "intercourse" meant. One girl admitted to having sex with a number of boys, with a resulting pregnancy, because "she thought if she refused, they would see her as a coward." Her social worker was almost relieved by this explanation, because it indicated naiveté rather than an "aggressive," enthusiastic embrace of promiscuity.[36] The authorities responded with particular alarm to girls who were found taking money to engage in sex with men, especially when the girls seemed to lack any understanding that this was "prostitution" or when they revealed a disconcerting lack of sexual guilt. One girl admitted to taking a dollar for masturbating an older man who lived nearby, and to drawing her sister into the business as well. "This condition of affairs is shocking," noted the crown attorney in court. "There are women old enough and willing to do that sort of thing without having little girls do it."[37]

Both parents and welfare authorities could bring teens who took "inappropriate" partners to court. During World War II, for instance, there was clearly anxiety that young girls would be enticed into sex by marauding, predatory older soldiers, though at times a girl was portrayed as the one doing the enticing. A judge in the Sarnia court, for instance, complained that the teen appearing before him was writing love letters to soldiers, "inviting them to go to bed with her."[38] Men already in conflict with the law themselves, older men, and occasionally men from different racial backgrounds were also perceived to be dangerous partners. But white girls involved with boys of colour raised particular concern. In one small Ontario town the CAS discovered a white girl who had twice spent the night with a "coloured boy in a car." Her promiscuity was made all the worse by her inability to see the danger of interracial sex. "These coloured boys are like tom cats that chase alley cats," warned the social worker, and the judge agreed that the girl did not "understand the seriousness of her actions."

Some parents, especially in the interwar period, but also afterwards, tried to use the courts to separate white daughters from men of colour. One Toronto mother complained to the family court that her daughter was "hanging around dance halls with coloureds," and she feared her girl would produce a "black baby." Even the social workers were a little mystified at this sense of grave concern, given that the daughter was going to stay with her own father, a heroin addict. Occasionally parents agreed to have their daughter removed to training school in order to wrest her away from an unacceptable partner. One well-appointed suburban family used this tactic after their daughter became involved with a young man with a criminal record. They complained that she was irrationally obsessed, even climbing out of her window and down a ladder to keep a tryst with him.[39] Daughters may well have seen these situations quite differently – perhaps as unrequited love stymied by overly strict parents.

The courts responded to girls' sexual misbehaviour by adopting a number of strategies. First of all they tried to aid responsible parents in establishing curfews, rules, and even compromises about dating and boys, all of which would allow the girl a taste of social life but presumably curb her excessive promiscuity. They also encouraged the girl to see her actions as dangerous, inappropriate, and, very crucially, a shameful blight on her moral reputation and that of her family. "I don't think you appreciate . . . the embarrassment [your parents] suffer coming into this court with you," a small-town judge lectured one teen.[40] In a memo to girls already in training school, a superintendent made it clear that shame and especially the fear of sliding into a life of prostitution were the psychological weapons that she would use to persuade girls to alter their ways. "You have done nothing to be proud of and much to be ashamed of. . . . Your poor work records and sexually delinquent behaviour is nothing to be proud of. Your associations with criminal men will only bring you misery and poor health – if you live to be 30, you'll be worn out hags."[41] As contemporary writers point out, "shunning and slandering" are common, and powerful, "everyday policing" methods that society uses to demarcate and discipline delinquent girls.[42]

A girl's attitude towards her sexual life was crucial to her fate. The court considered girls to be bad probation risks if they failed to understand the importance of shame, did not disguise the fact that they were "boy crazy," boasted about sex, or failed to indicate guilt and repentance. After one girl admitted to the psychiatrist that she now saw her previous sex activity as wrong, "quite outside the standards of her respectable family," she was considered "mature" and good reform material. Perhaps her insight was not as deep as the social worker hoped, because she later ran away and tried to elope with a soldier, even though she was underage.[43]

Yet both court personnel and CAS workers assumed a girl's ability to change her bad habits rested not simply on her willpower, but also on the example set by her family. A girl was considered high risk if family members were "sexually immoral" or had criminal records, if they lived in overcrowded, dirty, or impoverished circumstances, or sometimes even if they were uncooperative with the courts. Since sexual immorality was something that girls were presumed to imitate, mothers or other female relatives who lived common law or, far worse, had serial partners and illegitimate offspring were also signs that the girl would not change. "According to neighbours, mother spends time in beverage rooms and has man friends," said one pre-sentencing report on a delinquent girl, thus condemning both mother and daughter – the daughter, presumably, lacked a good role model.[44] The case notes for one girl made it absolutely clear how much the family became the evidence used against her. Only fifteen, she was sent to training school at the insistence of the local CAS, even though she said her illegitimate child was the result of her being raped. The rationale for strict sentencing related directly to her family. Her father had been in an industrial school and was now a "lazy, shiftless" miner not always employed; her brothers refused to go to school; her parents were separated; and the mother had deserted the family and had children with another man.[45]

At times families themselves pressed for court supervision, fearing the contagion of sexual immorality. One mother was persuaded to have her truant daughter, who was "running with a tough, boy crazy crowd in search of excitement," come under court supervision because she wanted her to "avoid the fate of her older sister, who was forced into an early marriage and much unhappiness."[46] More often it was the court authorities, sometimes prompted by the CAS, that focused on the contagion of family immorality – although definitions of what was immoral did change over the period. In the early years of the century, and even in the interwar period, some social workers saw common-law unions as de facto immoral; by the 1950s such relationships (especially if they looked like "respectable" marriages) were more readily, if reluctantly, accepted.

Definitions of immorality also often incorporated the inescapable effects of poverty. Families were criticized for taking in too many boarders, letting children sleep together, or living common law rather than divorcing (which for some of them was a financial issue). In one case parents in a rural area allowed their fifteen-year-old to mind the younger siblings while the parents travelled around looking for casual work. The mother also admitted to encouraging the daughter to have sex with the landlord, which gave the impoverished family free rent. While the emphasis of the courts was overwhelmingly on repairing troubled families, some families, like this one, were deemed unrepairable. "Home ties are thought best broken" was the conclusion court personnel came to when they decided to remove a girl, either to a foster home, or training school.[47]

Girls might also be suspect because of sexual abuse in the home, even if they had been victims of that abuse. The dominant medical and psychiatric discourses on incest over much of this period assumed that it was uncommon behaviour, situated primarily in the lower classes. Sexual abuse was often equated only with intercourse (so that girls sometimes had to undergo an internal examination to see if they were being truthful), and increasingly in the Freudian era of the 1940s and 1950s it might be seen as an unconscious or fabricated response of girls to difficult relationships with fathers and mothers.[48] Case notes often used the phrase "girl confessed to bad relations with father," language reflecting an assumption of girls' complicity. In a few cases girls were not even charged with delinquency but were whisked into training schools because the judge presumed this course would offer them the moral training required to overcome their "contamination." Yet, understand-ably, girls experienced this outcome as *their* punishment.

In a typical case, a fifteen-year-old runaway was found sleeping in a boxcar with a boy. As a result, her mother laid a charge of unmanage-ability against her. The court admitted that the father had been incarcer-ated for sexually assaulting the daughter, but the mother "felt sorry for him in prison" and took him back – though the family's economic status probably encouraged her actions. The daughter, Yvette, said her father was now attacking her younger sister, as well as threatening her; hence her attempts to run away. Yet the authorities attributed Yvette's delin-quency just as much to her immature, hostile behaviour. "She seems shallow," wrote one PO, "bitter and hostile." After the probation inter-view he described her as "rather aggressive." She "almost immediately discusses the incestuous relationship," he said, as though that tendency was in bad taste – and she was "placing blame for her behaviour" on the incest. "There is very little depth to her emotional content of these statements, as she is equally concerned that she missed a date in the detention home."[49]

Like Yvette, many girls who experienced sexual abuse rebelled not only against their families, but also sometimes against the dominant standards of sexual purity, which resulted in running away from home and illicit sexual activity with boys and men. Ironically and tragically, by running away, and thus rejecting their oppression at the hands of abusers, they found themselves labelled delinquent and came under the eyes of the law. Moreover, pressed into aiding other siblings, coerced or pressured by parents, ashamed and alienated, they might also return home – as Yvette did.

In the early 1950s a training school superintendent remarked both privately in her case notes and publicly, to reporter June Callwood, on the high number of incest victims who ended up under her care.[50] Yet the courts and the helping professions did not give sexual abuse signifi-cant explanatory power in their analyses of girls' conflicts with the law, even though some victims – the very young, and those who did not appear as subsequently promiscuous – were seen sympathetically as "more sinned against than sinning."[51]

Sexual abuse is seen very differently today, after more than two decades of feminist writing and politics that have led to a new openness to survivors' stories, and a new understanding of abuse as a corruption of power and control that is not rare and "lower class." Rather, we see abuse as mirroring and sustaining other forms of social and gender dom-ination in society. While some contemporary criminologists would argue, with good reason, that sexual abuse is still underestimated as a cause of young women's conflicts with the law, it is nonetheless addressed more directly than in the era before the 1970s. One girl who in the 1940s said she had been abused since the age of seven was at first simply dismissed, but she soon came into contact with the court when she had sex with boys in the schoolyard and older men, contacting VD. The CAS described Priscilla as "sex obsessed" and her committal sheet stated she was "immoral." But later events proved that she had indeed been the victim of incest, with more than one male relative involved. Social workers and doctors found it hard to get past their distaste at her "loud boastful" and amoral view of sex, but Priscilla's inability to adjust to any foster home and her recurring rages and depressions finally led them to concede that they might not know how to help her ever "get over her early traumatic experiences."[52]

While the apprehension and treatment of girls in the system undoubtedly reflected immense anxiety about their safety and sexuality – quite unlike boys – we should not forget that they did commit other offences. Next to incorrigibility, for instance, girls before the largest Ontario court, Toronto, were usually charged with truancy and/or theft. Ontario and Canadian statistics are similar. If simple truancy was the problem, parents might be amenable to a work permit as the solution. This was especially true until World War II, when teens as young as fourteen were easily able to join the workforce and, in some families, were encouraged to do so because more than one wage was needed to keep the family afloat. Even in the more prosperous post-World War II years, when the school-leaving age had risen slightly, early wage work was seen as an option for some perpetual truants and a necessity in some lower-income families. When a fifteen-year-old girl who had spent one and a half days at school over two months (preferring to hang out at Harry's Grill with her boyfriend, "Slug"), was before the court, she was simply issued a suspended sentence and a work permit, based on the understanding that her truancy was unlikely to change.[53]

Many girls did not see a future in education or had learning problems at school; at the same time, not much wage work was available that would allow them independence from their families. Until the 1930s, domestic work, with its low pay and insecurity, was almost all that was available, although waitressing and factory work were increasingly taken up as well. Probation officers were sometimes wary of waitressing because it might involve night work that put girls in contact with potentially tempting situations and strangers. They were less likely to see domestic work as dangerous, because it supposedly offered girls the protective cocoon of a private household – even though girls could just as easily be exposed there to sexual harassment. The courts often saw girls who did not want to embrace school or work as ambitionless or lazy, but work to these girls was not a "career" like the one that their social workers enjoyed. Rather, some came from economically marginal families in which continued education was not seen as normal or even possible, and their reluctance to jump into the workforce was predicated on their day-to-day exposure to their own parents' efforts to cope with difficult and unrewarding working-class labour.

Petty theft was also a persistent cause of committal throughout these years. Only seldom were girls involved in well-thought-out or gang-related robberies. One dauntless seventeen-year-old, Kathleen Boyle, played Bonnie to Cecil Irvine's Clyde in a 1930 holdup: she approached a Toronto bank teller asking for change for a five-dollar bill, then threatened her with a revolver, and along with Irvine (her brother-in-law) herded the frightened customers into the vaults. For her part in the robbery, she secured two years in the Mercer Reformatory. Girls might also dream up novel crimes. Another girl guilty of "babynapping" was sent to the Alexandra Industrial School after she made off with a sleeping baby that she had spotted in a carriage in Toronto's Eaton's store. Later, try as she might, she could not convince the authorities that she "just found it on her doorstep."[54]

More often girls were in court for stealing clothes or other small items from stores, and jewellery or money from employers or even their own family. In one typical case in the 1930s, fifteen-year-old Diane, already doing housework for wages, pleaded guilty to stealing a ring from her employer. She ended up in training school, not simply because of this one theft but also because the local CAS report charged that she was undisciplined at home, was "simple and easily led," and had been "immoral" with an older man.[55] In another case, two decades later, fifteen-year-old Harriet, from a poor rural family, was caught stealing a skirt and a pair of shoes from an Eaton's store in a nearby city where she had gone to visit her father, without her mother's permission. Although the items were small, the court became actively involved in part because the CAS had already been in contact with the family and deemed her impoverished mother to be "dirty and slovenly and repeatedly pregnant" and thus an inadequate moral example for her daughter.[56]

The cases in which theft was the only issue were rarer. One Toronto girl was charged in 1942 with two break and enters, and while she had gone to a lot of trouble – each time taking a ladder to the window of a house to break in – she had only carried off some clothes and, on the second heist, three dollars to pay back a friend. Another girl, Beatrice, was committed in a small Northern town for "stealing and lying." Beatrice had been moved repeatedly under CAS care from one foster home to another, often because she was caught stealing. While we should be wary of a stereotypical image of female kleptomania as the product of emotional or hysterical dysfunction, the items that Beatrice took, as well as her subsequent display of them, lend weight to the conclusion that she was less interested in amassing stolen property and propelled more by the unhappiness of foster care. From one house, for example, she stole the shoes of another girl, then promptly wore them in public. Most girls would have been put on probation for such minor thefts, but Beatrice's precarious status as a CAS ward made her more vulnerable to a training school sentence.[57]

Finally, one of the most troubling misdemeanours for the court was a girl's violation of probation. If a girl received a warning, agreed to new rules and curfews, was given a second chance with a work permit, or told never to run away again, and she disobeyed, her chances of securing a court appearance and even being removed to a foster home or training school were far greater. Indeed, because girls' crimes were linked to their self-destructive nature, possibly stimulated by deep emotional maladjustment, the authorities perceived a second or third transgressions as being even more alarming than boys' repeated thefts and vandalism. As one penal worker commented in the 1950s: "Girls are committed to training school for 'boy trouble' whereas boys are usually committed for theft, a more acceptable offence [in the public mind]."[58]

Class, Race, and Criminalization

While the immense anxiety about sexual endangerment might seem to have been applied equally to all females, this was not the case. As the expert definitions of delinquency indicate, the sexualization of female delinquency was shaped by class and race. Studies have shown again and again that working-class males were disproportionately likely to experience the criminal justice system. How did this streaming work for girls?

To understand girls' confrontations with the courts, we also need to survey the economic and social context of their lives, exploring how these conditions interacted with discourses about sexual endangerment to create girls' criminalization. A materialist and feminist framework remains an important guide as we consider how and why particular discourses about crime, gender, and race become powerfully embedded in social practices, state policy, and even human consciousness. However important the discourse of sexualization was, we must ask why it was most punitively applied to the poor, working-class, and racialized girl.

Girls' court files reveal a number of recurring themes. First, probation officers (and also the CAS) drew on neighbourhood knowledge – gossip – to gather information on girls. These networks were more circumscribed in affluent areas due to larger houses, physical distance of neighbours, less street activity, and patterns of more intense privacy. From the 1930s on, U.S. and Canadian studies mapped crime and delinquency by neighbourhood and then followed up with various theories about which factors – more immigrants, more transience, low income, social disorganization – were to blame.[59] A Canadian mapping study in 1966 admitted that areas characterized by poor housing and low income were the target of more intense policing, although the really crucial issue was police discretion, which "was much broader with juveniles." Usually younger children were reprimanded – unless they lived in a designated delinquency area, and then they were more likely to end up in court, charged with major delinquencies. Girls, this study also concluded, were more likely to secure the mercy of police at the initial stage and less likely to secure the mercy of the court once they were brought in. The taint of "bad neighbourhood" (or in the case of Native girls, "bad Reserve") was thus a central issue in the apprehension of delinquent boys and girls.[60] "That's how the police see [delinquency]," admitted the 1961 film *Youth and the Law*: as a question of "good and bad neighbourhoods."

Police discretion was indeed significant, because police made the initial decision about whether or not to deal with the case informally, refer the child to an agency, or immediately place her or him in detention. One Toronto study in the 1960s estimated that police screening meant that only 50 per cent of youth offences for which there was evidence ever resulted in charges.[61] Police could simply visit the home, assess the parents and surroundings, and possibly issue a caution, or refer the child and her parents to a social agency. Some advocates of police youth workers saw this arbitrariness as the virtue of the juvenile justice system. The anti-delinquency film *Youth and the Law* featured a series of dramatized typical encounters between delinquent teens and a stern but kindly Sergeant Clay, a police youth bureau worker. In one scene Sergeant Clay accompanies a teenage boy home after an auto mishap in which the boy had used his father's car without permission. Concerned that the boy was acting "withdrawn and strange," Sergeant Clay interviews the affluent, middle-class parents. The real problem quickly becomes apparent: the father "didn't run his own home." The mother, replete with heavy, dark glasses and sitting higher up than the father, is domineering and overprotective. "This was her big boy they were talking about," Clay narrates critically, "and when the father became too critical of the boy, she actually moved in to quiet him down!" With father's authority wrongfully usurped, the family was in disarray and the boy psychologically endangered. Sergeant Clay wisely saves them a trip to juvenile court by pressing them to go to family counselling instead. But in another scene with a noticeably "tough" working-class kid in tight jeans and greased hair, in trouble for tire theft, Sergeant Clay is not interested in recommending family counselling.[62] It was precisely this principle of "arbitrariness" that came to concern some witnesses testifying before the federal inquiry on delinquency in the early 1960s, but given that police were front-line workers, discretion – shaped by ideological assumptions of class, race, and gender – could never be totally reined in.

The welfare system, schools, and the courts were also becoming increasingly interdependent over this period, sharing information about their clients. Truancy charges brought one Hamilton girl to court in 1933, but once she was there the police discovered she was "peddling candy and perfume on the street" for her stepmother, and they suspected her of sexual immorality. This finding made her case all the more serious to the court.[63] Welfare officials passed on information, including knowledge of illegitimate children, to the courts, and visa versa. Moreover, this was not simply a case of the state and philanthropic institutions observing and controlling the less affluent. Many working-class or struggling middle-class families were encouraged to use the emerging family courts to broker family conflicts and secure counselling that they did not have funds to pay for privately. Women embraced the courts as a means of securing badly needed support payments from deserting husbands or dealing with violent spouses; parents used the courts to discipline children they could not control. The problem was that clients, then equated with "dysfunctional families," could become the focus of more censorial surveillance.

The process of probation had built-in biases as well. Although the method of talking through problems undoubtedly kept some girls out of training school and helped to mediate family conflicts, it also favoured the more affluent and educated. A solution favouring a talking cure, in which clients were supposed to examine themselves introspectively, was assumed to work better with "reflective" white, middle-class clients with "better cognitive skills and ego strengths."[64] This approach was also a problem for children whose parents did not speak English (in court translators were usually found, but this was less likely for the process of probation) and for Native girls, whose first language may not have been

English and whose cultural upbringing did not necessarily encourage this brand of psychological self-criticism.

Many probation procedures also involved proving respectability to the PO or judge, or they might also mean sending a daughter away to live with a willing relative, or even moving to a new neighbourhood. Although poorer parents used these strategies, sometimes at great cost, they were more readily available to the better-off. Moreover, parents who reassured the judge of their own law-abiding characters were more likely to secure agreement that daughters be allowed to come home under stricter supervision. The trappings of respectability and class, from living in good neighbourhoods to church membership to secure employment, reassured court workers that these girls could be reformed within their home situations.

It was not simply these very basic biases of the policing and court system that disadvantaged parents by class, but also the insecure conditions of labour, transience, and an inability to supervise children that came with the territory of low income. Parents who worked at jobs that appeared to be unacceptable (like two parents who worked in a bar) or jobs that did not conform to nine-to-five-hour days – including parents who had to board their children while they found jobs elsewhere – were disadvantaged in the probation process. Judges were sometimes insensitive to the economically insecure nature of parents' lives, assuming that those who did not appear in court, or did not change their jobs to fit their children's needs, might simply be irresponsible. "Why isn't the father here if you can't control your daughter?" a Toronto judge asked one mother whose husband was a travelling construction manager. "If your husband is not going to come, I'll have to send her away," he concluded, and he did.[65] Single working mothers were grudgingly accepted as a necessity, but those women with partners who worked outside the home might be accused, as one mother was in the 1950s, of failing to "realize a stable home life" for the child – and thus blamed for her delinquency.[66]

Economic instability also spiralled into problems such as transience, foster care, and sometimes neglect. Parents with inadequate incomes or those who travelled around searching for work sometimes placed their children in foster or boarding homes, particularly from the 1910s to the 1930s, though sometimes afterwards as well. Not only did this leave some children feeling rejected and alienated, but it also sometimes left them without adequate care and more likely to become engaged in the street life that occasioned contact with the police. Poverty sometimes overlapped with neglect, as children were deserted by parents unable and unwilling to care for them. These instabilities obviously enhanced the child's contact with the child welfare system. Current studies also suggest a connection between children who have experienced some form of state care and later conflicts with the law. Children who were placed in foster homes, or sometimes in orphanages, often carried with them scars of alienation, as the overwhelming idealization of the biological nuclear family left them out in the ideological cold.

Moreover, finding alternative homes for girls temporarily or permanently removed from their families continued to be a problem over the decades. In the years after World War I, many foster parents still had an image of a Barnardo girl in their minds when they imagined foster children – that is, someone who was going to do their domestic work. This image proved hard to shake, and so as one training school probation officer admitted with regret in the 1930s, if a girl was not going to help scrub the floors, many households did not want her. Despite some state efforts to inspect foster homes, and the fair treatment of many foster children, abuses, both physical and sexual, did transpire, resulting in further anger and alienation for these girls. Social workers inspecting homes could be persuaded that all was well by the foster parents' appearance of respectability or even profession of Christian aid. Much later, they sometimes admitted that girls' tales of sexual abuse, inadequate food, or ostracism had been true. Because most girls were unable to live on their own meagre earnings, and because it was assumed they would be better protected in a home environment, there were few options for their independent living, though by the 1960s group homes were emerging as the newest solution to this problem.

Although the school-leaving age rose during the century, teens working part-time or full-time were not an anomaly, especially in working-class families. In the 1920s many girls were working by age sixteen; as late as the 1950s, some fifteen- and sixteen-year-olds were required to work, at least part-time, shouldering major responsibilities that more middle-class girls would have been unlikely to face.[67] A judge in the 1940s castigated a CAS ward of fifteen for stealing a watch from the house where she boarded and decreed that "a big girl like her should be [out] working," making one wonder if he would have prescribed the same cure for his own daughter.[68] A lack of spending money or low wages undoubtedly provided a context in which petty theft was a temptation, particularly as consumer culture became more and more prevalent for teens by the post-World War II period.

Economic insecurity also accentuated illness, disability, and problems with violence. Poverty discouraged women from removing children from violent families, thus only increasing the risk of their running away. In one family during the early 1940s, for instance, the father was out of work after an accident. As a result the family was reliant on the mother's meagre earnings, while the teenage daughter cared for the home. The daughter became the focus of her father's anger, even his physical rage. The girl displayed her bruised leg – the result of being repeatedly kicked – to the judge, telling him that there was "something wrong" with all of her family – hence her runaway attempts.[69] Economic insecurity also made disabilities difficult to manage, and disabled girls found that the social service system did not adequately deal with their problems. One girl designated "deaf" in the 1930s was not outfitted with the necessary hearing aid. As a result she was not able to finish school or find work. She ran away and became involved in sexual activity, which in turn brought her into contact with the court. Her story of sexual abuse in the family was discounted, perhaps in part because of her disability.

While more runaways came from families in which there was little material incentive to staying, some middle-class girls also ran away from violent homes. The court often found it difficult to deal with the domestic violence the girls had encountered at home, not only because of the "stature" of the parents, but also because corporal punishment was socially and legally sanctioned. When did punishment become abuse? After her mother's early death, one daughter of a well-off insurance salesman was caught in a battle between her guardian grandmother and her father. After her grandmother complained about her late nights, the court became involved and suggested sending her to the father, which the grandmother initially supported because he had long refused to pay her any child support. Yet the daughter's behaviour only worsened. The court concluded that this was because she was "hysterical and wanted her own way." The father had no compunction about stating to the judge that "she needed a good slap now and then." Given this bravado, it is not surprising that the daughter and grandmother complained that he "strapped her . . . and beat her like a dog." She was removed from both homes, but the father was never charged.[70]

Violence was not totally ignored, but it could be easily sidestepped based on who was being accused, or the reputation of the accuser. In one incident that revealed the racist images held by court officials, an Afro-Canadian girl who complained that she had been raped by a group of young men in a church basement was simply disbelieved. "This is probably a fabrication," her psychiatric report noted; otherwise the minister who took the complaint would surely have investigated.[71]

Other girls, already deemed promiscuous, found that their charges of rape, like incest, were viewed sceptically. One working-class urban girl was picked up on the streets and charged with being drunk in a public place. Yet the police admitted she was "hysterical" as she claimed her mouth injury was due to an attempted rape by a man she had met at a party, and from whom she had fled. This violence, however, was less the focus of the court interview than her other "problems," namely her disobedience, uncontrollability, and "bad interpersonal relationships with parents."[72]

One of the most insidious social means of "policing" girls to conform, argue current criminologists, is girls' knowledge that poverty, a lack of privacy, homelessness, and unemployment can confront them if they reject the family or lose their claim to be "good girls." Yet a minority of girls did reject social norms, and the despair, anger, and resignation left by the taste and feel of poverty and insecurity, or by the fearful cloud of violence, were also factors in their criminalization. Their response to insecurity was not to embrace conformity or optimistic hope for the future, though some certainly struggled to find hope. Probation officers sometimes were at a loss to understand why some girls ran back to families deemed inadequate, uncaring, even violent. However, girls were caught in the confusion of conflicting emotions: they sensed that the economic and social cards had been stacked against their families, even if they also wanted to escape from them.

One teen, Rona, was removed as a child from her family because she was "neglected" by "abusive, alcoholic parents" who had their own conflicts with the law. By age twelve she found herself in juvenile court on charges of sexual immorality and carrying venereal disease. When she was released on parole from training school, she was encouraged to secure work as a domestic. She disliked the work, not the least because one employer would never let her forget her family background or sentence, "always throwing it back in her face." She returned to her family, to care for her younger brothers, of whom she was very fond. Trapped between feelings of affection and sympathy on the one hand, and anger and resentment on the other, she cooked and cleaned for the boys but sometimes called the police on her father or walked out and lived temporarily with friends.[73] Such conflicted feelings might also characterize more affluent girls who came into contact with the juvenile court, but their parents could also use other temporary solutions, such as sending them to a convent or relative, that were unavailable to poorer families.

Responding to Court Supervision

It is a mistake to see the process of court supervision as a monolithic exercise of power by court workers and judicial authorities over girls and their families, as did some earlier works emphasizing the class oppression inherent in the justice system. Still, this scholarship contains a kernel of truth, because there were concentrations of power within the system: favouring judges over parents, social workers over children, and parents over daughters and sons. Judges did not always agree with probation officers or with psychiatric assessments; they might incarcerate a girl against the advice of the medical report or occasionally allow more lenience than was suggested. But judges, court workers, and the child welfare workers they co-operated with were more often in some agreement about the basic causes and cures for delinquency, even if their strategies to "normalize" the girl differed.

Because parents used the courts to warn their daughters, control them, or re-establish lines of authority in the family, their relationship to these professionals was complex. They professed fears for their daughters' futures, or invoked their own respectability, sometimes even claiming an excessive religiosity that court workers suspected was more act than reality. The very fact that parents were *in* court, however, signalled their failure to some experts. Nonetheless, a minority of parents did challenge the courts' negative assessments of themselves and their children. One father from a reserve took issue with the Indian Agent's testimony, first pointing out that his daughter could not be sent away, as he had arthritis and he needed her to help him with his work, and, second, that he disputed her repeated immorality. "There are so many rumours about her," he countered, "that to be true she would have to be a woman of 50."[74] Other parents hid their daughters' pregnancies or sexual activities, or took issue with the court's moral condemnation of their own lives. A probation officer tracking down a seventeen-year-old who had already been in the Ontario Training School and was now suspected of living with a man faced down the girl's mother on the street. The mother "offered the usual copious tears," the worker noted sceptically in her report. But the mother had the final word on her daughter's supposed immorality: "Well, they've had their nights together so you might as well let them alone."[75] When a judge blamed a father, who was living common law with his housekeeper, for his daughter's immorality, the father countered indignantly, "I'm not the start of this trouble."[76]

The most difficult responses to probe are those of girls themselves, and no wonder. They were often highly vulnerable in the legal process. It was assumed that adults were better equipped to make decisions for them, and the culture of the courtroom was more likely to induce acqui-escence than confrontation. If they were in conflict with parents, foster parents, or guardians, girls had to convince the court of the truth of their side of the story, particularly if their parents or guardians appeared to be reliable and respectable. Only a minority flaunted an unabashed rejection of all authority. One middle-class teen facing the Toronto court in 1947 for lack of discipline, late nights, and a refusal to continue in school (though she was working) told the investigating officer that "all adults are stuffed shirts." According to the officer, "She hates every-body." Admitting that this was in many ways a case of "typical adoles-cent rebellion" rather than any "mental illness" did not stop the court from trying to press the distraught parents into institutionalizing her.[77]

A few girls openly challenged the court process; more often they voiced disagreement in private hearings with social workers and medical examiners. Disputing the court's right to judge her, one girl in the 1930s announced defiantly that the older man she slept with "was not the first man in my life and won't be the last."[78] Girls who ran away with men or had sex with them justified their actions with statements that they were in love or old enough to handle independence, or they pointed to adults engaging in the very same behaviour, with no similar censure. Girls also lashed out at family members, even probation officers, who they believed had betrayed them. "If you had kept your trap shut I would not be here," said one angry daughter to her mother, who had filed the complaint (and the girl was right). Another girl threatened to "put her mother in bed for three weeks." According to the "nervous" mother, the daughter had already threatened to kill her.[79] Big Sisters might also come under fire. "I thought she was going to help me, not prosecute me," one girl snapped to an unsympathetic judge when she realized her Big Sister had informed on her bad behaviour.

Girls also complained to investigators about their sexual abuse at the hands of relatives. As in the case of Yvette, the fifteen-year-old runaway who had been abused by her father, they expected some retribution for the abuser, not for themselves. They also complained about mistreat-ment at the hands of their own parents or step-parents or foster parents. One girl told the CAS officer that her foster parents "beat her with a horsewhip."[80] Others complained that they were denied any affection, made to work hard, or given inadequate food. Given the emphasis placed on sexual purity, the most astute among them knew that they should attempt to assert their virginity. One girl accused of hanging around disreputable "bootleggers and a thirty year old woman with a bad reputation" as well as an older man who lived nearby, repeatedly denied the sexual activity that the court doctor had implied in her report. "It is not true," she tried to counter. "I just went to say hello . . . he is only my friend . . . I know my mistakes [now]."[81] Others accepted past misdeeds but tried to put them in a sympathetic context, arguing that they ran away because they were "picked on at home," or locked out of the house, or that they were "going with bad company" who egged them on, daring them into thefts, runaway attempts, or sex experimentation.[82] Certainly, the less naive girls knew that a "pardon tale" to prevent them from being sent to training school was in order. "I'll come out ten times worse," pleaded one girl to her judge to avoid such a sentence.[83] It was an astute plea because it might well have been true.

For the girls, facing down a judge was certainly a less common experience than trying to explain their life to an interviewer from the CAS, a probation officer, or even a psychological or psychiatric examiner. And though the girls' stories sometimes seemed unbelievable, subsequent events might indicate that their accounts of abuse or neglect carried more weight than the parents' denials. In one case, for instance, a fifteen-year-old girl ran away from home, stealing a car with her boyfriend and making it as far as the U.S. border. The CAS was somewhat suspicious that the mother who had sworn out the complaint did not want her daughter at home, but disregarding the CAS report and the psychiatrist's recommendations entirely the judge sent her to training school. Once there, adamantly believing her sentence to be unjust, she only became more disturbed and, placed in detention, drew "macabre pictures of girls, with their heads cut off, and axe nearby, and the words 'you did this.'" When she was released social workers initially cited excellent treatment by her mother, but later they admitted that they had been hoodwinked. The girl was being locked out, pushed out of the home by the mother.[84]

Juvenile Courts: Apparent Successes and Troubling Realities

Open resistance on a girl's part was less common than accommodation; even girls' intermittent objections to being defined as delinquents were usually quelled over time. The majority of girls altered their behaviour during probation and did not reappear after a suspended sentence. They tended to strike out on their own as soon as they could, or perhaps they simply hid their activities far better. Indeed, the belief that "age is the best cure for delinquency"[85] had a strong resonance for girls in particular, because many of the status offences they were charged with – truancy, incorrigibility, promiscuity – were not defined as crimes in the adult world. The process of normalization, one might conclude, was effective, though there was enough sporadic rebellion on the part of girls and their families against the moral norms laid down by the courts to suggest that the results were not uniform.

One of the main objects behind the establishment of the juvenile courts and the JDA was thus achieved: by in large, girls were kept out of institutions like training schools. They were warned off "bad behaviour" or treated through some kind of probation, though sometimes removed temporarily from their own families in the process. Historians such as D. Owen Carrigan have pointed to the use of probation as proof of the JDA's positive success, and in one sense he is right. Yet other historians have been critical of the JDA and the "private technocratic" justice of family courts, which "eroded clients' legal rights" in favour of critical scrutiny of the working-class family.[86] Probation can also be read as an increased surveillance of the morals of working-class families, and an intrusive regulation of the sexuality of their daughters.

Behind the apparent successes of probation lay more troubling realities. Despite its legal justification as a child-saving institution, the juvenile court system reflected and indeed reproduced class, race, and gender inequalities. In a myriad of ways, material factors shaped, mediated, and legitimized the criminalization of delinquent girls. The insecurities of poverty and working-class life, the experience of violence, the perpetuation of racist ideas: all of these forces shaped the apprehension, sentencing, and treatment of young offenders. Even the sexualization of these girls, so clearly articulated in the court records, was intertwined with class and race: the ideological construction of "good" as opposed to "bad" girls cannot be disentangled from the material and social context that incited girls' conflicts with the law.

Integrated into the courts was a growing legion of new experts, educated in medical, social work, or social science disciplines, who saw themselves as the helping professions, aiding the rehabilitation of girls who had rejected dominant social norms. These experts did not overtake or subsume judicial authority, but rather worked hand in hand with the law to regulate delinquent girls, often through a process of encouraging them to create a new moral "subjectivity," to feel shame, repentance, regret, responsibility. For some girls, probation provided them with a chance to voice their dissatisfactions, protest the neglect or the traumas of violence they suffered, and demand better treatment. Parents and guardians also used the courts for their own purposes, to stabilize family life or reassert control over girls who were driving them crazy. Yet the agency of these clients seldom matched the power invested in the court, and in the last instance court personnel would most likely impose their expertise and solutions.

There is thus good reason for historians to cast a critical eye on the operation of juvenile courts and on the JDA's arbitrary powers and the way in which they were used. The paternalism of the courts, no matter how well-intentioned or protective in tone, also had the effect of criminalizing sexual behaviour that was not a crime for adults, and stigmatizing girls who were sometimes victims of violence or neglect. Feminists especially have criticized the manner in which juvenile justice created a sexual double standard of criminalization. Moreover, the family was portrayed as a private domain, with bad parents producing bad children, thus obscuring the way in which family both acted as a shock absorber for capitalist social relations, and itself became the site of unequal relations of gender power and oppression.

Girls before the courts had often seen the dark side of family life; many had coped with poverty or economic insecurity, though some, admittedly, just hated the imposition of every instance of adult authority. Still, offering these girls the ideal of a reconstituted family, even if it was temporarily acceded to, was often a superficial solution for more deep-seated social inequalities, alienation, and oppression. It was not simply that these problems were beyond the mandate of the courts. Rather, the juvenile justice system and the process of constructing "moral" female citizens were predicated upon a implicit tolerance of structures of economic inequality, deference to paternal authority, and racialized and sexualized images of delinquency. The process of normalizing girls thus had some short-term successes, but it could not halt the tide of girls who continued to run away to the streets.

Five

Treating the Intractable: Training Schools for Girls

While probation, removal from the home, or simply fear of incarceration resulted in most girls adapting – at least superficially – to the demands of the juvenile courts or other child welfare officials, some of them were deemed to be so disobedient, immoral, or high risk that they had to be isolated in institutions designed to change their behaviour. From the late nineteenth century, child-saving reformers and governments across Canada collaborated in efforts to construct industrial schools and, later, training schools for girls. As these institutions evolved they incorporated new ideas about curing so-called juvenile delinquents, adding services linked to medical, psychological, and social work aid, and they altered their physical structures and educational ideals to accord with current, progressive thinking on juvenile justice. Still, some telling continuities remained across the decades: most girls sentenced to industrial and training schools came from poor and working-class families; many had already experienced violence or debilitating economic and social insecurity; many were being isolated in hopes of altering their sexual morals; and, often, the prospect of turning them into moral citizens was seen as more precarious and difficult than the alteration of boys in conflict with the law.

Although only a small number of girls were incarcerated in this "closed custody" option, the treatment offered in these institutions tells us much about the definitions of, and attempted cures for, female delinquency – for those girls deemed most dangerous and intractable. Indeed, the treatment highlights in bold relief both the dominant definitions of "bad" girls and the prescribed ideals for "good" girls. To some extent, the institutions offered much the same strategies for dealing with delinquency as did the courts, child welfare workers, and even families. Rewards were juxtaposed with punishment, and shaming with positive encouragement: the velvet glove was an ongoing motif in the operation of juvenile justice. For teenage girls the experience of such institutional isolation was often dramatic, life-changing, and sometimes destructive. Their histories should not be forgotten, particularly given current debates on the benefits and drawbacks of isolating girls for YOA infractions.

Industrial and training schools – sometimes referred to generally as reform schools – assumed three closely related goals: preparing girls for responsible wage work, containing their sexual activity until marriage, and creating a new, subdued femininity. Although treatment was always the rhetorical motto of these schools, more direct, coercive forms of regulation were still part of the correctional equation. Nowhere is Foucault's writing on how discipline "makes" individuals, on how modern penal techniques are designed not only to regulate inmates but also to create their own self-regulation, more fitting than in the discussion of reform schools. Inmates were subject to "hierarchical observation" (the knowledge of always being under the gaze of the authorities), "normalizing judgements" (setting ideals as guidelines within which one is encouraged to act), and "examination" (the conventions and rituals that establish that the inmate is objectified, surveyed, scrutinized).[1]

That these institutions often drew on a rhetoric of both maternalism (at least until the 1960s) and treatment made the practice of regulation – and girls' resistance to it – even more complex. The system often depicted matrons and superintendents as surrogate mothers providing kindly everyday guidance as well as implementing discipline, yet, as in the case of Big Sisters, this approach also comprised a form of regulation or power, even if it was "naturalized" as an "ethic of care." As Kelly Hannah-Moffat argues vis-à-vis the history of women's prisons, a range of ideas, forms of power, and disciplinary regimes can co-exist, overlap, and intersect in a correctional institution.[2] Indeed, the "non-expert" advice and feelings that matrons imparted to their charges in industrial and training schools were intercut, first with religious belief and later increasingly with "scientific" and medical expertise. The simultaneous use of praise and punishment, incentives and lectures, social events, and the cruel punishment of the "hole," solitary confinement, epitomized this overlap in strategies.

Whether or not this regime succeeded, and what forms the actual feelings and responses of the girls themselves took, are the most difficult questions to answer. Nonetheless, even if the conclusions are limited both by the inadequate sources (left primarily by those in authority) and by our distance, in time and experience, from the incarcerated, the attempt at understanding remains important – especially if we are to sustain a political project of gaining knowledge about and empathy for those whose conflicts with the law continue to place them in closed-custody environments.

"Taming Rebel Souls": The Evolution of Industrial and Training Schools

Industrial schools for boys came first, a reflection of the dominant social fears of male criminality. Ontario's 1874 Industrial Schools Act first laid out the means of and rationales for sentencing boys to these schools. Children found begging or without jobs, "wandering" without "proper guardianship," habitual truants, or those who were growing up without "salutary parental control or education" due to neglect, drunkenness, or other vices on the part of their parents: all of them could be removed to industrial schools.[3] The Victoria Industrial School for Boys, established in Mimico in 1886, was supposed to differ from the existing reformatory for convicted criminal boys under twenty-one by *preventing* crime, taking in "homeless and neglected" Toronto boys who were likely to fall under the spell of criminal ways. The Victoria Industrial School was to be a midway point between a school and a reformatory. Rather than prescribing hard manual labour, it was to provide the pre-delinquent and delinquent children with "industrial training" and lessons in "moral character." It would offer a second chance for working-class boys caught in the web of poverty, family disintegration, and delinquency.[4]

Other separate juvenile institutions quickly followed. In Toronto a Refuge for Girls was placed initially within a separate space in the adult Mercer Reformatory for Females, but a new Industrial School for Girls, the Alexandra, was established in 1893. Catholics, concerned with ministering to (and maintaining) their own, quickly followed suit, establishing the St. Mary's Training School for Girls, located on the northern edge of Toronto. Similar institutions sprang up across the country. In Nova Scotia, Presbyterians and Methodists created the Maritime Home for Girls in 1914, and in Vancouver the Industrial Home for Girls opened in the same year. Child-saving advocates presented industrial schools as part of a broader progressive agenda, which included improved parole services and firm school attendance laws, though not all reformers were keen on the institutionalization of children. Some saw foster or family care as a preferred solution, arguing that putting first offenders or neglected children alongside more adept delinquents would simply double the number of delinquents.

Nonetheless, pro-foster care organizations, such as the Children's Aid Society, could, and did, take part in committals to reform schools. CAS agents had the same powers to arrest as did the police in child welfare matters, and they often advised magistrates on sentencing. Under the later Ontario Training School Act (1931 and 1939), for instance, child welfare officials could sidestep the courts, committing the child on their recommendation through the Training School Advisory Board, comprising appointees who advised the minister responsible for the operation of the schools. This long and well-entrenched tradition of combining court/legal sentences with admission through child welfare intervention reinforced the overlapping, blurred connection between poverty and crime, the welfare and correctional systems.

Ontario's industrial schools for girls and boys had common aims and promoters. The Alexandra and Victoria schools were both overseen by a philanthropic board, the Industrial Schools Association of Toronto. Composed of both wealthy benefactors and professionals from the middle classes, the board prescribed a program of basic literacy, religious and moral instruction, and gender-specific vocational training. Boys got lessons in trades such as carpentry, metal-working, and barbering, while girls were instructed in the domestic arts, as well as in the moral lessons of "true womanhood." In both industrial schools, the lines between poverty, delinquency, and dependency (for example, orphans, or those whose parents were in jail) were often hazy. The authorities assumed that most of the children came from the "unfortunate classes" and needed to be rescued from their undisciplined, immoral, and impoverished upbringing – "lifted out of the low sphere in which they lived" – and prepared for more respectable working-class life and labour.[5] As Susan Houston argued, for many of these reformers the main difference between the categories of neglected and criminal was that the neglected were "potential" rather than "actual" criminals.[6]

Girls, again, were more likely to be sent to industrial schools for "victimless crimes"[7] such as disobedience, incorrigibility, and sexual immorality, though some were also accused of petty theft. Most of them came from impoverished or working-class families, and often their disobedience was related to a refusal to partake in wage or domestic work combined with nights out or runs from home. In some cases, it was not simply the lust for pleasure that motivated the girl's escape into the urban streets, but violence at the hands of a family member; in other cases distraught single parents placed their daughters in the school as a temporary emergency measure in the face of financial or familial problems, believing that they could reclaim them when the home stabilized.[8]

Modelled on the latest in correctional fashion – that is, the cottage system, with matrons as surrogate mothers – the Alexandra Industrial School offered its "rebel souls" a cure for their profligacy based on basic literacy, religious training, practical domestic skills, feminine deportment, and, of course, the inculcation of good work habits.[9] Transforming girls from those who "preferred to loaf and gossip" to "honour citizens" was the goal, to be accomplished through both recreation and the redemption of hard work. Alexandra girls sewed hundreds, indeed thousands, of garments for the state. Central to its reform agenda, argues Iliana Arapis, was the understanding that wayward girls needed "a healthy dose of domesticity."[10] They were trained to be domestic servants or homemakers, simultaneously reshaping their inner lives to accommodate the values of co-operation and conformity, maternity and piety. The Alexandra's annual reports recounted its success stories, sometimes lauding girls who took up a calling such as nursing, but more often pointing to girls who worked as domestics to create a trousseau and marry respectably. Indeed, the same picture of an Alexandra inmate in white wedding garb, titled "Leaving the School as a Bride," appeared year after year in the annual reports to advertise this symbol of success. Despite the heavy use of benevolent maternal rhetoric, however, the "structure, organization and operation" of the Alexandra functioned in a more coercive manner, "much like an adult reformatory."[11]

By the late 1920s and early 1930s, both the Victoria and Alexandra faced severe criticism, though not simply because of the coercive nature of their governance. Even though industrial schools were managed by a philanthropic board, government grants increasingly sustained them, and government inspections decried their crowded conditions, buildings in disrepair, and autocratic administration. An Ontario royal commission of 1930 on public welfare recommended that the decrepit Alexandra be relocated to a modern building in a rural area, with more careful winnowing out of the mental defectives who were a detriment to the functioning of the school. After years of wrangling and various government reports, some industrial schools were finally taken over by the provincial government in 1934. The Industrial Schools Association Board recognized that it had "outlived its role," though its members felt somewhat put out that the government didn't thank them more profusely for their years of labour on behalf of "children of the worst type, feebleminded, hardened offenders from the most depraved homes."[12]

Moreover, by 1934 the government had opened its own training schools, which became the newest solution to cure delinquency. In 1925 the government, drawing on volunteer aid, opened its first model training school (originally called the Home and Welfare School) for boys in Bowmanville, and provincial legislation again clarified that children who came under the Children's Protection Act (that is, children who were neglected, or abused, or those under CAS care), the Industrial Schools Act, or the federal JDA could be committed to a training school. Eventually this legislation was replaced by the new Training School Act (TSA), passed in 1931 and amended in 1939. The TSA could be applied to boys and girls. Its mission statement bore telling similarities to earlier industrial school advertisements about their work: training school inmates were to absorb a "mental, moral and vocational education and training and profitable employment" as well as adopt a "change in attitude" so that girls and boys would adjust "harmoniously" to the community and be able "to earn a livelihood."[13]

Nonetheless, government-run training schools marked a shift in policy.[14] Industrial schools had been private, philanthropic institutions, supported with hefty doses of government money. Training schools were government institutions, aided by private volunteer aid. If the government was footing the bill, it would rather be in charge, guarding efficiency and competency – though it still allowed private Catholic training schools to operate with government grants. At the time the government's assumption of this role as child custodian was controversial. Some politicians and child-savers, such as the prominent child welfare leader Charlotte Whitton, feared that the role would discourage private charity – though Whitton was adamant that trained social workers should oversee all such endeavours, whether they were in the public or private sphere of social welfare.

Training schools also ushered in the increased use of social science, medical, and psychological experts. They were known for their emphasis on the streaming and segregation of children by intelligence: the aim was to segregate the feeble-minded child from the teachable delinquent. By the post-World War II period the system was placing less emphasis on mental defectives and more on the mentally ill as unreachable problems, but in both cases medical categorization and specific professional treatment were key themes. Religious instruction, though present, diminished; the new training schools were Protestant in general orientation but lacked the evangelical fervour associated with some of earlier institutions like the Alexandra.

In the 1930s training schools had become the latest in progressive penal thinking, delivering medical classification, psychological therapy (even more important by the 1950s), education, and vocational training, all under the banner of "treatment." Yet a cynic might comment on the striking similarities between industrial and training schools. Like the earlier industrial schools movement, the lobby for training schools emphasized that unfortunate children were being saved by community action; bad parents had caused the problem, but society had a responsibility to children who were innocent, malleable, and trainable. There was still a blurring of lines between neglect, dependency, and delinquency, as girls from all these categories ended up in training schools. Moreover, the categories were assumed to be the province primarily of the working classes and the underclass, despite public rhetoric maintaining that the schools were for all children. In a sentencing address in 1933, a Hamilton judge told a frightened girl that she was going to the Alexandra, a school with the same "advantages" as a "boarding school for the better off." In the early years the Ontario Training School for Girls, too, was also portrayed as a "very fine school" for "lucky girls." This absurd rendition of reform schools as veritable private schools for the privileged was soon discarded, though some judges tried to balance the shame of the sentence with reassurances to the parents that the girl would be trained for useful work.[15]

A reform rhetoric of protection and education masked the reality that these were closed custody institutions, correctional in nature. Although industrial and training schools were at first bounced from one ministry to another, they came to rest in the later 1940s with the minister responsible for correctional or "reform institutions," probably the most apt place for them. The earliest title used – Refuge for Girls – denoted a place that girls could run to for protection. "Industrial school" denoted useful education in industrial work; and "training school" had the connotation of a place for vocational learning. But these were not schools. Girls could not simply walk away from them, because they were incarcerated, made wards of the state. When parents subsequently tried to secure their release, or when children decided that they wanted no part of the training offered, they discovered that, bars or no bars, a training school also functioned as a prison. Finally, both the earlier industrial school and the later training school adopted common tactics for reform. Girls were quarantined socially and medically on arrival, their "past slowly erased" until they were placed in the curative surroundings of familial cottage life.[16]

Adjusting to Cottage Life

Perhaps the usefulness, drawbacks, and impact of institutionalization can best be drawn out through a case study of one of these institutions, the Ontario Training School for Girls – looking at its school regime, the girls' reactions to their incarceration, and the patterns of their eventual parole.

In its inception OTSG, situated in Galt, Ontario, was an equal opportunity project for more affluent rural and urban women's organizations: Big Sisters, Local Councils of Women, and Women's Institutes pressured the government for a girls' training school modelled on the same lines as the boys' school in Bowmanville. These women reformers did not want to see girls left behind as training became the recommended panacea for combatting delinquency. Perhaps the reigning Ontario government was astutely aware of the female vote-getting potential of establishing a new training school. It also knew the value of drawing on private philanthropy for the project; it secured private donors who purchased the land for the construction of the school.

When the school was opened by the wife of the Ontario premier on September 7, 1933, it was portrayed as a modern, model enterprise. The local newspaper lauded this "door of opportunity for underprivileged girls of Ontario," taking care not to overly stress the word "delinquent." Since committals could be made through child welfare organizations, this caution was understandable, but it also underscored how OTSG was promoted as a charitable, and thus publicly popular, project. "This is not a reformatory," the minister declared at the opening, "but a place where underprivileged children may be taught. . . . The new approach to juvenile delinquency is to take growing girls starting life with the wrong ideas and by guidance and useful training change their whole concept of life until they are established in the path of rectitude and they take a profitable place in society." The minister stressed the philanthropic goodwill behind OTSG, and its important place within the *educational* system of the province, but not its importance to the juvenile justice system.[17]

Bureaucrats had made the usual junkets abroad to study the latest in juvenile institutions, and the result was a multibuilding complex based on the cottage system, with a reception/hospital section, administrative offices, an assembly hall, classrooms, and two cottages. Each of the cottages had twenty-five single bedrooms rooms, as well as its own kitchen and dining room (later expansion substantially increased the number of residential rooms). Architecture and environment were part of the process of reformation. OTSG was placed within a semi-rural area, close to a small city, but far away from the corrupting temptations of Toronto streets. Idyllic rural peace and tranquillity had been prescribed for female correctional institutions since the late nineteenth century,[18] as the kind of environment equated with new beginnings and curative healing. Ample outdoor areas allowed for healthy sports, the possibilities of garden care, isolation from prying, voyeuristic male eyes, and, of course, fewer possibilities to escape easily to the city. The original buildings were red brick with white trim, and the cottages resembled large houses, conveying the image of a welcoming, domestic dwelling. Both spatially and psychologically, the cottage system was meant to evoke the notion of a comforting family. Each cottage had a house mother or matron, and girls contributed to the domestic functioning of the unit by cooking, cleaning, setting tables, and otherwise helping to take care of things. The very word "cottage" contradicted the notion that this might be a prison. After all, weren't cottages the retreats of the idle rich in the Muskoka lakes north of Toronto?

The reception/hospital area was crucial to the modern image of the school. On entry, girls were placed there for orientation and for medical and psychological examinations. The emphasis on diagnostic testing was considered a major step forward, and, indeed, it stood in contrast to some Catholic institutions for girls in Quebec that still stressed the power of faith over the power of psychology.[19] OTSG was lauded as the "first institution of its kind in the British empire" where the girls were all in the "normal mental range."[20] This aspect represented the triumph of testing, streaming, and segregation. Even though the methods of testing intelligence and personality changed over time, the diagnostic centre was crucial linchpin of the school's work. In later years the centre would not only sort out girls' programs within OTSG, but would also be used to assign them to other institutions. By the mid-1960s, girls could also be sent to Trelawney in nearby Bolster; it was a place for the youngest and most promising charges, and was more akin to a group home facility. Or they could be sent to a new training school in Lindsay if their academic scores looked good. If their tests were less promising, they were kept in Galt for vocational education. No wonder the girls themselves quickly understood the epithet that emerged for Galt: the "last chance school for girls."[21]

The average stay in OTSG varied from nine to eighteen months. Superintendents constantly chided the government when there was overcrowding and girls had to be pushed through the program quickly, because longer sentences gave them more time to modify the girls' character. But for most girls, the earlier they could go out "on placement," a form of parole, the better, though some still had to wait years until they were fully released from state surveillance.[22]

Most of the girls sent to OTSG were fourteen or fifteen (although they could come in as young as ten), and their committals noted problems with petty theft, incorrigibility, truancy, running away from home, and sexual immorality. Ultimately, though, sexual activity – perceived, possible, or real – was often the lightning rod that attracted incarceration. Moreover, the vast majority of these girls came from working-class and poor families, often households facing crises and tensions such as unemployment, disability, contact with the CAS, and violence. Economic insecurity was so prevalent in these girls' lives that the funnelling process in the juvenile justice system became eminently clear. Middle-class or more respectable working-class girls in conflict with the law were more likely to avoid incarceration; the poorest children were less likely to. The government's own statistics on why girls were incarcerated, however, did not categorize the material as much as the disciplinary problems precipitating incarceration: the top three reasons for a training school sentence point invariably to parental inadequacy, noting "poor home, no control," "parents separated," and "fair home, no control," among other factors. (See Table 5.1.)

When new girls arrived on the OTSG doorsteps, their first stop was the medical exam, including a psychiatric interview and TB and VD tests. Like some girls forced to undergo court-ordered internals, a few OTSG inmates objected strenuously to the mandatory medical. When one girl returned from a placement outside the school and faced her required internal, she refused the procedure, initially accepting her punishment of solitary detention and floor-scrubbing rather than undergo the examination. Orientation was also designed to teach a girl the rules and routines and to begin the process of resocialization – separating her from previous bad associates and habits and encouraging acceptance of the new lines of authority. Psychologists often described a transition process in the school in which the girl's previous self was reinscribed, rewritten, perhaps only after an initial rebellion against the rules: "She needs to go through a process of disillusionment with her past associates, then rebellion, then perhaps she may see the light."[23]

Statements in girls' files also indicate the traumas of separation, isolation, and anxiety as they struggled with an alien environment. She is "sullen, rebellious resentful, and does not want to be at the school," remarked one assessment. Another girl's initial reaction was retreat: "She cries easily, is full of self pity and does not mix with others."[24] Girls' responses ranged from quiet adaptation to immediate disagreement with the medical examiner, even pleading for his help in securing release. One girl complained to the doctor that "she had only run away from the [CAS] shelter because she was afraid of coming here. She feels her committal was unjustified and has found no congenial girls. She does not want to be a domestic and feels doomed to this if she stays. [She maintains] she should not have been sent here . . . saying her uncle ill-used her."[25] A few girls took drastic measures, such as the one who "took an overdose of pills to try to get home, as she said she was lonely" (though her response had the opposite effect). The

Table 5.1
Top Five Factors Contributing to Delinquency of
Those Committed or Admitted to Galt, 1935-64

Year	Top Factors Contributing to Delinquency	Number of Girls Cited	
		N	%
1935	Poor Home, No Control	18	34.6
	Either Parent Immoral	9	17.3
	Mother Dead	6	11.5
	Either Parent with Mental Defective	4	7.7
	Fair Home, No Control	4	7.7
1941	Parents Separated	21	19.8
	Either Parent Immoral	15	14.2
	Father Dead	13	12.3
	Poor Home, No Control	11	10.4
	Either Parent with Mental Defective	10	9.4
1947	Parents Separated	22	25.0
	Poor Home, No Control	14	15.9
	Fair Home, No Control	12	13.6
	Alcoholic Parents	12	13.6
	Father Dead	5	5.7
	Either Parent Immoral	5	5.7
1953	Parents Separated	40	38.5
	Fair Home, No Control	21	20.2
	Either Parent Immoral	9	8.7
	Poor Home, No Control	7	6.7
	Alcoholic Parents	6	5.8
	Either Parent with Court Record	6	5.8
1959	Associations	27	22.1
	Poor Home, No Control	17	13.9
	Fair Home, No Control	15	12.3
	Parents Separated	14	11.5
	Either Parent Immoral	10	8.2
1964	Associations	23	24.7
	Parents Separated	23	24.7
	Fair Home, No Control	20	21.5
	Poor Home, No Control	13	14.0
	Father Dead	4	4.3
	Stepfather	4	4.3

Source: Ontario, *Annual Reports on Ontario Training Schools.*

superintendent complained that one twelve-year-old "had only recently got over the childish habit of playing with dolls," and that another girl was "afraid of storms and the dark" – vivid reminders that these were, after all, still young girls coping with an extremely difficult incarceration.[26]

In contrast to these common experiences, in a 1940 public report the superintendent wrote about the uplifting orientation story of "Mary," an inmate who was quickly awakened to the joys of the school's possibilities. The story stressed girls' exercise of choice about their activities, the kind maternal care and expert advice they received, and the support from other students. Mary was first invited by the house mother to her "sitting room" for a friendly chat about the opportunities and activities in the school. She was provided with some clothes, told that she would be allowed some say over her clothing in the future, and was delighted to find that the "food cooked in her cottage was very tasty," though some of the girls were "counting their calories." After a medical exam she was promised needed dental work and then escorted through the school routine by a friendly girl who pointed proudly to the common room. The girls had painted it themselves. Mary found that everyone shared in the work, that girls appreciated the advice of the medical staff (one girl was "cured" of her temper tantrums by keeping a "temper-diary"), and that there were opportunities for music, handicrafts, and many other diversions. Indeed, the girls were taken to the circus in town on her first night. By the time Mary "crawled into her comfortable bed her first night, she remembered that she had expected to be homesick, but there really hadn't been time!"[27]

The public story of Mary was not necessarily the private story relayed in girls' files. The superintendent did, however, quite accurately recount the training and educational options accorded Mary. Girls generally received academic training for the morning, and then turned to vocational training in the afternoon, though academic training was also geared to age and IQ results. When the school was set up in the 1930s, vocational training was essentially domestic training, with emphasis on four areas: preparation of food, sewing and clothing, laundry, and household management. By the 1950s home economics was described with proliferating subcategories, including baby care, interior decorating, and table setting, yet aside from these seeming refinements, it remained centred on the basics of cooking, sewing, and cleaning.

Other kinds of vocational training gradually emerged, including beauty parlour work, "commercial" (that is, typing), and power-operating in the laundry room. Still, these segments were less common than the two basics: grade school education and domestic vocational. In the 1950s the superintendent complained privately to the government that the beauty training was almost useless, not providing girls with real apprenticeships: "The beauty salon is a problem; it neither trains the girls and certifies them, [any more] than it teaches individuals how to do their hair. . . . When they do each other's hair, they are not learning self reliance."[28] Moreover, most girls were not able to train fully for white-collar or secretarial work within OTSG: it is finally possible this year, said the 1944 report, to give "a few girls commercial training." OTSG's reports on how girls spent their time in the school highlight the importance of basic education, followed by domestic and vocational training. (See Table 5.2.)

Table 5.2
Activities of Residents during Year,
Galt Training School for Girls, 1935-64

	1935	1940	1945	1950	1955	1960	1964
Educational Activities							
Full time – Classroom	0	24	62	91	126	158	160
Part time – Classroom	44	98	76	107		119	
Full time – Vocational Shops	2	96	87				
Part time – Vocational Shops	44	98	76	108			
Occupational Activities							
Part Time – General Work					6	5	
Cooking and Sewing[a]	29						
Culinary		194		47	49	41	11
Sewing		194	40	22	4	4	6
Gardening[b]	1						
General Domestic	7	73	72	154			
Hairdressing	4	23		6	29	12	15
Laundry			71	154	1	7	8
Nurse's Assistant			7	4	7	13	6
Farming/Horticulture		32	47	65			
House Maintenance		218	40		12	29	
Office and Commercial[c]	5	6	2	39	17	2	39
Woodworking and Hobbies				129			
Piano				50			
Maintenance and Paint Shop							30
Stores[d]							5

a. From 1940 on, cooking and sewing listed as two separate categories.
b. Gardening was replaced with "Farming and Horticulture" in 1940.
c. Of the 39 girls reported as receiving occupational training in "Office and Commercial" in 1964, 34 were full time, and 5 were part time.
d. Part-time training only.
Source: Ontario, *Annual Reports on Ontario Training Schools.*

Vocational training might be undertaken along with academic education (the pre-vocational, as the classes were sometimes called), or it might be girls' *only* education. A group of girls referred to as the "specials" emerged in the 1940s. The name was something of a misnomer, except that they worked *especially* hard. Their practical training in the household arts essentially meant that they spent all their time working on the school's domestic upkeep: helping in the kitchen, cleaning, tending the garden, even removing snow. This facet was also common to adult correctional institutions, where inmate labour reduced the institution's costs, paid back the government, and satisfied those who worried that idle hands were dangerous and believed that labour was a cure for the troubled soul.

In the 1930s and into the 1940s most girls were seen as benefiting primarily from a grade school education, and in an era when learning disabilities were not part of the scientific lexicon it is not surprising that some students did not fit easily into the academic routine. Superintendents continued to complain about the low mentality among some of the students (though as much as possible such students were sent to Orillia, or later Smith Falls, institutions for "mentally retarded" children). Those complaints may have reflected students' difficulties in learning, not simply their inability to learn. Only a small number of them were educated in high-school subjects; a few attended the local collegiate, though their overseers admitted that those students had a hard time socially. They were "pointed to and giggled at," marked out negatively because of their connection to the OTSG.[29]

Even when they were sent on placement outside of the school, few girls had their board fully paid so that they could finish high school. More often they were sent out to work. Some had to combine the two. As one placement officer noted realistically, a fifteen-year-old who was trying to go to high school, do her homework, and do domestic labour in the home where she boarded was so exhausted that she would most likely give up trying to better herself. Perhaps, the officer feared, the girl would soon be "taking up with undesirables" again.[30] Symptomatic of the government's view of further education was its refusal to provide the paltry funds needed to send girls to high school. In 1936 the OTSG superintendent went to bat for permission to fund two "outstanding" students who were already doing well in commercial courses so that they could continue in high school. The response from Deputy Provincial Secretary C.J. Neelands was swift and short: "By 16, they should be earning their keep, not on the taxpayers' bill."[31]

Although by the 1950s and 1960s the authorities saw at least some high-school education as a useful endeavour, the emphasis on training girls for their assigned class/gender place in the labour force remained strong. Placement reports clarified the fit between OTSG training and working-class labour. Although live-in domestic work was less common in the postwar period, girls were trained to be mother's helpers, and the channelling of the less academically competent into this option provides a telling comment on the qualifications perceived as being useful for child care – and this in the era of supposed glorification of motherhood. By 1960 more girls were listed as spending full-time in the classroom, but they were still being educated with an eye to taking on early wage work in areas such as retail work, waitressing, mother's helpers, factory work, or a category simply described as "miscellaneous" work – an indication of its uncertain and probably low status. (See Tables 5.3, 5.4.)

Table 5.3

Placement Statistics (percentages), Galt OTS 1937-61

Type of Placement	1937	1940	1943	1946	1949	1952	1955	1958	1961
Returned Home	6.0	5.7	13.7	13.4	14.0	42.0	38.6	61.8	43.3
Foster Homes and/or Boarding Homes	22.4	33.0	14.6	28.7	7.7	10.7	11.4	5.7	19.4
Work Placements	26.9	53.8	33.2	32.3	26.8	29.5	30.0	10.8	25.0
Other Institutions	4.5	3.8	18.6	7.9	11.1	10.7	19.3	19.1	10.6
Absent without Leave	40.3	3.8	19.9	17.7	40.4	7.1	0.7	2.5	1.7
Totals	100.0	100.0	100.0	100.0	100.0	100.0	100.0	100.0	100.0

The format of the placement reports changed completely as of 1962.
Source: Ontario, *Annual Reports on Ontario Training Schools.*

Table 5.4

Summary of Placements, Galt OTS 1937-62

Type of Placement	1937	1942	1947	1952	1957	1962
School	19	33	12	30	17	33
Employed	68	128	177	224	53	77
Other Institutions	1	39	17	0	2	2
At Home	23	28	26	5	10	21
Unknown/AWL	0	0	12	3	3	16

Source: Ontario, *Annual Reports on Ontario Training Schools.*

While many girls were sent to OTSG to alter their sexual and moral characters, the inculcation of the work ethic was an essential part of their cure. "Our philosophy," said the superintendent, is to "develop proper work habits, girls who appreciate the value of work, teaching them acceptable deportment, cleanliness, neatness."[32] Raising the underclass to the level of the respectable working class was deemed a laudable goal of the institution. Making the case for OTSG's good works, one superintendent argued: "I know there is a curve in the living standards of our released wards. They grew up in the sordid slums and now they live in respectable working-class districts."[33]

In the eyes of government bureaucrats and penal workers, their role was to make girls more self-sufficient, and to prepare them for jobs that befitted their skills and were readily available – all practical goals. When a government official once frowned on girls driving tractors as "unadvisable,"[34] he had a realistic sense that jobs for female tractor drivers in the 1950s were non-existent, while those for mother's helpers were plentiful. This realism, however, revealed underlying assumptions about the girls' having limited abilities, and that some even deserved limited options. It unfortunately resulted in girls being pressed into the lowest paid, most insecure jobs, precisely the kind of work that many girls had witnessed bringing their mothers and families to levels of poverty. In decades when the options for working-class women were expanding slightly to include more white-collar and blue-collar work, many OTSG girls were being trained primarily for the isolated drudgery of being a maid.

Girls who had unusual ambitions – to be doctors, lawyers, or writers, for instance – were seen as unrealistic, if not unbalanced, and were urged to substitute their crazy dreams for practical goals. One girl, admitted in the 1930s, complained bitterly and repeatedly that her father (who had laid the complaint against her for incorrigibility) had not let her continue in school past age thirteen. She wrote poetry and managed to place one of her poems in the children's page of *The Globe and Mail*, but her dream of becoming a writer was discouraged as being unrealistic. Instead, she was released for domestic or factory work. Her psychiatric appraisals worried that she might be a "schizoid personality" in the making, for she had vivid fantasies and she made up stories. Her favourite was one about becoming a cowgirl on a Western prairie ranch. The report described her as "fanciful, wild, forgetful," and its recommendation was to "curb her fantasy life," even though there was some realization that she might be constructing stories to counteract her "frustrated ambition for an education." But was she actually unbalanced as they feared, or simply an imaginative, potentially creative young women with no outlets, role models, or encouragement for writing in her stark working-class life?[35]

Training was a word that encompassed more than education and vocational skills: it was also implied in OTSG's goal to create a femininity that was co-operative, polite, unaggressive, and certainly not sexually assertive. This goal was to be accomplished through extracurricular activities, as well as through many rules governing social interaction. The OTSG used social life to erase the taint of girls' inadequate upbringing, especially families whose "physical appetites" and leisure were low-class and unacceptable, focusing on booze, sex, or other vices.[36] The school offered healthy alternatives, in much the same way as the recreational movement offered role models and alternatives to pre-delinquent children.

Public reports on OTSG often made it sound like a summer camp, noting Halloween parties, handicrafts, singing, piano playing, clay modelling, knitting, basketball, skating, weekly swims at the YWCA, and much more. Yet the girls did not pursue all these activities, and some had to earn them as privileges. Team sports and physical education were considered very important (although girls could also lose privileges there as well), and in the late 1950s Superintendent Ruth Bentley clearly loved to see her cadet corps parading through the grounds, surely a sign of discipline if ever there was one. The school also encouraged religious activities – as long as they were not too fervently "emotional." As well as requiring girls' attendance at chapel service, the school allowed some proselytizing by local good Samaritans. "Christian businessmen come in once a week at night," reported the superintendent, and "the local Baptist Church sends cars every Sunday" to take girls to church.[37]

Girls were also allowed a certain contact with the community, though not on their terms. Exceptional athletes, for instance, were occasionally permitted to play on community teams, and the sense of accomplishment these talented girls gained helped them cope both with school regimentation and their own past hurts. But, again, these privileges could be cut off if the girl was disobedient. One talented ballplayer was allowed to join a local team, travelling with them to games, but her later parole problems were chalked up to "being spoiled" by this experience. She was unusually multitalented, doing well at sports, music, and school, and she even talked about being a lawyer. This ambition, of course, was completely discredited, even though she had committed no criminal offence and was not even "immoral." It was her total lack of respect for authority that had condemned her to OTSG. The superintendent seemed almost pleased (vindicated, at least) when she landed in the Mercer Reformatory after breaking parole at age seventeen.[38]

Some girls also attended a two-week summer camp, staffed by volunteers from the Macdonald Institute, a "household science" college in Guelph, and they might be taken into local cities for entertainment. The school used these activities to further emphasize the arts of domesticity and femininity, and to introduce the girls to good role models. When the school temporarily moved to Cobourg during and after World War II, the girls made sandwiches for the local business and professional women's club teas. They also put on plays for community groups, including a musical, "Sunbonnet Sue," and a work they penned themselves, tantalizingly titled "The Tomboy Girl." But mixing with the locals also held out the temptation of boys. While the opposite sex was supposed to be off limits, the superintendent herself admitted, "There is hardly a girl in the school over 13 who is not interested in boys after several months incarcerated in the school and if we are to keep all potential sex problems in school until 16, we will need room for 300."[39]

Contact with the community thus posed security dilemmas. On one entertainment trip in the 1950s, the girls were escorted to a YWCA-sponsored "circus" with local acts. Several men, complained the superintendent to the Ministry of Reform Institutions, incited the girls by posing "almost nude" in one act, with one of the culprits a member of the notorious "Pearl St. gang in Brantford" and a "recent release from Guelph [reformatory]." There was a flurry of quick note-passing in the lobby, and some girls quickly went "awl" (or AWOL), supposedly aided by Brantford's gangland. To make matters worse, one of OTSG's own, a demure ballerina, who danced at this occasion, also went awl. If the penal workers did not count this as a resounding success for community contact, the girls, bored with their circumscribed single-sex lives, probably enjoyed the diversion.[40] The girls, then, were not completely cloistered, and they were even photographed by local papers, although school policy supposedly declared such exposure off limits. They put on fashion shows and once entertained the Galt locals with a "successful minstrel show" in which forty girls posed as "pic-ci-ninnies in black-face," and one played the role of Sambo. The superintendent proudly passed on the newspaper clipping reporting on this event to the minister. The local paper, surprisingly, also made no comment on the racially derogatory nature of the presentation, congratulating the girls on keeping "the audience laughing."[41]

Extracurricular pastimes were not just for fun: they were to be learning experiences. In all activities, students were encouraged to be their own monitors, "developing orderly habits."[42] They were also encouraged to monitor each other, and the penal workers clearly drew on student gossip as a means of locating disobedience and rebellion. By the late 1940s a student council was in operation, helping to "plan parties and harmonize the routine of the school."[43] In the 1950s the girls began to publish their own paper, "Echoing Halls." A surviving copy contains poems, interviews, and short stories, including one on the origins of the Easter Bunny and one, perhaps written by a child with some experience of family addiction, warning that alcohol will "either leave you a nobody, homeless on the street, a parent now, or one who will ruin your children's lives." A poem dedicated to "Mother" also contained a mixture of disciplinary warning and love: "Be kind to your mother and don't sass her back, for it you do, look out for a slap." While the paper provided an outlet for feelings and creativity, it also provided the administration with another means of reinforcing the rules. In one piece, "How to Improve Your School Habits," students were told to "keep your clothes pressed, hair brushed, skin clean. We must always smell nice. Do not be insolent to staff, never start rumours. Do not talk in line up."[44]

One of the major aims of OTSG was to transform girls deemed too tough, rambunctious, loud, and boisterous – all words used again and again – into more polite, passive, feminine young women. It was a transformation also linked to class, for the loud and boisterous were presumed to be the working class and underclass, whose less than Waspy ways would make them less-than-ideal domestics and service workers. Understanding full well the change of persona expected of her, and how irrelevant it was to her subsistence life on a reserve, one young Native woman simply retorted in response to the demands for more demure behaviour: "I'm no lady!"[45]

The school thus ran on an intricately balanced system of rewards and punishments: visits home, visits from home, movies, and other pleasures were earned through good, and lost through bad, behaviour. According to later observers in the 1960s, even basics such as blankets and toilet paper could be removed.[46] Girls' progression through the school program was marked by different coloured bows, worn on their uniform; they could lose bows through backsliding for pushing another student in line, passing secret notes, talking back, or swearing. In short, behavioural modification though the "carrot and the stick" was an essential part of the regime. While this same approach held true for many ordinary classrooms in the province, the OTSG rules were often excessively strict, imposed on girls who had no recourse to complain, no parents to defend them, and, at worst, could end up in solitary if they disobeyed.[47]

The image of solitary was not what came to mind for most community members when they thought of training schools. Even if a rhetoric of treatment prevailed, there were moments when the public protested the "soft" lives of training school inmates. Their complaints were not unlike those heard today about the need for less fun and more punishment for incarcerated young offenders. In the early years of World War II, for instance, when OTSG buildings were handed over the to military, the school moved temporarily (for almost a decade, as it turned out) to Cobourg, to smaller, less adequate quarters, with limited dormitory beds, forcing the school and courts to put more children on probation. The public outcry that followed called for discipline as the only cure for delinquency. In a letter to the newspaper, an upstanding member of the Protestant Women's Federation said her volunteer court visiting had shown her that "probation was a farce, [with] very little supervision," and that "most repeaters think court is a joke as they will only get a suspended sentence." Other individuals and welfare and educational groups urged the ministry to restore training school places to inculcate children's obedience, discipline, and "respect for the law."[48]

About a decade later a legislature Select Committee on Reform Institutions gave law and order MPPs and the public another chance to voice similar concerns. "Swimming pools [at Bowmanville], TV, and [nice] clothes are . . . ruining the lives of inmates," reported *The Globe and Mail*. "The Chair of the Committee says luxurious living is spoiling inmates for [future] life outside."[49] That luxurious living could be equated with scrubbing floors would have been amusing to many girls in OTSG. Penal workers defended their work, and privately OTSG Superintendent Isobel MacNeil condemned the committee's failure to criticize the "deplorable homes, no decent housing, irresponsible parents" causing delinquency, and also attacked the suggestion that her girls did not even deserve the same "decent food, clothing and recreation" as other children had. The symbol of training school luxury became the cigarette: three a day were offered to some girls of sixteen and over who were already smoking. Law and order types protested the cost, saying it was $6,000 a year, clearly an exaggeration. What was perhaps more revealing was that the superintendent's defence of the policy only revealed again how pathetically young these incarcerated girls were. The younger ones without a cigarette ration, she said, got candy instead.[50]

Adaption, Accommodation, and Therapy

What did it actually mean to be sent away to an institution, at as young an age as eleven, but more often at fourteen or fifteen? Girls responded in a variety of ways. Some quickly accommodated themselves to the regime, astutely recognizing that fitting in would secure their release. Some, it would appear, internalized prescribed norms of cleanliness, deference, and politeness as being superior to their former values. Others certainly suffered from loneliness and anxiety, showing obvious physical reactions, from bedwetting and insomnia to crying. Superintendents were fond of saying that OTSG offered the girls security and care that had not been provided at home. Some girls did come from such impoverished families that they had been pilfering on the streets for food; others knew the barren texture of life shaped by parental unemployment, insecure jobs, and paltry welfare payments. Girls might remark that they had "better lives at the school than at home," with more food, privacy, and security, if economic want, violence, addiction, or parental mental illness had made their previous lives difficult to predict, or worse.[51] This new experience did not always lead them to reject their families. A girl from the North, who had at home supposedly been sent out without any food to "sell flowers in the streets," defended her sole-support father, saying he "was sick and unable to do the best for the family. . . . He was punished for not getting relief."[52]

The youngest girls, or those open to emotional connection, sometimes bonded with matrons or the superintendent no matter how strict the regime. Some sought structure after having none previously in their lives. The case of "Donna," who came to OTSG at only ten years old, reveals the neediness of such young children as well as the painful inadequacies of institutional and foster care and the presumptions, based on class and family, that clung to many girls even after they left the school. Donna, who lived in a small city in Eastern Ontario, had been taken away from her mother by the CAS when she was only one year old. She went through five foster homes in the early 1940s before being committed under the Training School Act for being "incorrigible," which in her case meant "temper tantrums" at home and at school, accompanied by the all too vague charge that she had "recently attempted sexual experience" (which could have been kissing, for all we know). The CAS offered the scientific equation of "like mother, like daughter," declaring that "she was trying to be like her mother," who despite her "good family" had become an alcoholic and had a "vile tongue."

After a stay at OTSG Donna was sent out again to a foster home, only to be judged negatively: the foster parents and teachers determined that she was "attention seeking and jealous," that her intelligence was low and her school work problematic, and she was rude. Not surprisingly, her temper tantrums worsened after she heard that the authorities were shipping her off to Orillia. The final explanation that social workers gave for her problems laid bare the racism that occasionally surfaced in their reports: "She is very dark skinned, appearance suggests Indian heritage." Yet Donna's letters back to the current OTSG superintendent were often polite, and certainly searching for approval.

> Dear Miss Pender: Did you enjoy Xmas? I did. I got lots of presents, I will try to be a good girl. . . . Could I have my pink taffeta dress? . . . I wrote this [letter] to my mother too . . .

> Dear Miss Pender
> I think of you always
> Though I'm far from home
> Every day I'm near you
> From your side I'll never roam
> May God Bless you dear Miss Pender
> And I will always pray
> That I'll be very near you
> Through Life's darkest way.[53]

Who is to say that the child who penned this letter and poem at age eleven or twelve was not simply disturbed by her precarious status as an "undesirable" foster child with no certain home?

Other girls also sometimes wrote back to the school, professing their desire to maintain a good record: "I'm contented now, Miss Pender, I'm working hard to get my name back in red ink in your black book." Or they could be even more contrite: "Miss MacNeil . . . I cannot explain my actions [but] I am ashamed of how I treated you and others."[54]

Girls who did adopt the much-encouraged OTSG persona still found it difficult to wipe the past away. One astute superintendent noted that no matter how unhappy her family life had been, an inmate "began to think her family was a paradise" after being incarcerated for some time.[55] Girls who came to believe that their families were immoral still had to wrestle with their tortured feelings, as in the case of one girl whose mother had "chosen" the immorality of a common-law mate over securing custody of her children: "She has considerable affection for her [mother], but still says the home was erratic. . . . There was an emotional leave taking in which the mother said she would commit suicide without her children. . . . She knows her mother is unstable, but worries about her health." Perhaps the real question is why the mother was forced to make this choice, and how girls, so young, were to cope with adult anxieties, responsibilities, and problems over which they had little control.

The most emotionally troubled girls were supposed to receive psychological and psychiatric care. The staff and a psychologist usually selected those they believed needed a psychiatric interview, yet the resulting session was never carried out with a resident doctor. In the early years OTSG drew on people from the Hamilton Mental Health Clinic for a half day of interviews a month. Later the school used doctors from Kingston or Toronto, but this sometimes meant sessions of one or two days a month for all the girls. Despite the emphasis in the public promotional literature at the time on "treatment," and even the academic reflection since then on the "overmedicalization" of women, in reality it proved harder to see a shrink than not see one. Psychiatrists often had little time other than to listen to girls' confessional stories involving past sexual abuse or mistreatment, or to their current complaints of unhappiness and bad treatment by staff. One psychiatrist noted that an incest victim was "plagued by her past" and needed "extensive psychotherapy . . . so Training School will not be a help," revealing how meagre were the services offered.[56]

Nowhere were the limits of medical care more clearly revealed than with sexual abuse victims. Some psychologists and doctors prescribed the cure of "forgetting the past" (even if the girl had to go back to the same household). Since this repression seemed to work for some, they didn't understand why it failed for others. When a girl appeared who seemed truly disturbed by sexual abuse, doctors and psychologists alike were limited by their training in the dominant medical discourses of the time (which downplayed sexual abuse and incest), and sometimes by an underlying suspicion that girls in training school were less than reliable storytellers, especially if they were supposedly promiscuous. The results for girls already traumatized were often tragic. In one case a girl who was deemed promiscuous, a runaway who had been caught lying about certain exploits, was cast as a likely "fabricator" of her incest accusations. After she made two suicide attempts and said she wanted to "kill her parents," the doctor initially downplayed her behaviour with the diagnosis of "immature but no psychotic behaviour." He was subsequently forced to backtrack, but was still inclined to see allegations of abuse as a fabrication because the girl supposedly heard voices too. And no wonder: her descriptions of being "tied up with an ironing cord, held down with a pillow on her face, tied to her bed when her mother went out" while her father raped her were seen as impossibly inhuman. Today, given what we now know about survivors' stories, her account would seem far more credible. One cannot but wonder: if she had been believed, would she have avoided her eventual destination – a mental hospital?[57]

The institutional regime also revealed other contradictions in the delivery of medical and psychological care. Despite – or perhaps because of – the profession's claim to be uplifting the underprivileged, medical care was extremely basic to the point of being miserly. Some girls whose families could not afford dentists got cavities filled; others had free tonsillectomies. But girls were expected to be grateful (as charity cases should) for the basics, and not complain or demand more extensive services. When one girl had a cast on her leg, and kept complaining of pain, she was dismissed as an attention seeker. When the cast was removed, the staff found that her leg had gangrene.[58] Girls with disabilities were clearly penalized by government parsimony, for it took ages to get something as simple as a hearing aid. One time, when they were making no progress with a hearing-impaired girl, the school pointed out realistically that if the government was not going provide instruction in lip-reading, there was little use in the girl being there.

Aside from the paucity of psychiatric time, tensions and disagreements could develop between the head doctors and penal workers. The penal staff members were far more likely to concentrate on order, and the doctors saw themselves as administering to the soul – even if they did agree on the need for some discipline. One point of tension was the practice of detention, with shrinks often warning that this punishment made a girl more bitter, angry, and hostile, and penal workers ignoring the advice. Doctors were also called on to help sedate the more violent or rebellious inmates. The use of drugs was not common until the 1950s, but at that point tranquillizers and sedatives made a striking appearance – as did a scientific electroencephalogram survey in which brain waves were studied as clues to delinquency. In one particularly glaring case, the superintendent wanted the resident psychiatrist to commit a difficult, violent young Native women to a mental institution. The psychiatrist refused. He did prescribe tranquillizers, but this especially authoritarian superintendent went to the government asking for permission to have massive "intramuscular" doses prescribed for her and a few others in order to calm them down – and make her own job easier.[59]

Rules and Resistance

Keeping order in an institution of girls already noted for their dislike of authority was never an easy task. The exact blend of verbal persuasion, kindness, discipline, and punishment varied from one superintendent to another. Indeed, OTSG went through five superintendents in its first decade, which indicates that the position was not the most popular job.

One superintendent resigned in the late 1940s after public charges that she was locking inmates in basement cupboards and flogging them. Another resigned a decade later amidst bad relations with the ministry and clear antipathy for some of her charges. She absconded with the detention (or punishment) book.[60] Yet, despite their strictness, other superintendents defended and protected the girls, and sometimes claimed their affection – as the poem sent from "Donna" indicates. To generalize about decades of rules and resistance is thus difficult, even more so because at first glance the girls' rebellions appear to have been unfocused and sporadic. However irrational it appeared to those in authority, resistance to their order nonetheless did assume certain patterns, emerging especially from girls' frustration with the school regime and their anger with past and current mistreatment and injustice.

Many girls verbally protested their incarceration to school officials or, more often, in the psychiatric confessional. Families also tried to get girls released. Some parents did not originally understand the full consequences of giving over wardship to the state, fully expecting a short three-month sentence. A few regretted their participation in the court case and engaged lawyers to try to extract their daughters from the system. Others enlisted the help of local notables or politicians. When one couple tried this approach they pressed their claims as respectable "British citizens," protesting that their daughter was "not training school material."[61] During World War II a Forest Hill matron wrote to the provincial secretary, citing her social contacts (including with his wife), while trying to secure release from OTSG of a working-class woman's daughter, who she said was suicidal and had been precipitously incarcerated because she simply fell in with a group of "bad Italian" boys.[62] Girls, understandably, tried to obtain parental aid in securing their release, arguing that they were terrified by the "rough and tough matrons" in charge and the "evil talk" of the fellow inmates.[63] Many parents petitioned for release because they needed their daughters' help at home, or their wages, and in few cases their motives seemed more mercenary than affectionate. Most parents, in return, were treated with some measure of paternalism by the penal officials, who believed they knew what was best for the girls – and it was rarely their families.

On the inside, most girls also engaged in some kind of rule-breaking. Sauciness and insolence to teachers and matrons were probably the most routine forms of rebellion, and extreme defiance, such as swearing, might lead to detention or a strapping. But simply maintaining a loud, boisterous character or boasting shamelessly about sexual exploits could also lead to chastisement. Refusing to stand silently in line, or smoking secretly, or talking or singing after lights out: all of these and more minor infractions were noted in the files. Girls also focused their anger on each other, and a few unpopular girls bore the brunt of hostility. Some pilfered small items, argued with each other, or even physically intimidated foes. One girl admitted to striking another girl so hard that a gash appeared; the argument was over a staff member whom she thoroughly disliked.[64]

Rather than adopting direct argument, the girls often used more passive forms of resistance. As anthropologist James Scott argues, those who want to avoid direct confrontation with an authority that has immense power often take up mundane, muted "everyday" acts of resistance, such as silence, foot dragging, claiming ignorance, or even gossip.[65] Some girls followed the rules, but with such reluctance that both the matrons and the superintendent knew full well that they were not internalizing the school lessons about purity, femininity, and work. Aboriginal girls were especially suspect in this regard because they were-supposedly "unreachable," but others were also accused of hiding rebellion behind silence or of feigning acquiescence to rightful authority. The superintendent described one twelve-year-old girl as a "smooth" inmate, "just earning her promotion in a lazy way," without a true metamorphosis. The girl had been committed on the rather flimsy pretexts of "hanging out with an older crowd" and suspected sexual activity.[66]

Girls also established their own countercultures within OTSG, with their own rules governing social interaction. Groups were based on ties of friendship, but some were also tightly knit units resembling nuclear families. These "pseudo-kinship" groups, allowing girls to play roles of mother, father, sister, brother – the very family ties they had been cut off from – were common in other correctional institutions for girls and women.[67] While penal workers were happy to see girls develop leadership skills through the officially endorsed student council, they were unhappy with girls whose leadership was derived through these alternative cultures and peer-related rebellion. "She gains security by being a planner – of runaway attempts," noted the reigning superintendent critically. The school described another talented organizer as "one of our best instigators [of runs] in a dumb blonde kind of way."[68]

Girls also established intense same-sex relationships, for which they could be reprimanded. One girl was punished simply for sleeping with another inmate, while another teen, who supposedly admitted to sexually "pursuing" other girls aggressively, was eventually sent to the Mercer.[69] Girls were warned about the dangers of same-sex sexual "abnormality" by their psychologists and psychiatrists, who used penal staff as informants to uncover these relationships. Ignoring the authorities, girls established "love lights," special intimate relationships with other girls, representing love, loyalty, and intensity; these were not usually sexual relationships, though in some cases they might develop into "sex lights" or sexual relationships. In one letter that the matron seized, a girl in detention wrote to her love light, separating her from a sexual liaison, but pledging devotion and escape:

> Ask Miss B if you can do your two months up here [in detention] it will be long and boring, but at least you know you will be with me.... I'm suggesting this because I care about you and want you in my plan.... I love you chic, but don't get the wrong idea, I mean like a sister or partner, I have been through the queer business and I know it is stupid once you get past the first stage.... I could get some money and clothes, and we could go up north to a cabin.[70]

The "love light" relationships were seen as dangerous not only because they established close bonds that countered institutional lines of authority and could stimulate other rebellions, but also because they might lead girls down the dangerous path to lesbianism. "The institution is demented with love light troubles," complained one superintendent in the 1950s. "I don't know how to discourage [them] ... movies will be suspended until the whole institution settles down."[71] Psychiatrists and psychologists had some sympathy for girls' search for intimacy, but drew the line at sexual desire. Like doctors writing about prison lesbians at this time, they believed that women's emotional nature and the absence of men could lead to a craving for love, but that only a minority of women having sex were truly "pathological homosexuals."[72]

Close friendships and love lights were also integrated into one of the most prevalent means of rebellion, namely "awls" (AWOLs). Many girls had been incarcerated to begin with for running away, so that they were quite adept at running; others used awls to cement relationships and establish their bravado and leadership. But running was also an understandable reaction to loneliness and frustration. Some runs were spontaneous, unplanned, and the girl was returned quickly, by police or family, or she turned herself in if hunger got the better of her. Other girls were more melodramatic, leaving notes saying they "would kill themselves if followed," or taking physical risks, as with one desperate girl who "swam across a river and nearly drowned" trying to get home.[73] The more resilient and resourceful among them remained away for long periods of time, if they could find shelter – sometimes at a sexual cost – and anonymity in large cities like Toronto or Montreal. Girls often ran in response to initial arrival or reincarceration, or to punishment, or when they were denied holidays at home. "All three detention cells are full of girls trying to take Easter holidays without permission," wrote a superintendent in the 1950s. She conceded that girls often ran "on impulse to see their families," sometimes prompted by letters and visits from troubled family members. Families might also protect runaways, and one superintendent tried to get the ministry to be harsher with such "harbouring" families. She cited the recent case of "G," who had run away and was only spotted by police when she went to a dance with her boyfriend. The officers followed her home and a melee ensued; her uncle helped her out the back window, while her father started a fight with the police. Extra reinforcements had to be brought in to "avoid a brawl."[74] Other runaways who resisted arrest had their sentences lengthened. A girl sent back by train from the North, where she had run to her mother, "fought, kicked and scratched police" when they tried to apprehend her, leading to further charges of incorrigibility in court and time in a local jail.[75]

Some OTSG workers understood the desperation that led to awls, and they often distinguished between the truly "bad" and the merely "lonely" girl: "There is a difference between a girl who runs away irked by authority or concern for her family and one intent on immorality. . . . Bonnie is the latter as she ran away . . . and lived with men in the carnival."[76] In the early 1960s the superintendent also advanced an explanation that attempted to promote an image of the school as a "haven" rather than a prison. Some girls ran away, he told the federal inquiry on juvenile delinquency, because they "unconsciously . . . did not want to go home and therefore ran away to ensure return to the school."[77]

Over the decades awls were a persistent, but varying, irritation. Official statistics show they peaked in 1945, yet around that time, when the school was in Cobourg, the superintendent also claimed that they were more easily halted, with co-operative police intercepting girls on a nearby highway. Later on they were also apparently undermined when the school encouraged a self-policing culture in which inmates discouraged, and told on others. But the official statistics on this question seem suspiciously unreliable.[78]

The more contentious issue became the punishment for awls; this was usually detention, a form of solitary confinement. Psychiatrists argued that detention would at least partly provide a cooling-down period, but penal workers saw it more predominantly as punishment and deterrence. Detention rooms were sparse, sometimes having grilled or painted-over windows. Those inside received no mail, got no outdoor exercise (though floor scrubbing was allowed), had limited reading material, and perhaps had only a mattress on the floor. Sometimes only pyjamas were allowed, since some girls had torn up their clothing as well as damaged furniture. Continued defiance might lead to a restricted diet of milk and bread. Girls could remain in detention for days; in one year in the 1950s, an average stay in detention was fifteen days per stay, although one girl spent sixty-seven days or 55 per cent of her sentence there. Girls, the ministry admitted, were more likely to end up in detention than were boys in Bowmanville, which probably reflected more social horror at girls' aggression – a trait more likely seen as "normal" in boys.[79]

The use of detention went on public trial in the late 1950s. Supported by its own psychological experts, and fearful of pressure from public opinion, the ministry officials argued with the reigning superintendent, trying to make sure girls had some reading material, normal clothes, and regular food. In contrast, Superintendent Bentley saw detention as a means of isolating girls who might "infect the rest of the school" with bad behaviour, and as pure punishment: "There is no reason for staff to be spending time seeing a bunch of psychopaths when they could be doing more important things . . . [and] detention can't be a yakking ball for these psychopaths."[80] The matter was worsened by the government's decision to build a new detention unit at Galt, for the most difficult, supposedly violent girls, who had previously been sent to the special OTSG wing of the Mercer Reformatory.[81] The Elizabeth Fry Society vigorously protested the virtual prison design of the unit and the notion of solitary for such young girls, wrestling with the minister for support of other women's groups on the issue.[82] Despite the attempts by Elizabeth Fry (and parents) to protest conditions at OTSG, the new detention unit was created, and by the 1960s some of its inmates were being bused to breakfast because they were not even trusted to walk to the dining hall. When an opposition MPP brought the subject up again in 1965, after a visit to OTSG, he said that girls were still being left in detention cells, framed by three concrete walls and a bare floor, without even a cot to lie on in the day, and only a Bible to read.[83]

Strapping did not engender as much controversy. In the 1930s and 1940s girls could be strapped for running away, insolence, or physical rebellion. A misdemeanour as small as swearing at a matron could earn a girl a strapping, but it was used more often to punish awls on their return, which explains why some girls went to great lengths to avoid returning to the school. In some cases doctors were brought in to oversee the punishment, as in the instance of four girls who "were behaving foolishly in the yard." After they were told to stop the girls managed to get up onto a roof, where they were sprayed with water from fire hoses as encouragement to come down. Afterwards they were placed in detention and strapped, with two attendants required to hold one girl down. When they continued to resist, smashing glass and light bulbs, the superintendent responded that "she was glad to get permission to strap them again . . . with an additional ten strokes . . . a sufficient deterrent for a while."[84]

Girls themselves also sought out detention, using the isolation as a form of passive resistance – like the fifteen-year-old who came from a background of abuse and firmly believed in the injustice of her sentence to training school (see p. 100). She soon ended up in detention, drawing disturbing pictures of girls with their heads cut off. Apparently, she had made it clear soon after her arrival "that she wanted to live in detention." Psychiatrists claimed that the proclivity for detention was a sign that the girls were emotionally disturbed, and masochistic. Indeed, that was also the interpretation of another form of girls' anger and rebellion, writ large on their bodies: namely, carving (or slashing), which was accomplished with everything from safety pins to shards of plaster.

Many head doctors – especially in the Freudian 1950s – analysed carving and other self-destructive reactions to institutionalization as a form of female masochism, in which girls "yearned for punishment."[85] Girls' self-inflicted violence was supposedly subtle and masked, just as some popular, fifties-era criminology portrayed women's crimes more generally as masked, subtle, and devious – a view that even some advocates for women bought into.[86] By the 1960s a voluminous expert literature existed on carving, and much, though certainly not all of it, focused on institutionalized females. Many explanations saw carving as the product of individual psychopathologies – retaliation, depression, attention-seeking, sexual dysfunction – though others also noted the social dynamic of carving, which was often integrated into other rituals of initiation and rebellion against authority. Carving was seldom mentioned in OTSG in the 1930s but had, according to the records, become a generalized practice by the 1970s (with one famous study stating that over 80 per cent of the girls in OTSG carved), which would seem to indicate that it was a new, emerging form of protest.[87] But surveillance and expert intervention were also far more detailed and intense by the 1970s, so that carving either might not have been all that new, or might simply have replaced other forms of rebellion.

Like love lights (whose names and initials were often carved into arms and legs), carving was an unsolvable problem for penal workers, whose strategies of disapproval, deprivation, detention, hiding the scars, and even behaviour modification with rewards seemed to do little good. Punishment only seemed to make it worse. In the 1970s, two well-known psychologists confidently announced that they had solved the puzzle of carving, though almost by accident, in their intensive research with OTSG (by then called Grandview) girls. They surmised that their successes only came when they gave power over to the girls and co-opted "wheels" (girls who were already leaders) to set up their own therapy groups. A more cynical Foucauldian might note that having girls become "their own prison wardens" was far more successful than having prison wardens issue orders against carving.

Girls, this study claimed, slashed in order to counter feelings of helplessness in a situation over which they had little power. Rather than being masochistic, they were seeking control over their lives, making carving an "interaction of psychopathology with social interaction," though, ironically, researchers contended that those who carved were often considered the "least disturbed" and most "socially acceptable" to begin with (surely a sign that the institutional context was the problem). As one girl supposedly told the researchers, carving drew strong reactions from the matrons and superintendent – reactions that girls could predict down to the second, thus indicating that the girl was the one in control, especially of her body. Given the sexual abuse or violence that girls had already experienced, this aspect was surely significant: "It's my body and I can do anything I want with it. It's mine – it's the only thing I control completely. I'm its boss. . . . Your rules can't stop me from doing anything if I want to do it. . . . You guys can punish me – so what – I'm in control."[88] Even though some experts in the 1970s gradually reinterpreted slashing as a sign of anger, a search for power, defiance of authority, or even an indication of allegiance to peers, the popular literature contained a lingering suspicion that what was really at work was female masochism.

Both detention and slashing were related to the last, most extreme, means of rebellion: violence and rioting. Girls' violence was sometimes directed against the authorities in OTSG or, more often, simply against the physical plant. Girls tore out radiators, smashed windows, set fire to mattresses, pushed matrons down stairs, and stabbed them with forks. Violence might be individual or collective. It could erupt into disturbances that the authorities called riots, though the actions rarely involved more than five girls. There was no one predictable model of causation for violence – individual personality did matter – but there were repeated patterns and provocations. The files of disruptive inmates removed to Mercer Reformatory indicate that these girls often came from contexts, both community and family, in which physical violence, and occasionally sexual abuse, had been a part of their daily lives. Many also came from economically marginal backgrounds, in which economic insecurity was matched with tremendous emotional and social instability – desertion, transience, and foster care, for instance. Recent research indicates that girls' physical rage could be a product of their "internalization of the dominant, patriarchal culture which valued violence" as expressions of power and control.[89]

At the time the authorities portrayed girls' violence as sporadic, irrational, and pathological, and totally out of keeping with true female nature, although some observers noted the therapeutic value of girls externalizing their anger by "kicking things and breaking furniture, writing obscenities on the walls."[90] Like more recent cases of girls designated as violent, there was probably some perceived purpose to their rebellion as the girls attempted to mete out punishment to others or alter what they felt were intolerable "imbalances in their hierarchical world."[91] Clearly, girls often reacted to crisis points or dead-ends in their lives, sometimes to protest the injustices they believed they were suffering. One girl who was out on placement was determined to support her baby so that it would not be put up for adoption. She was caught drinking underage with some men and was reincarcerated, losing her baby and her freedom. She threw the washstand through the window and slashed her wrists.[92]

Possibly, other outbreaks of violence were simply the cumulative products of a troubled history. One "riot" of OTSG girls in the Mercer was instigated by Kate, who the authorities said planned to murder the sewing instructor, though more likely the attack with sewing scissors was an attempt to escape. Often, when the girls were finally cornered, they broke glass and slashed themselves. Yet the crucial fact about Kate (and almost every other girl like her) was that she had *not* been incarcerated to begin with for violence, but for incorrigibility and sexual immorality. She had run away from home with an Afro-American boy, and probably for good reason since she had been excessively physically punished and perhaps emotionally abused. When she finally got out on placement she lost her job and was reincarcerated, and after a number of rebellions at OTSG was sent to a cell at the Mercer at age seventeen. The final attack was a culmination of years of anger, frustration, rejection, and violence.[93]

Some of that anger undoubtedly came from the experience of incarceration itself. The use of strapping and detention made some girls more disobedient; the impact of humiliation and stigmatization, and the racism encountered by Native girls, accelerated the spiral downwards into violence. Older girls were usually more prone to group revolt; they were frustrated with their isolation, and their years in OTSG gave them an opportunity to form small gangs bent on physical intimidation and rebellion. The group hosed down from the roof was described as a "gang of five" older girls who purposely planned trouble to fulfil their exalted role as "bad girls of the School."[94] When it came to violence, for some girls incarceration was far from a solution: it became the problem.

The existence of violence also contradicts recent sensational accounts of girls' and women's violence that say it is entirely new – the result of feminist demands to be the same as men – and tolerated, as Patricia Pearson claims, because feminists have erroneously constructed women as helpless victims of violence.[95] On the contrary, feminist analyses have recognized the history of female violence, and rather than explaining it away, as Pearson maintains, we have tried to situate it within circles of social, economic, and familial relationships, comprehending its individual tragedies without dismissing these as simply the product of pathological, evil personalities. Moreover, the way in which girls' violence in the past was described and analysed also sends a telling message. Because it was seen as abnormal and unfeminine, it was probably exaggerated, and it was certainly treated with some panic. Similarly, reactions to girls' violence today suggest that minor assaults are being portrayed as major assaults, and sensational cases are extrapolated to encompass all delinquent girls. Even minor assaults should not be condoned, but instead of letting them spiral into major ones, we need to ask how and why they came about in the first place.

Escape through Placement

Placement approximated adult parole, although supervision of the girls' homes, work, and social life was more protective, intense, and invasive than in the case of adults on parole. Some girls returned to their own families, some were placed in paid foster situations (where they attended school, with board paid by the government), and many boarded while working as a domestic either in a home or outside the home. By the late 1950s more girls were being sent home, though most of them were employed in some manner. (See Table 5.5.)

Placement officers wanted to show girls the curative and positive example of a good family, and some girls, especially the younger ones, did manage to find care and affection in new families. One twelve-year-

Table 5.5
Work Placements by Type, Galt OTS 1937-64

Type of Placement (General Categories)	1937	1940	1943	1946	1949	1952	1955	1958	1961	1964
Domestic	63	47	46	51	69	188	17	17	40	29
Factories	2	20	64	33	42	7	11	18	4	13
Business	2	2	7	11	27	18	7	9	11	3
Waitresses	0	2	6	4	12	5	0	10	2	0
Hospital	1	5	0	14	12	3	2	0	0	0
All Other	0	8	4	2	1	3	8	12	43	23

Note: Domestic includes laundry; Business includes shops, offices, clerks, cashiers, etc.; Hospital includes ward aides; All Other includes unemployed.
Source: Ontario, *Annual Reports on Ontario Training Schools.*

old, sent to live with a recently immigrated Scottish family while she continued at school, was made welcome – the parents insisted they wanted to adopt her, and the placement officer said she was so thoroughly integrated into the family that she was now speaking with a Scottish accent. Even those who ran into trouble on placement might find unusual support. One girl working as a domestic hid a pregnancy until she suddenly gave premature birth in her employer's home. The woman insisted she stay to recover, and to protect the girl's reputation she told the neighbours the medical crisis had "just been appendicitis."[96]

Unfortunately, many of those who took in OTSG girls were interested more in the girls' abilities to do domestic labour (indeed, the school got phone calls asking for domestic workers). Understandably, girls had trouble adjusting in more affluent, middle-class families in which they would never be part of the family circle. Placement also reminded some girls, who had already been in foster care, of past unhappiness. One "terrified" girl asked her psychologist if everyone would know she had been "bad" and if she would be allowed to eat with the family.[97] When a troubled young woman went to do domestic labour for a prominent university professor and his wife, she was immediately accused whenever something petty disappeared from the bedrooms of their teenage (school-going) children. A girl could simply not easily escape the past.

No wonder, then, that one girl, who had already been through the trauma of two illegitimate pregnancies, quickly rebelled with bad behaviour when placed with her aunt, whose own daughter of exactly the same age was nothing short of a goody two-shoes. The cousin, said the placement report, was "intelligent, attractive and church going" and probably seemed self-righteously superior. The OTSG parolee wanted out. She did much better after being placed in a boarding house and in a well-paying factory job, although her placement officer's comments reveal a basic suspicion of such charges: "When I suggested that she not go to certain dance halls, she agrees too readily." Yet surely this nineteen-year-old, who worked at a welding job and insisted on paying for her own appendix operation, had shown a high level of independence and maturity.[98]

In contrast, placement officers took at face value the claims of prospective boarding families about being keenly concerned with the girls' welfare. Placement officers could apparently be fooled by the trappings of middle-class respectability, religiosity, and affluence. Their inspections of the physical environment symbolized this tendency. Their descriptions reveal that some of them would have made excellent real estate agents, selling a home beautiful: "a lovely old home in a good residential neighbourhood, rooms are spacious and imposing, ceilings are high which keeps house delightfully cool in summer, very tastefully furnished."[99] In the saddest cases, superficial markers of respectability hid mistreatment. One time, for instance, a teen who had suffered abuse and was deemed quite disturbed was sent on placement with a fervently Christian couple. The two hosts not only physically punished her, but the man also made her pregnant. He admitted to this but was never prosecuted because both the CAS and OTSG thought the girl – previously accused of promiscuity – would simply be discredited on the witness stand. School officials also privately admitted to making a mistake with a young twelve-year-old who had been sent out to a rural, churchgoing farming family, in which the father was a respected "church elder." The girl didn't even get enough to eat, a fact her school teacher recognized as well. Nor was mistreatment limited to foster families, as some girls returned to face seemingly unsolvable problems with violence or addiction in their own families.[100]

These cases were negative examples of placement, but they highlight the contradictory ideal of the good family held out as a cure for delinquency. Not only had many of these girls already experienced the dark side of family life, but they were also unlikely to be welcomed with open arms into more affluent families, or foster families less likely to tolerate teenage rebellion and rudeness. Placement could be lonely, especially for girls in rural areas – and those placements were popular in the early years because farms were considered wholesome places – or in isolated domestic jobs. Moreover, attempts to cope with life on the outside were set back by the rule that forbade socializing with other former inmates – precisely the people who understood what they had been through and what they could feel comfortable with. Girls broke this rule anyway, and placement officers might look the other way if they could use one girl to secure useful gossip on another ex-inmate.

If a girl was to have wardship terminated, she had to prove she could hold down a job. Some of the more ambitious and persistent girls resisted the emphasis on domestic training and pursued factory or retail jobs because of the freedom those jobs provided after hours, the higher wages, and the more sociable work cultures. They would rather have a factory foreman than a middle-class matron watching over them – especially if the matron came with twenty-four-hour supervision. Some of the girls also obtained training as nurse's aides or secretaries, and the school was extremely proud of their accomplishments. This is our "most successful graduate to date," they enthused of a young woman who had become a stenographer and had the attributes of "a real lady" to boot.[101]

But many girls found alternative avenues closed to them. They lacked the requisite education, and they could not muster the immense determination needed to oppose the school's incessant training chorus of "domestic, domestic." One "bright" fifteen-year-old in the 1930s was trained for domestic work, even though she told the school that her ambition was to be a stenographer. Sent out to work as a domestic, she was soon in trouble and was sent back for breaking parole. On a second parole she applied to nursing school, and after initially saying yes the school officials mysteriously changed their minds on her admission (perhaps because they found out about her record). When she was finally released at age twenty-one, her ambition was apparently still to be a steno, because she was saving for business school. Her experience with the nursing school was not uncommon. Former inmates were often teased, shamed, and treated suspiciously by employers. One girl quit her nurse's aide training when her past was revealed and she "lost face."[102] Another girl found it only took two days as a grocery clerk at a Dominion store until her employer discovered her past and fired her.

Given these stresses, some parolees not surprisingly ended up breaking the rules. Insolence, breaking curfews, or running away could bring them back to the OTSG, and the high level of returns and re-placements every year indicate that many girls found it hard to adjust. In many years, at least a quarter to one-third of girls on placement were returned to the school at least once. With some exceptions in the late 1940s, girls were also more likely than the Bowmanville boys to be returned from their placements, and occasionally 50 per cent of the girls found their way back to OTSG.[103] Promiscuity and pregnancy were obviously central concerns, and penal workers often believed that a girl had absorbed nothing if she returned pregnant. Yet in those days birth control advice was out of the question. A young fifteen-year-old managed to escape as far as Saskatchewan, where she found steady work as a waitress, but she was discovered and brought back in protest. She was pregnant, which was a sign of failure to the superintendent, who branded her "a very pregnant psychopath who will long be both pregnant and psychopath." Yet this "psychopath" was clearly intelligent ("too smart" for the penal workers), and determined to keep her baby. She later found work in an old-age home and attended Bible College.[104] Given the centrality of sexual containment to placement success, the officers involved heaved a massive sigh of relief when girls married, even at sixteen or seventeen, as long as the man appeared somewhat respectable. Presumably the girl's sexuality would now be properly restrained, and she would be looked after by someone else.

To guard against reincarceration, placement officers closely investigated an inmate's social life, looking for signs of respectability in dress, deportment, and sexual decency. Some must have felt like private detectives as they trailed girls across city streets to favourite hangouts. They worried about the girls wearing too much makeup or "extreme" (that is, sexualized) clothing, or having dyed hair, and they urged girls to save responsibly for necessities like practical winter coats, rather than blowing wages on fun and fur coats. They warned against beverage rooms, riding in cars with men, and dance halls. Instead they favoured joining the YWCA, churchgoing, and other suitably sedate pastimes. They even surveyed reading material. With a barely disguised class bias, one placement officer complained about the "low cultural plane" of an ex-inmate who "likes movie magazines and . . . crime stories on the radio." She was forbidden to read crime comics.[105]

Placement officers sometimes offered girls much-needed moral support in their new lives or rescued them from unhappy living situations. Occasionally they even looked beyond the makeup to the girl underneath. Commenting on one ward who went back to care for siblings in a family racked by alcoholism, the placement officer commended her for playing "social worker" with her less than moral parents. She was a "peroxide blonde who seems hard boiled," the officer pointed out, "but she has a code of her own and is outspoken and honest."[106] Placement officers knew that financial insecurity was a major obstacle to these girls' independence. One superintendent tried to secure withheld family allowance monies for girls on release, and as more girls opted for factory and retail work in the 1950s and 1960s, she pressed the government for a small fund that could be used to advance money to girls on placement, knowing they desperately needed funds for clothes and rent. That every penny had to be fought for reveals the low priority put on rehabilitation, rhetoric to the contrary.

Once a girl had been in OTSG she thus faced continuing suspicions about her character, even though only a few of them ended up in the adult criminal justice system. More than one penal worker harboured the view that some girls by age sixteen or seventeen were already lost to criminality, and wanted to drag others down with them. As one superintendent warned, there were "disturbed" but good girls who wanted help and then there were the unrepentant "vicious" ones who wanted to "boast about their indulgences in sex delinquency, booze," and escapes. There are "Jekyll and Hydes," commented an even more cynical superintendent: "girls who are not helped by mental health and foster homes. . . . Not all delinquents come from troubled homes. Some are just born that way." A few girls, in one final rebellion, disappeared on placement. A couple of them were eventually found, integrated into petty crime and street life, but one or two managed to "disappear without a trace."[107]

Emerging Critiques

OTSG, renamed Grandview, did not close until 1976. However, by the mid-1960s the institution, like the broader juvenile justice system, was coming under critical scrutiny. The detention controversy, initiated by the Elizabeth Fry Society and others, opened the door to questions about the penal nature of training schools. Although Elizabeth Fry reformers, like many bureaucrats and OTSG workers, agreed that girls would be aided by medical, psychological, and social work experts, they believed that these services were meagre, educational offerings were half-hearted, and incarceration overly punitive. Needless to say, some OTSG superintendents were nervous about Elizabeth Fry "having access to our girls," because they were used to having a free rein over OTSG inmates in the quest for institutional order.[108]

By the mid-1960s, others were interfering too. Responding to internal and external pressures, the provincial government revised the Training School Act in 1960 and 1965. In the first round the ruling Progressive Conservatives removed the word "incorrigible" as a rationale for incarceration, and in the second round they raised the minimum training school age to twelve, removing the minister's power of committal (making admission possible only through the courts), and supposedly safeguarding the child's rights by requiring judges to hear the child's evidence and ascertain in writing the basis for a training school sentence. These changes reflected growing criticisms of the lack of legal due process in the juvenile justice system – criticisms voiced to the federal inquiry on juvenile delinquency.

Nonetheless, the 1965 bill was still portrayed by the Ontario Conservatives as a measure to look after the "welfare" of children, focusing less on their offences and more on their "social and emotional needs."[109] Many experts already involved in juvenile justice, including some straddling both academe and government employment (such as Dr. Tadeusz Grygier, a long-time researcher at OTSG), were consulted on the bill and marshalled to defend it against the critics who persisted with a biting civil rights critique of the Training School Act. As one indefatigable law professor argued, the new bill still allowed arbitrary judgments, tied to concepts such as "protection" and "environment," rather than being based on legal principles and the rules of evidence to decide incarceration. "Would our society allow emotionally disturbed adults who had not engaged in anti-social conduct to be sent to reformatories or penitentiaries?" Professor Bernard Green asked rhetorically.[110] New Democratic Party critics in the legislature focused their critiques far more on the need for a more serious "welfare" approach to delinquency. The speeches about children's welfare meant nothing, they argued, if alternative diagnostic, social, and psychological services needed by the "emotionally disturbed" children sent to training schools were desperately lacking across the whole province.[111]

In March 1968 another NDP member of the legislature, with connections to Warrendale, an institution for emotionally disturbed children, visited OTSG again and still maintained publicly that it was a "child prison" with girls treated like "rats in a maze." Some investigations by the popular press treated the school administration sympathetically, but others questioned the value of having girls scrubbing floors for hours, or only receiving a mattress in detention for good behaviour. One reporter effectively quoted an unhappy inmate in detention: "In the hole I just sit there and hate them. It doesn't do me any good." A study of self-mutilation published in 1979 noted that the researchers walked into a dreary, authoritarian, if not military atmosphere at OTSG: "Drab uniforms, barrenness of the rooms, teenage girls forced to march from place to place ... forced to sit in silence in common rooms, not even allowed to cry. . . . This was discipline in its most Dickensian sense."[112]

These descriptions were a far cry from the public happy story of Mary issued two decades earlier, and much worse was to come. Charges of physical and sexual abuse eventually emerged, sparking a number of criminal trials (though not all were conclusive), a civil suit, and finally a government apology for the abusive treatment that girls received in the school. In the early 1960s some of the government's psychological experts ventured that one problem was the surfeit of women overseeing training schools; they suggested that more men needed to be hired to compensate for the fatherly (Freudian) role models that girls lacked. Not only was it unlikely that having men in charge was going to solve the problems within the institution, but some men made the problems far worse: one of those who did plead guilty to sexual assault in a later trial was a male guard. Many Grandview survivors today believe that justice has still not been done.[113]

Why did this experiment, once the favoured project of Big Sisters, now find itself, thirty years later, under the scrutiny of Elizabeth Fry? The historical records may seem to reinforce the polarized, simplistic view promoted by penal workers at the time, of girls either sadly troubled or irretrievably bad. As a consequence, penal workers argued, the uninitiated became corrupted, while the troubled did not have enough access to medical and social resources to change. Indeed, a disjuncture does seem to exist between girls writing about the Easter Bunny and girls attempting to push matrons down the stairs. Admittedly, both were part of OTSG, but I believe we need to avoid pigeonholing and polarizing girls in the way that the exasperated, overworked, and discouraged penal workers did.

One underlying structural problem was that no institution, so meagrely funded, so lacking in rehabilitative services, and so clearly stigmatized as a place for the impoverished, could deal with issues that had deep roots and had already taken an immense toll on many girls: poverty, alienation, racism, violence, and abuse, with the latter two worsened by economic insecurity. Moreover, in the case of sexual abuse, the expert discourses shaping rehabilitation were themselves inadequate, never fully exposing and confronting the abuses of familial power that girls had experienced. Treating the family as a contained psychiatric problem rather than examining broader issues of power and poverty, simply blaming the girls' "immoral" families, while holding up an ideal "good" family as the cure: all of this created a contradictory and inescapable impasse for the girls. Encouraging girls to wipe the past away and attempting to inculcate a new feminine persona of middle-class morality and demeanour were simply too superficial as an approach to solving the problems.

Moreover, fundamental questions were never asked about the sexual regulation of these girls, which was understood and rationalized as protective, but also became coercive and stigmatizing. Even during the 1965 debate about the Training School Act, politicians of all stripes persisted with the assumption that sexual immorality was an adequate reason for "treatment" in a training school, although they tried to put a sympathetic spin on this stance, portraying the girl as a victim – as someone either following the example of immoral parents or turning to prostitution because she was "emotionally disturbed."[114]

Many girls were incarcerated primarily for running away and promiscuity, which were not crimes in the adult world. As one superintendent astutely noted, the young teenagers arrested saw the eighteen- or nineteen-year-olds receive suspended sentences, while they themselves were incarcerated, which only added to their sense of unfairness and cynicism about the institution. It is not enough to say that this ideology of sexual protection was altruistic; it was also the product of a class-based and ultimately patriarchal image of normal marriage, sexuality, and family, which simply did not work for everyone. Nor did the authorities explore the connections between social and economic disadvantage and sexual endangerment and rebellion. Why did these girls, overwhelmingly poor – and, in the 1950s, increasingly Native – end up with so few options other than a sentence in training school? This was a question answered by the causative link between class, colonialism, and criminalization.

Although protection from violent families undoubtedly did aid some girls, the means of delivering that protection could feel like punishment. And the project of segregation and reform easily slipped into a project of penal correction, despite the good intentions of many women and men working in the juvenile justice system. Some girls left OTSG better fed and educated, temporarily rescued from abuse. But others left having absorbed a sense of shame, with unresolved traumas, with limited education and skills, making it just as difficult – perhaps more so – to face the outside world as when they were admitted.

Six

Race, Gender, and Delinquency:
The Criminalization of First Nations Girls

A rguments that youth criminality is linked to race and racial identity – with Black, Hispanic, and Asian youth the primary negative scapegoats – are now commonplace in North America, even if they sometimes appear in muted forms, designed to mask charges of racism. Popular press renditions of crime are sometimes less circumspect, directly implying that Afro-Canadian or Asian youth are especially prone to violence and crime, or that a dispossessed underclass of Native youth, often pictured as young addicts, have little regard for law or even their own well-being.[1] In the 1990s, even a scholarly overview of delinquency in Canada noted a connection between an alarming proliferation of male gangs and the influx of immigrants: "Although the Chinese have been the dominant Asian gangs for some time, they are now being challenged by other ethnic groups from Latin America and Viet Nam. Ethnic gangs . . . carry weapons and do not hesitate to assault, maim and kill." Police find immigrant youth gangs difficult to deal with, D. Owen Carrigan continues, because those youngsters are used to "harsh and repressive conditions in their own countries" and to them the Canadian criminal justice system appears "tame" – yet another subtle implication that the YOA is soft on offenders.[2]

Some fifty years ago, police and social welfare workers in urban areas like Toronto and Vancouver were also concerned about violent gangs, portraying them as marginal, dispossessed youth who exhibited their "status deprivation" in anti-social ways.[3] Because they were white, though, race was not the issue; rather, their deviance was thought to be the product of dysfunctional families, pathological personalities, and poor social environment. In a similar vein, writing on juvenile delinquency by legal and social work experts in the 1940s seldom discussed Aboriginal peoples; yet today virtually every study of delinquency includes an article on First Nations youth and the law. Race and ethnicity, then, have taken on different meanings over time in definitions of, and explanations for, delinquency, though there is no doubt that, in the last two decades, race has become more salient, more heavily invoked in Canadian public and expert discourse on youth criminality.

Race, as other scholars have argued, is a socially and culturally constructed category rather than a firmly designated scientific or biological designation. These categories can nonetheless assume immense ideological weight and negative power, with the result that some groups are defined as "deviant" outsiders, even non-citizens. Analyses of race and racism do vary. Some scholars urge us to explore the discursive constructions of race and to start from the "standpoint" of those who are deemed outsiders by virtue of racism.[4] Others, like Vic Satzewich and Li Zong, stress the importance of locating race within wider structural "political and economic contexts associated with state formation and economic exploitation." Since the nineteenth century, they continue, changing constructions of "race" in Canada have drawn less on genetic heredity and more on the determinants of culture, history, and environment. The "race question" in nineteenth-century Canada was assumed to be the French-English clash of cultures, while European depictions of Aboriginal peoples became *more* heavily racialized (and racist) over time as securing military and economic alliances with the First Nations became less important than securing their land, isolating them on reserves, and defining their subservient relationship to the Canadian state.[5]

Although race may be culturally constructed, it is not merely ephemeral. Racism, an ideology denoting superiority/inferiority and power/subordination, has thrived in Canada as an ugly reality, and historically the law implicitly and explicitly sanctioned white superiority through discrimination, exclusion, and segregation, all of it articulated through public policy, statute law, and judicial interpretation.[6] The law, and social thought more generally, may reproduce ideas about race, and racism, through unstated, subtle ideological, as well as more directly coercive physical means. Racialized constructions of, and explanations for, Native delinquency, for instance, are implied in the mainstream media's portrayal of Native youth as "unreachable," perhaps unsalvageable, victims of cultural impoverishment with an inability to cope with the modern world. Race is thus used as a reified, culturalist explanation for alienation, dispossession, and crime, sidestepping the more basic question of the legacies of inequality, underdevelopment, and cultural oppression created by colonialism.[7]

Historically race has also intertwined with gender and sexuality,[8] a condition not immediately apparent in the writings of those concerned with male gangs and delinquency. If race became more routine in discussions of delinquency after World War II, how was this articulated for, and experienced by, young women, even if the dominant concern of law enforcers and criminologists was male criminality? Feminist critical race theorists have argued that we need an "intersectional" approach to class, gender, and race that looks at their mutual interaction over time.[9] Taking up this general goal, in this chapter I explore a specific example of race, gender, and delinquency: the emerging over-incarceration of Native girls. First Nations girls – both Aboriginal and Métis – comprised a small percentage of girls deemed delinquent in the period from 1908 to 1965, but what was significant was the *escalating* numbers of Native girls in the juvenile justice system and training schools after World War II – a trend that parallelled the growing over-incarceration of Native peoples in post-World War II Canada.

The diagnoses of Native girls' conflicts with the law often approximated those accorded to non-Native girls. Both groups were supposedly victims of cultural impoverishment, and both were often targeted for sexual promiscuity. However, the diagnoses also revealed the increased use of "race" as a category of analysis in expert discussions of Canadian delinquency, simultaneously exposing ethnocentric stereotypes of an "unreachable" Native cultural persona. At the same time, we cannot attribute the increased sentencing of Native girls to the simple triumph of race over class as the means of regulating young women. Definitions of delinquency and the experiences of Native and non-Native girls both overlapped *and* differed. Gender and class inequalities, already well entrenched in the juvenile justice system, interacted with the social construction of race and patterns of colonialism to create distinct, and sometimes destructive, experiences for First Nations girls.

Native Peoples, Advanced Colonialism, and the Welfare State

When industrial schools were proposed in late nineteenth-century Canada, reformers and government officials initially saw them as a common solution for the working-class boy of the urban slums, and for the Aboriginal boy in need of similar education, discipline, moral, and vocational training.[10] This undertaking briefly advertised the twinned aims of Canada's nation-building project: to civilize and acculturate both the poor and the colonized to middle-class, Western, white, and Anglo norms. These nation-building projects soon diverged. Native children were increasingly sent to residential schools, where the state intended to replace the language, culture, and work skills of reserve children with "superior" Western and white values. Non-Native delinquent and neglected children were sent to industrial and later training schools, but by the 1940s and 1950s more Native children were being sentenced to those institutions as well. Their increased presence in the juvenile justice system was the result of more interventionist state welfare policies for Native peoples and of increasing urbanization, material and social stresses, and transience, all of which led Native youth into conflicts with the law.

The notion of "race" as historically and culturally constructed becomes absolutely transparent in the Ontario government's changing designations of the "race" of training school inmates. In statistical records government officials first coded differences as "race" and then later entered them as "nationality." The government did record the number of "whites" as opposed to three other "races" – Hebrew, Negroes, and Indian – sentenced to training schools.[11] What is clear amidst these changing categories is that the number of Native girls in training schools in the post-World War II period increased. In the 1930s, just after it opened, OTSG admitted one or two (sometimes no) Native girls every year; by 1958 the number had climbed to a high of fourteen girls, or 9 per cent of the admissions, although Native peoples were officially less than 1 per cent of the province's population.[12] A similar pattern existed at St. Mary's, the Catholic training school for girls. Moreover, the government's own figures may have underrepresented the numbers of First Nations girls. In the 1950s, for instance, OTSG admitted an urban girl whose family, though solidly blue collar, had official "Indian status" under the Indian Act. But the record described her with far less reference to her Native heritage than it did in other cases for girls from reserves (whether Métis or status Indians) because the reserve, and particularly the hunting and trapping subsistence, were equated with a racialized culture of backwardness.[13]

Native children's conflicts with the law and placement in correctional institutions were also complicated by a persisting jurisdictional issue: the federal responsibility for Native peoples and provincial and local responsibility for courts and correctional institutions. Native teens could be charged under sections of the federal Indian Act and dealt with by the Indian agent, but they came under the legal view of the Juvenile Delinquents Act and the Training School Act, as well as local Children's Aid Societies. The Ontario government initially opposed having Native girls in its correctional institutions; it argued that Indians were "federal wards," not provincial responsibilities (a position clearly taken up for largely financial reasons).[14] The Ontario government's Training School

Advisory Board repeatedly asserted that Indian children were rehabilitation problems and belonged in federally financed residential schools for Indians. When training schools were overcrowded during World War II, efforts to segregate Indian children were again heartily endorsed by the nationally prominent social welfare leader Charlotte Whitton.[15]

Playing the age-old game of squabbling over federal and provincial jurisdiction did not last long. An agreement was reached by the late 1940s, with the federal Department of Indian Affairs paying the upkeep of status Indians in OTSG. This did not stop some bureaucratic bickering over who was an Indian; in one case the parsimonious province tried to argue that the daughter of a status mother who had moved off the reserve to live with another man had forfeited her Indian status.[16]

It was not simply bureaucratic policy changes that resulted in increased incarceration of Native teens. Broader social, cultural, and economic forces were also crucial. This period of "advanced colonialism" was characterized by intensified material and social dislocations for many Native families and communities. Reserves were not able to provide adequate levels of material security for an expanding population, and now previously isolated areas of the North were becoming resource-developed, industrialized, and urbanized in ways that directly disadvantaged Native communities that relied on more "traditional" forms of subsistence. The legacy of residential schooling was taking a toll on family health, and although the majority of Native peoples continued to live on reserves, more and more of them were moving off in search of work. In urban areas, however, Native peoples found little opportunity and considerable racism. Their conflicts with the Euro-Canadian criminal justice system, shaped by paternalistic suppositions of police, court, and penal personnel, and by their own cultural distance from these institutions, exacerbated the problem, making penal time more likely.

At the same time the state was taking a more interventionist approach to child welfare in Native communities, resulting in more and more removals of Native children from their families, creating traumas that are still with us today.[17] After World War II the social work community urged governments to integrate Native peoples into the welfare state, offering them "equality" through assimilation. Addressing the Senate and House of Commons Committee on Indian Affairs in 1947-48, the Canadian Welfare Council and the Canadian Association of Social Workers called for an end to "discriminatory practices" and for the extension of provincial social services, such as education and health, to Indians, "thus effecting the full assimilation of Indians to Canadian life."[18] Social workers pleaded for the right to help Native communities deal with problems such as delinquency. "Indian juvenile delinquents, apprehended off the reserve," they lamented, "were in most cases returned forthwith without any attempt being made for their treatment and reform."[19]

Framed within this rhetoric of equal rights and citizenship, the pleas for the equal "protection" of Indian children, just like "white children," brought results.[20] In 1955 the Ontario government agreed to extend Children's Aid Society services to Native peoples across the province, and the federal Department of Indian Affairs also increasingly deployed social workers to service reserve communities. Even though the federal Hawthorne report of the late 1960s conceded the problems that had ensued from these policies, including Indian antagonism to adopting out of their children, it deemed these problems not entirely "unique" to Indians and blithely recommended further integration into the Canadian welfare state.[21]

The pressure that social workers put on governments after World War II reflected a new interest in their own research and practice with the First Nations. Social workers assumed that the "cultural backwardness" they saw in reserves resembled the backwardness of "lower-class" families, and that both situations could be altered with education, material aid, and character reformation. Delinquent Indian girls, noted one 1949 social work study, were a "welfare as much as a juvenile delinquency" problem, with their "antisocial behaviour," like that of white girls, often emanating from inadequate family life. Indeed, one researcher argued that there were "universal causes" of delinquency, regardless of race: "neglect, unhappiness, ignorance and poverty."[22] Social workers stressed the social and environmental causes of Native delinquency, often making trenchant criticisms of government neglect and Native impoverishment. One prominent Canadian social worker noted that poverty, disease, and even "supposed character traits such as indolence and shiftlessness" among Indians were most likely caused by malnutrition. Another study pointed critically to the racial "prejudice" against Indians and to their "low standard of living," especially the poverty and disease plaguing reserves. Criticisms of residential schools and indictments of federal Indian policy as "disastrous" were fairly bold for the time.[23]

Some social work studies, though, also had trouble shedding an underlying cultural denigration of Native peoples. The legacies of colonial contact, they suggested, had created disintegrating Native cultures, with no moral compass. They are not "inferior," said one social worker, but their customs, somewhat "childish and savage," were destroyed by missionaries who offered little in return, save a religion "too abstract for them to grasp." Her conclusion that Indians were "backward, yes" but the problem was "more environment than native intelligence" summed up this paternalistic cultural denigration, and was not unlike anthropological studies of the time that also stressed Native family disintegration and social dislocation.[24]

Commentators saw illegitimate pregnancies, for example, as a common sign of delinquency for both white and Native girls. While conceding that in some Indian communities a more "permissive and accepting" attitude resulted in the integration of these children into extended families, one U.S. study claimed that Indians still looked on illegitimacy with a measure of disapproval, and that absent fathers resulted in the child's failure to enjoy a "normal psycho-social development."[25] The federal government had for some time urged that Native girls in residential schools be given lessons in sexual purity. Just as poor and working-class girls were assumed to be more likely to fall prey to sex delinquency, Native girls were presumed to need extra moral surveillance to curb their amoral inclinations. These concerns were taken up by the new cadre of CAS and reserve social workers whose worries were sometimes grounded in fears about the vulnerability of Native girls. Social workers objected, for instance, when impoverished and underage Native girls were taken in and sexually "used" by an older white man; in some cases Native girls, aided by female relatives, also complained to federal authorities about sexual abuse by Native men in their communities.[26] The problem was that a desire to protect could easily slide into condescending and coercive surveillance.

Social workers often cited the failure of Native parents to discipline their children forcefully as evidence of cultural inadequacy leading to delinquency. They are "fond of children," admitted one agency worker, "but apathetic about their training and discipline."[27] Indian agents often agreed that "parental laxity," including apathy about truancy, led to "no sense of responsibility and discipline" for Native girls.[28] Native parents may have seen the issue differently. As Dr. Clare Brant, a Mohawk psychiatrist, later wrote, many Native cultures allowed a large measure of choice and independence for youth: they did not impose discipline through parental coercion or external control as much as through "indirect" learning, exposure to community controls, or rituals.[29]

Social workers and Indian agents ultimately deemed their own white, middle-class, and Euro-Canadian child-rearing norms to be superior (even though these norms, ironically, sanctioned physical punishment, which Native families generally did not). Both social work organizations and reform groups such as Elizabeth Fry, which also lobbied for integration of Native women into the welfare state, believed this mainstream practice would counter racial discrimination, prevent Native incarceration, and offer Native peoples equal opportunities. As in the work of the Big Sisters and other reformers, their goals vis-à-vis girls in conflict with the law were well-intentioned, reflecting the dominant, liberal notions of "citizenship" of their times. But despite their good intentions, these advocates did not question the professional self-interest and cultural superiority often underlying their definition of, and solution for, "the Indian problem."[30] Social work practice and government policy, which presumed the value of "assimilation for equality," had become another unintended instrument of colonialism.

Initial Court Conflicts

Native girls usually came into conflict with the law for much the same reasons as other girls did. They were considered high-risk teens because of sex, running away, truancy, disobedience, alcohol use, and, to a lesser extent, theft. Moreover, Native parents were often deemed morally or financially unable to care for their children – they were sometimes even excused for producing delinquent daughters because they were supposedly unaware of the community's moral standards. One magistrate paternalistically informed two parents that "had they been white, there might have been a charge of contributing to juvenile delinquency laid against them." Presumably, they escaped because they knew so little about controlling their children.[31] Native girls, stated an Ontario government official, were really "unmoral rather than immoral." They were childish, naive, and ignorant; therefore it was a "good thing to have them in protective custody up to the age of marriage or 18, whichever is earliest."[32] Poverty and a lack of privacy, authorities also maintained, resulted in the visibility of adult sexual encounters, and thus sexual immorality in children. The same argument had been used for many years to scapegoat the rural and urban poor for problems of incest and sexual violence.[33]

To police and court officials, Native parents appeared to be apathetic and irresponsible – again, the same criticisms made of many non-Native girls' parents. In court Native parents might concede that they had problems with their daughters, but they then refused to "manage" them according to the courts' wishes. These parents seemed to say that they *could* control these girls, but they chose not to. Such responses were certain to disappoint judges who were looking for declarations of more, not less, discipline. One father agreed that his daughter should "go to school," and when asked about her drinking he simply responded, "I don't give it to her." When the judge asked, "Why don't you punish her?" the father's response indicated a "hands-off" approach: "Well, I can't do anything else other than tell her to go to school. If she does not want to listen to me, what can I do?"[34]

Girls' conflicts with the law also reveal the very real burdens of work, family care, and poverty that limited the ability of parents to control their daughters' conduct. Parents with transient, insecure work lives were not able to oversee their daughters' school attendance. Thus, when a young girl whose parents worked in Southern Ontario tobacco fields broke her first probation rules, remaining truant, she was sent to OTSG despite her parents' desire to keep her at home. Similarly, a Native mother confronted by a judge about her inadequate discipline seemed puzzled at the suggestion that she should physically restrain her daughter from wandering through the reserve. She added practically, "I can't go looking for her when I have many other children to look after."[35] Families were themselves often used as evidence against girls; indications of arrests for alcohol use, criminal records, illegitimacy, or sexual immorality in the family all condemned the girl and could be rationalizations for her incarceration. The court saw sexual promiscuity especially as contagious, passed on from other female relatives, with girls imitating their sisters and mothers.

Some First Nations girls, like their non-Native counterparts, had already encountered state care as CAS wards or foster children, and a small number of Native girls sentenced to OTSG had attended a residential school, an experience that could provoke deep alienation and anger in young girls. One girl sent to OTSG in 1939 explained that in "Indian school" they had told her she could take a bath for ten minutes, but "after 5 minutes, they came and strapped her." She hit back, and continued to do so when the principal came to strap her. The violence she encountered at residential school resurfaced in her actions when she returned home. Her mother began to complain to the authorities that "she could not control her," and the police became involved.[36] After government policies facilitated the admission of status Indian girls to training schools in the 1940s, some residential school principals tried to send "problem" girls to training schools, arguing that residential schools were never meant to be correctional institutions. Yet the punishment at most residential schools was as harsh as, if not harsher than, the treatment at OTSG, and the only reason some girls preferred to be sent to "Indian school" was to be "with their friends" and thus escape the linguistic and cultural isolation of OTSG.[37]

As with other girls, sexual promiscuity was a central concern of the courts and a major reason that judges resorted to secure custody sentences. Sexual misconduct might become the central issue, no matter what the original charge or concern of the Indian agent, CAS, police, or the family might have been. One Native orphan who had been placed in a residential school and was engaged in petty theft from other schoolmates was sent to OTSG for "her own protection" – not only to curb her stealing, but also because she had "run away with a man and spent the night in his cabin."[38] Insinuation, gossip, and the suspicions of Indian agents and others intent on regulating reserve morality were enough evidence for a magistrate or judge to prescribe training school. Court personnel were concerned with how much sexual intercourse had taken place, when, and with whom; multiple or inappropriate partners (older married men, strangers) and a lack of sense of guilt were indications of the need for the girl's retraining in sexual values through strict probation rules, removal from the family, or incarceration.

The refusal of girls to accept rules set by parents, teachers, or Indian agents (who also sometimes acted as probation officers) or to desist from petty theft also occasioned conflicts with the courts. In distinction to white youth, however, Native girls were more likely to encounter surveillance and punishment for underage drinking, in part because promiscuity was assumed to be the inevitable outcome of intoxication. Alcohol consumption was a concern not only of the police and Indian agents but also sometimes of community members near reserves, people who wanted Native youth controlled. Occasionally parents also worried that their daughters were falling into bad drinking patterns. Reflecting a prevailing stereotype of Natives being prone to alcoholism, one judge sentenced a girl, arrested only once, to training school, noting, "She has to be protected from alcoholism, if she is drinking at fourteen." An Ontario government official privately noted that communities close to reserves often wanted to "get rid of" Native youths who were drinking, thus indicating one of the reasons for the increased incarceration of Native girls in this era.[39]

Just as working-class and poor families sometimes participated in the criminalization of "delinquent" daughters who refused to contribute to the family economy, obey rules, or were deemed to be out of sexual control, some Native families also asked police, court, or federal Indian authorities to intervene when their daughters misbehaved. "I cannot control her, she will not listen to direction," testified one distraught grandmother in court after her granddaughter was arrested on alcohol charges. Two other parents said they wanted their daughter, who had run away and been arrested with a prostitute, sent away to "Indian school," though their wishes were disregarded and the judge opted for training school instead.[40] Like many respectable working-class families, Native families frowned on youthful sexual relations outside of marriage, whether these were customary or Christian, and generally endorsed marital monogamy, though extended kin networks, especially on reserves, would also adopt illegitimate children.

Tensions and power struggles within families were not only exacerbated by the precarious if not impoverished conditions of living, but also by ill health, alcohol use, violence, and the transience or desertion of some family members. Girls who told the authorities about violence perpetrated against them by family members or strangers, however, were viewed sceptically, especially if their own conflicts with the law involved insinuations of promiscuity. When one girl said that her brother-in-law had raped her, the authorities dismissed the story as a case of consensual sex. Another young Cree teen from Northern Ontario, a fourteen-year-old in residential school, went to the police after she was gang-raped on the streets. They did not believe her story, simply because she later admitted that she knew the men, and because she refused a medical exam.[41]

Unhappy with their families or their lives, a few Native girls themselves asked to be sent away, no matter where. One girl arrested because of "late nights, drinking and intercourse with boys," declared in court that there was a "man at her aunt's who she does not like." She told the judge, "Just send me to Training School and I'll go." Another girl said she confronted "strapping" at residential school and did not want to return there, but she also declared that she wanted to be sent "a million miles away" from her mother, who she said abused the younger children in the family.[42] More often, parents complained about their daughters. Even if Native child-rearing practices traditionally tended not to be coercive, some parents, whether more acculturated or simply overwhelmed with worries, drew outside authorities into their attempts to regulate their daughters' conduct. Indeed, this was part of a longer tradition of First Nations selectively using Euro-Canadian law and the Indian agent to deal with perceived problems within their communities.[43]

In a classic case involving familial power struggles, one teen fought for independence from the authority and discipline of her guardian grandmother. Almost sixteen, Patricia had been taken in by her grandparents after her widowed father left home. The grandmother alleged that the father had a drinking problem and had deserted his two remaining daughters. Patricia had long been enjoying considerable independence: her father had frequently been absent, and she had left school at thirteen to look after the household. After she moved to her grandmother's, she went to work as a babysitter for a local teacher, but the teacher discharged her, saying Patricia was sleeping on the job (which Patricia did not deny). But it was her grandmother who pushed the issue into family court, complaining that she had heard that Patricia "drinks," and, more important, that she "stays out all hours, [even] overnight," refusing to say who she was with. She said that men in cars drove up to the house and honked to lure Patricia out, which seemed to symbolize for the grandmother the lack of sexual respectability and dangerous independence that her granddaughter had assumed.

Once the family court became involved, Patricia was on precarious ground. In an interview, the probation officer managed to wrest out of her the damning fact that she had once had intercourse with a seventeen-year-old, and that she drank beer. The judge offered a three-week reprieve, with a strict curfew. Given the antagonism between grandmother and granddaughter, the curfew was bound to fail. At a second court appearance Patricia admitted to staying out all night at a friend's (even though she was with her older brother), and her grandmother testified eagerly about her missed curfews. Patricia was sent to OTSG despite her desperate pleas to avoid that fate and her brother's offer to pay his army salary to Patricia so that she could go back to their father's house and live by herself.

At every turn Patricia expressed resentment of her grandmother's control, which was hardly surprising because she had already exercised considerable independence at a young age. Aided by her lawyer, she defended her own actions and explained that she and her grandmother could not see eye to eye on any issue, including religion: she apparently refused to go to her grandmother's evangelical church. Indeed, this one reference to her grandmother's religious affiliation may well explain the grandmother's actions; and the juvenile court, however much it claimed to defend children's interests, often placed more stock in adults' testimony. The judge's closing remarks could well have been made at countless trials of girls in the 1950s:

> You have brought this on yourself by not following orders. . . . Do you not see what you are doing to your grandmother? . . . You only live for yourself. You don't have any notion of discipline. Intercourse with one boy might be the beginning of very improper conduct . . . leading you into real trouble and sorrow. You are redeemable . . . but we will send you to Training School.[44]

Not all family members were so firmly committed to exerting control as Patricia's grandmother was, but some families did initiate complaints or testify against daughters. Few of these families actually wanted the girl removed to training school, but once the case went to court the process often moved very quickly beyond their control.

Despite the overlap between the origins of Native and non-Native girls' conflicts with the law, there were also some important differences. Like their mothers, girls who did come from reserves were also subject to an extra layer of surveillance from the federal Indian agent who monitored their truancy, alcohol consumption, sexual "immorality," and illegitimacy in their families. He could initiate a legal complaint or testify for or against a girl in court. On some reserves, systems of social control shaped by First Nations customary law did persist, so that conflicts were dealt with internally without the intrusion of the state; but by the mid-twentieth century the destructive impact of colonialism had eaten away significantly at the cultural autonomy and equilibrium of many First Nations. The Euro-Canadian assault on Native culture had led to their partial integration into and use of the state's criminal justice system. The result was never the complete cultural and legal subordination of Native peoples, and many First Nations are now discussing how to recover First Nations customary justice practices suited to current needs.[45] In this earlier time period, though, the immense power of the Indian agent to survey and judge reserve inhabitants, and the Native communities' own use of state law to deal with community problems, were both factors shaping the outcome of girls' conflicts with the law.

The decision to incarcerate Native girls also reflected anxieties about their "primitiveness" that exposed deep-seated denigrations based on racism. Native girls were slightly younger than non-Native girls on admission to OTSG, and the majority of them were originally reserve inhabitants.[46] The authorities saw Native families involved in hunting and trapping for subsistence as especially problematic because the parents were more transient, sometimes leaving children alone to look after themselves, or because they lived "in the Indian [nomadic] fashion" in a tent for part of the year.[47] Indeed, the whole reserve environment was seen as retrograde. An Indian agent or probation officer would sometimes note the positive aspects of reserve life, such as the collective concern expressed for children or the community's sharing of meagre resources, but those benefits were overshadowed by the view that children were neglected and undisciplined. An image of lawlessness and excessive drinking characterized many of the committal and probation reports of girls from reserves. As one probation officer noted, "Her behaviour is common for the Reserve. . . . She is out late on weekends, and may not return home for a day or do."[48] Girls might explain that they were simply travelling around the reserve, staying with various friends or relatives – understandable in such small, contained communities – but this point was ignored. Police often testified that reserve youth were hard to control, and that the mere sight of a cruiser led them to "hit the bush" – perhaps an understandable response. The reserve environment, legal authorities also believed, hindered the cultivation of a work ethic in children. "As with the custom of the Indian," noted a probation worker, "Mary works for a few days or weeks, then takes a holiday until she needs money again, or is ready to return to work."[49]

Once before a court, some Native girls were also given little chance to redeem themselves on probation. After only one incident in which she was arrested for drinking underage in a car, fourteen-year-old Anne was sent to OTSG. The police urged her sole-support father to lay a summons against her, and in court the RCMP testified that Anne was not adequately supervised in the home, a statement certain to influence the judge's decision to send her away – which he did. Such rapid incarceration was undoubtedly facilitated by the racist notion that Native girls, with laxer morals and less willpower, required immediate protection. However, reserve girls also came up before rural or smaller city courts that lacked the more highly developed probation system offered in large cities like Hamilton or Toronto. The result was "justice by geography," with girls offered fewer options or chances before incarceration. This condition became painfully clear in the case of the Cree girl from the North who was at residential school but was deemed a problem because of truancy and staying out at night; her statements about being raped when on the streets were viewed sceptically. Because her single-parent father was working in the bush, and with few foster care options nearby, she was immediately sent to OTSG, despite a warning from the residential school principal that the father would probably prefer her to be sent to him.[50] Significantly, the Native girls sent to OTSG rarely came from large cities but were more likely to hail from areas close to reserves, either in the North or from Southwestern Ontario, close to Lake Huron.[51]

Culture Clashes

The most trying traumas for Native girls came not in the courtroom, but within the walls of the training school, where the experiences of Native girls often differed markedly from those of the other inmates.

Compared to some U.S. reform schools, where issues of race and segregation were noticeable in the early twentieth century, Ontario institutions, with their predominantly white clientele, were less concerned with race – although this is not to say that the few Afro-Canadian girls admitted to OTSG did not encounter racist treatment. OTSG made efforts to place these girls in "coloured" families to sidestep cultural alienation, but if a girl of colour said she was looked on "differently" or discriminated against, penal workers usually chalked this up to another delinquent fabrication. Native girls too encountered vestiges of "biological racism" from penal workers. " 'Anne' is dark skinned and shows her racial characteristics," wrote one penal worker of a Native girl. "She is childish, likes to play with dolls and be outside."[52]

When Native girls became more numerous in the school, government bureaucrats and OTSG staff more often designated them as "cultural problems." The OTSG superintendents, particularly Ruth Bentley, who took over in 1952, repeatedly objected to Native girls' admissions: "Indian girls are a problem in the school. Their cultural patterns are not understood and they appear unreachable." Her reluctance to take Native girls came not from any particular respect for Native cultures, but from a feeling of white supremacy and her certainty that Native cultures were inferior and unalterable. Fellow students played a part in the denigration as well, sometimes mocking Native girls whose first language was not English. A thirteen-year-old raised in the North by her Cree-speaking grandmother confided to the medical examiner that "she was unhappy in the school and says the other girls tease her about her accent."[53]

Psychologists and doctors admitted that for Native girls, especially those from the more remote North, depression was sometimes the result of the "tension of living in OTSG."[54] In the case of the "dark-skinned" Anne, the girl sent to OTSG after one alcohol offence, the psychiatrist who examined her said he found "nothing really wrong with her except that she was homesick." He even criticized the judge's sentence (which doctors rarely did): "One would consider this [one offence] a questionable reason for sending a girl to reform school." Once a girl was incarcerated in the training school, however, the real trouble could begin. The OTSG superintendent noted critically of Anne that she was withdrawing. She "seems to wish to stick to her own culture."[55] For many Native girls, complete withdrawal was their only defence in an regime designed to alter, indeed assault, their very inner being.

The more recent work of Mohawk psychiatrist Dr. Clare Brant has reinterpreted the process of withdrawal, a process recognized at the time by doctors and penal workers. Combining his mainstream psychiatric training with the writings of anthropologists and his own experience as a Native medical practitioner, Brant developed theories delineating how the psychological process of "identity creation" took on distinctive contours in Native (primarily Ojibwa/Cree and Mohawk) cultures. Emotional restraint and non-interference, Brant argued, were key values conveyed in Native child-rearing: "Gratitude and approval are rarely verbalized . . . joyfulness and enthusiasm [may be] repressed along with anger." When these values clash with other child-rearing practices, he continued, the result may be "paralysis and frustration" for the child.[56] When medical experts examine Native children, they often find them "passive, difficult to assess and not forthcoming," a condition that clinicians unfamiliar with Native culture often misinterpret "as evidence of psychopathology." For Brant, such passivity "reflects patterns of conflict suppression, conflict projection and the humiliating superego," all of which are "techniques of ensuring group unity and cohesion." It was the "failure to recognize and understand such cultural influences" that could "turn what was intended as a helpful encounter into a destructive one."

The emphasis in many Native communities on teasing, shaming, and ridicule to secure social norms, Brant also believed, could produce children with a "humiliating superego" – that is, fearful of criticism, to the point of retreating, "avoiding trying anything new or apologizing for error."[57] Faced with the clash between her own culture and the dominant culture of the white colonizers, the child's coping mechanism might well produce a weak sense of self-esteem.

Brant's characterization of the medical and social work misunderstandings of Native children captures the encounters between reform school experts and Native girls with tragic precision. Unfortunately, the staff interpreted the emotional restraint that served the girls as a defence mechanism in an alienating and racist environment as a sign that the children were either mentally "slow" or "lackadaisical," exhibiting a moral and emotional emptiness at their core. "She makes little real progress . . . an Indian child on whom the school will make little basic change. Goes along, creating no real trouble, but absorbs little from the environment. She contributes little and takes little," the superintendent wrote disapprovingly of one girl. Failure on placement was then predicted as inevitable: "In the community her prognosis may be poor. Under 24 hour supervision she is ok, but when left on her own, her judgement will be faulty and attitude lazy." The school workers also interpreted the Native girls' retreat behind a wall of restraint as "sneakiness," as they employed a common racist stereotype. "She is quiet, deep and cunning," the superintendent said of one girl. "She has no conscience and is not progressing. . . . She appears cooperative, but is deceitful."[58] As Brant notes, the white authorities' "obsession with eye contact" and direct engagement was used in the courtroom and in OTSG to cast Indian girls as shifty and "secretive," or "smooth" and deceitful.[59]

In the training school, hiding emotions behind a façade of either toughness or silence was a safety valve for many girls who had to cope with an alien and strict environment, as well as with memories of poverty, violence, neglect, or unhappiness. For Native girls, though, the strategy was especially noticeable. The Cree girl who said she was gang-raped on the streets was questioned by a psychiatrist, who noted that she "looks blankly at the floor" and in testing "only answers in one or two words. . . . She can't relate to the other girls, can't even remember how long she has been in here."[60] She was undoubtedly frightened – and a mere fourteen – but her responses were nonetheless taken as a sign of low intelligence. Today a more affluent white girl displaying the same signs would be diagnosed with post-traumatic stress disorder. But then even the interviewing techniques of medical and social work examiners would have been alien to many First Nations girls. The emphasis in Native cultures on "reciprocal" rather than one-way encounters and especially an aversion to "direct requests, instructions, or disagreeing openly" meant that the girls were unlikely to communicate openly with social workers trained to use interviews as a means of instruction and forthright "problem-solving."[61]

Although their keepers often cast Native girls within a homogeneous, and negative, cultural mould, the girls did not uniformly adopt a strategy of restraint as a coping mechanism. Their reactions were more varied, with some adapting to OTSG's expectations and a few rebelling with a fierce determination. Those who did not fit the penal workers' and doctors' preconceived images of Indians were always described as exceptions to the rule. This is a "materially indulged Indian girl, who on occasion adopts a superior air," the school noted about Grace, who did not approximate their image of the impoverished Indian (and presumably was arrogant for *not* being one). Her probation report continued in this vein: "This is one of the more intelligent better educated Indian families" on the reserve.[62] The staff and assorted experts saw the "typical" Indian family as being poor, "living in a tar shack" surrounded by dirt, and drinking to excess. To staff, the model Native inmate (though seldom found) did not disrupt their image of slowness but conveyed the requisite appreciation for the school's care: "She is dull . . . [but] always happy, *grateful* for her clothes, obedient, and gets on well with children."[63] A "grateful" Indian child fit nicely into the colonial mindset, which believed that Natives should be thankful for the paternal/maternal care offered by institutions like OTGS – a view that itself justified and replicated colonialism.[64]

Nowhere is this cultural dissonance more glaring than in decisions made about girls' intelligence, sometimes resulting in their transfer to institutions for the mentally retarded. Historians have documented the class and race bias of intelligence tests and forensic theories used by medical experts in North America, as well as the increased role of such "scientific" advice on sentencing decisions in the later twentieth century. The difficulties presented by language and cultural differences often compounded the problem for Native girls.[65] Doctors and psychologists who tested the girls when they were first admitted to OTSG used standardized IQ and personality tests, including the Binet-Simon, Roestch, and Bender-Gestalt, even though by the late 1950s they were sometimes admitting that these were inadequate measures. "She can barely read or write, has no general knowledge, does not understand the consequences of her promiscuous action," and is therefore "retarded," noted one doctor in his appraisal of a girl in the 1950s. Yet a year later the same doctor admitted that an IQ test was not a good measure for Native girls. In examining a girl named Ellen, he initially concluded that her "retardation" and "IQ of 72"were due to her "cultural patterns." Yet he noticed that she was carrying an Ojibwa bible and asked her to read from it. "She reads quite well," he acknowledged, which led him to note that the IQ test was probably inadequate.[66] This finding did not, however, lead him to abandon such testing.

Ellen's case as well seemed to represent a fundamental problem that was lost on the experts: they were testing girls whose first language was not English and whose language – in this case Ojibwa – did not contain exact words for some of the concepts, such as guilt, that the assessors were looking for. The case of two Ojibwa/Cree girls from Northern Ontario exemplified the potentially drastic outcome of such testing. The girls, ages thirteen and fifteen, were supposedly sent to OTSG for a break and enter, but clearly concerns about sexual promiscuity were also key to their sentences. They had been arrested after breaking into a house, with their younger brother in tow, and stealing some groceries. The "victim" of the theft then acted as a translator at their trial. Because they were destitute, seldom at home (their parents were supposedly transient), and spending time "in the bunkhouse" with local miners, they were sent to OTSG. The younger of the two girls had a "minimal" English vocabulary, and limited schooling, the psychologist admitted, so that those in charge had to rely on "basic tests" and the "views of school teachers" at OTSG. The girl, they found, could not do arithmetic and subtraction, and when asked to draw a person she produced a "stick person," which was deemed "primitive." "Regardless of language and primitive background," the doctor concluded, "she appears to be a high grade mental defective."[67]

Her sister's artistic test and fate were similar. The superintendent concluded that Susan was more intelligent; the doctor disagreed. Her stick person was more sophisticated, "with details like fingers" indicating "border line intelligence," but, like her sister, she was still deemed "defective." Thus OTSG would be "wasted" on her because she could not be integrated into its educational program. Despite language difficulties, and despite the doctor's admission that the older girl was extremely tense when examined, the tests were taken as "scientific truth" and the sisters were transferred to the facility for the "mentally retarded" in Smith Falls. The doctor's musings on what to do with these sisters reveal the experts' racist equation of the "primitive" reserve with low intelligence: "We have two solutions. 1. return her to her primitive culture and accept that we can't modify her behaviour or secondly, consider her functioning as a high grade mental defective and certify her [for] one of Ontario's Hospital Training schools."[68] In his eyes, the two solutions were synonymous.

How many Native girls were similarly transferred, under medical orders, thus making it difficult to release them? In one instance a father from the North urged the federal Indian agent to use his "authority" both to "make his [deserting] wife return" and "release his daughter from Smith Falls." The daughter had been sent from a residential school to St. Mary's Training School for Girls, then transferred to Smith Falls. Replying with some condescension, a DIA social worker told him that "specialists" with far greater knowledge than him had recommended this institution, and that he would have a difficult time "managing" his daughter anyway with her mother gone. When the father persisted with his demands for the daughter's release, he was chastised for failing to value his own daughter: "A year in this institution – one of the best in Canada – will mean a great deal to E. . . . I realize you want her home, but we are often called on to make sacrifices for our children." Rejecting this paternalism, the father persisted still, with no apparent effect.[69]

Some of the social work and medical experts assessing girls in training school were aware of the discriminatory testing of Native girls, but

they still remained trapped within their overall acceptance of the juvenile justice system or their own professional training. One psychologist
tried to argue with the penal workers that they were not cognizant
enough of the "cultural differences" that had caused a Native girl to
periodically "blow up" in rage. She believed that the girl did badly on
the IQ test because of her "social-economic background," and that the
girl's life on the reserve had been so completely different that she could
not cope with OTSG. She too believed that Native families were undisciplined, but she at least sensed that cultural, environmental, and spatial
differences were leaving girls profoundly estranged in OTSG:

> She has grown up on a reserve where there is a different way of deal-
> ing with things that you don't like. . . . [Family] controls are at a mini-
> mum. . . . From twelve on, she was on her own to do as she pleased.
> Here, she has to conform to standards she has never known before.
> Also she has to live in close contact with others. At home, she simply
> took herself away physically if she didn't like someone, even her
> mother. Here, she doesn't like two staff members, and she keeps the
> problem inside until she blows up.

Her analysis was a sympathetic attempt to make penal staff – who
focused on order and control – understand the alienation of this inmate
and the discriminatory consequences of the school regime on her. The
psychological assessment, however, carried with it no power to send the
girl home. She could only weakly recommend counselling to help the
girl "handle difficult situations." Perhaps there was no easy resolution.
The girl initially rejected parole with her family because "there was too
much drinking" there.[70] Ultimately, though, she chose her father's house
over a work placement outside the reserve, opting for a culture she
understood over one she did not.

Accommodation and Resistance

Girls' practice of "conservation-withdrawal" was undoubtedly one form
of resistance, as well as a coping mechanism. It was a strategy that some
girls had already used in their court hearings. When a thirteen-year-old
was queried in court about her runs from home, she answered yes when
asked if she liked her home, but refused to answer any questions about
why she ran away for four or five days, and where she went.[71] Such
silences did not aid the possibility of probation, but as in the case of
many other girls before the courts, the withdrawal of Native girls into
silence probably displayed an astute intuition that they could exercise

only minimal control over the court's decisions. Those girls who did protest the evidence or their sentences found that pleas for another chance had little effect on the judge once his or her mind was made up. When Patricia, the girl whose grandmother had taken her to court, begged the judge not to send her away, and worried about being placed with girls she did not know at OTSG, the judge's firm response offered not even a hint of a second chance.

While silent withdrawal was more common among First Nations girls, other strategies adopted to cope with their incarceration bore strong similarities to the approaches of their fellow inmates in OTSG. Certainly, the best method to secure release was to accommodate oneself, at least superficially, to the school's lessons concerning social purity, femininity, and the work ethic. This was ultimately the strategy of most girls, both Native and non-Native, though they often engaged in considerable foot-dragging along the way, only reluctantly accepting the strict school regime and the attempts to remake their morals and character into a new femininity. The distinct problem that Native girls faced was the stereotype of their unreachable nature. Even if the girls were classified as "quiet" or "not very much trouble to the institution," matrons and the superintendent harboured resilient doubts that they had truly internalized the lessons of the school and could be sent out on placement.[72]

Some girls did rebel, using the same tactics as their fellow inmates: talking back, running away, creating same-sex intimacies and countercultures, carving themselves and otherwise becoming violent, with their anger focused on both property and other people. OTSG officials also asserted that Native girls were more likely to engage in awls, especially if they were very young when admitted, and far away from their homes.[73] By and large, none of these tactics were embraced by Native girls more than by others, and both Native and non-Native girls found their runaway attempts and angry outbursts rewarded with time in detention, a strategy of behaviour control that penal workers liked but psychiatric and psychological counsellors sometimes conceded was self-defeating. The girls emerged contained but unaltered – bitter, until the next outburst.

For the Native girls who appeared to be withdrawn, such outbursts of anger must have seemed all the more incomprehensible to training school staff. As Clare Brant put it, if children raised with the "hands-off" principle of non-interference find their existing community norms gone and their identities under assault, they may understandably become "aggressive," unable to appreciate "the needs and rights of others."

Under some conditions, he warned, emotional restraint can also "explode into the open as repressed hostility or violence, projected onto those near to us."[74] Moreover, as many anti-racist writers have noted, those who are taught to hate their own "self and identity" may respond by becoming "traumatized and self-destructive."[75]

School placement workers often tried to place rebellious First Nations girls in foster homes with other Native families as soon as possible, even if this meant sending them to a different reserve. Indeed, one girl refused to go to a non-Indian home when she was to be sent out. "I hate the way you people live," she told the placement officer, "always washing and going on. We do not live like that." Concluding that "she would only fit into a home with her own race," the worker found a temporary foster family for her on another reserve, only to run into problems because the girl lacked status with that band and her mother had lost status on her own reserve. Returned to the school because of "promiscuity," the girl soon went awl. She broke through windows to escape, then fled in search of her father, leading a group of other inmates as far as Detroit. Eventually she was placed on parole in the keeping of her own sister, prompting a provincial official to reiterate the concern that the school should simply not take Native girls.[76]

If OTSG placed a girl out in a Native home and the probation was unsuccessful, this result only reinforced the preconceived notion that Indians were unreformable. Admitting that Ellen, who came from near Dryden, was very "unhappy," OTSG placed her near a reserve in Southern Ontario to be schooled with other Native children. A pregnancy ensued, confirming the superintendent's view that she was a "typical Indian who does not understand our moral standards." Sent back to the training school, as almost all pregnant girls were, Ellen was designated as being too "stubborn" to be helped, particularly because she was often in detention. Once she tore a cast off her broken leg in rage. Yet a letter she sent to the superintendent after her release, and following further conflicts with the law and a suicide attempt, revealed not stubbornness, but despair:

> Miss B if you felt the way I do, you would want to kill yourself. I tried it. But I still woke up in the same house. Everyone around me making my life miserable. They know I want to get hold of sleeping pills again. I have never had anyone to talk to about why I do these things. I guess I never will. . . . If I was dead then I would not have any more worries. . . . I wish you would ask Mrs H to write to me. I want to go some place where I will get help, and where I can't see my mother [who] calls me a whore. . . . I was for awhile, but I had to get some money. . . . I want someone to help me out of this problem.[77]

When her wardship was terminated at age eighteen, Ellen had already also been in the local jail and mental hospital.

Ellen's later suicide attempt offers a rare and foreboding glimpse into a life that became far more unhappy after her institutionalization.[78] Her self-destructive actions were surely a consequence of the broader social and cultural context of her life: the traumas, the unnamed "powerlessness, poverty and alienation" created by colonialism. As Brant suggests in a more recent analysis of federally incarcerated Native women and suicide, the very success of correctional institutions in inculcating a sense of guilt and shame in women who have no method of dealing with these immense blows to their sense of self sometimes results in suicide appearing to be "the only way out" – as it may well have appeared to Ellen.[79]

At least one OTSG doctor argued that girls from mixed-race backgrounds suffered especially difficult cultural adjustments. In one case his diagnosis of a girl's cultural alienation led to his (rare) recommendation of release as a solution for dealing with a violent inmate. When Jane, a young thirteen-year-old Métis girl, was sent down from the North for promiscuity and running away, and proved to be one of the most difficult girls in the school, resisting at every point, the doctor suggested sending her home to her Native mother, even though the local CAS in the North refused this direction because the mother was supposedly "promiscuous," impoverished, and incompetent. "No counselling will work," disagreed the doctor emphatically: "I have pointed this out many times . . . a mixed cultural background causes this."

Jane became involved in repeated runaway attempts and violence not only against others, but also against herself, including slashing herself with broken glass. "When not awl, she spends most of her time in detention," commented the superintendent, who suggested that the solution was to give Jane massive doses of tranquillizers. The authorities also resorted to a temporary transfer to the OTSG wing of the adult Mercer Reformatory after Jane's "runs and promiscuous" behaviour and an attack on a matron proved to the superintendent that the girl had to be pacified. To the psychiatrist's credit, he resisted the pressure from the OTGS superintendent to certify Jane so that she could be transferred to a mental institution. His assessment ultimately pointed to the loneliness, alienation, and difficulty of coping with denigration and self-hatred that had propelled Jane to slash herself and run away: "She feels frustrated in a desire to be with her mother and this periodically involves her in [runs]. She feels quite desperate when she thinks of her mother and the simple surroundings she is used to and becomes angry at staff and destroys property. . . . Send her home."[80] By the time Jane was sent home, though, her spiral downwards had left her violent towards her own family, drinking heavily, and desperately unhappy. Her OTSG sentence was a disaster. Her self-punishing and violent outbursts were expressions of anger, or unanswered calls for help, or both. The potentially tragic effects of institutionalization could not have been more conclusively evident.

Families who remained in close touch with their daughters sometimes attempted to speed their releases by arguing (as many other poor families did) that the girls' labour or domestic aid was needed in the home. One father admitted that there was a "problem" with his daughter, but protested her incarceration from the very beginning. He said he needed her help in his job as school janitor on the reserve because he was arthritic and his wife was disabled. "I could have brought half the reservation to testify" in her defence, he noted at her trial, but "I did not have the money."[81] After their daughters were released from OTSG, families sometimes pushed for parole for them at home – despite meagre incomes and small houses – rather than placement elsewhere.

In a few cases families and friends tried to protect released girls by hiding their behaviour from the prying eyes of probation workers. "The parents are protective and won't tell you anything," grumbled one probation officer doing follow-up.[82] Occasionally a girl was able to disappear from sight, a strategy accomplished fairly easily if the reserve community was sympathetic to her or if she lived in a remote area. "We can't trace this nomadic family, so terminate wardship," a superintendent finally conceded reluctantly of one Northern family. Another placement officer searched high and low through all the "local Indian cafes" near a Southern reserve with an Ontario Provincial Police officer, then gave up. Her resignation reflected a particularly racist view: "It appears she is good at hiding . . . and I cannot tell her apart from any other Indian squaw."[83]

When placement officers came calling, Native families might also successfully resist their intervention. When a young girl out on placement on her home reserve became pregnant by a neighbouring boy, the families announced to the OTSG worker that they wanted "to settle it in their own way . . . in the longhouse tradition." The boy's parents did not rush the couple into marriage, but waited until after the baby was born, and even then the paternal grandparents expressed a strong desire to adopt the child. They expressed concern that the girl was not yet ready to settle down and marry. The father assured the OTSG worker that "they would do what is right," and even though girls were routinely reincarcerated for such pregnancies, the placement officer walked away, agreeing that it was far better to let the families settle things in their own manner than force the girl back to OTSG.[84] In a few instances, then, social workers' sense of cultural distance from Native communities provided the space that Native families needed to exercise their own methods of social and familial control.

The resolve of these families to solve their own problems was testimony to the persistence of the traditional means of social control in Native communities, despite the attempts of the Canadian state to impose new legal and welfare measures on Native peoples. The extent to which communities selectively used Euro-Canadian law, or their own traditions, or both, varied from one reserve to another, but a small number of parents and certainly the girls clearly resented the intrusion of the Canadian criminal justice system into their lives. Other families did make use of family and juvenile courts to try to maintain control over their daughters, though their aim was rarely incarceration in training school, and their use of the criminal justice system clearly fell within the context of the times: the immense material, social, and cultural stresses on Native families. Unfortunately, when social workers pleaded with the federal government to let them "help" Native juvenile delinquents in the late 1940s, they failed to consult the key constituency: the First Nations themselves.

Gender, Colonialism, and Criminalization

The specific experiences of Native girls in conflict with the law indicate how race, gender, and class intersected over a period of three decades. The interaction shaped a process of legal and moral regulation that both resembled and differed from the legal governance of other female delinquents. While explanations for delinquency remained closely tied to social marginality and familial failure, the racialization of delinquency was also emerging in post-World War II Canada. Ideas about race, as well as racism, are not timeless historical constants; in this period Native culture was seen as backward, impoverished, and in need of assimilation to the "modern" world, all of which played into girls' conflicts with the law. But questions of "race" were also linked to the unfolding and debilitating experience of colonialism: girls' encounters with the courts and their experiences in correctional institutions were indelibly marked by their marginalization as "federal wards" whose land, livelihood, language, and culture had been either appropriated or suppressed.

Native girls became more involved in the juvenile justice system as they and their families came into more day-to-day contact with an encroaching, urbanizing white colonization, and as social, emotional, and material stresses on Native families and communities – also the product of colonialism – created problems that were taken to the courts for adjudication. Ironically, too, Native youth found themselves in the courts and training schools because the government, often advised by well-intentioned social workers and political activists, tried to integrate Native families into the welfare state. Although Native communities undoubtedly wanted to share in some benefits of the welfare state, the families also found themselves the subject of increased surveillance and intervention, leading to a loss of control over their children's lives. Despite well-intentioned calls for an end to discrimination, the integration of Native peoples into the welfare state was governed by an ideal of assimilation. Social work discourses and government practices urged intervention, intervention slid into surveillance, and surveillance sometimes became the first step to incarceration. Ironically and tragically, by the 1950s Native girls were increasingly being offered the equal "right" to be confined in training school with white girls.

Native girls were deemed to be in need of probationary protection or removal from their families and communities when authorities saw their promiscuity, absences from home, truancy, drinking, and petty theft as being out of control. As in the case of most girls facing the courts, the officers involved had a dominating concern with their sexuality, and the girls often came from families coping with internal conflicts, immense poverty, and sometimes violence or addiction. Indeed, the sexual regulation of these girls was never separate from this material and social dislocation.

While the nation-building projects of assimilating the poor, the working class, and the First Nations overlapped in design, in practice those different undertakings might also diverge. White girls were usually seen as being at least more easily transformed into new, model citizens. Colonialism in the later twentieth century increasingly created a context in which Native girls were vulnerable to state surveillance, through the Indian Act as well as the Criminal Code, but once incarcerated those girls were assessed through a racist lens as being more primitive, unreachable, unreformable. Cultural differences were ever-present in the contact between white experts and Native girls in OTSG, but the treatment of Aboriginal girls was never simply a question of cultural misunderstanding.[85] Subsuming the judgements made about them were the social relations of colonialism and racism, interlocked with the gender and class biases already inherent in the juvenile justice system.

While many girls coped by accommodating themselves, at least superficially, to the make-over demanded of them, for some girls the school regime could be profoundly tragic. At its worst, institutionalization created alienated, angry, and sometimes violent or self-destructive girls. In their attempts to deal with the denigration they faced, Native girls drew on the cultural resources at hand, practising "conservation-withdrawal," although a small group also spoke and acted out against a regime they found alien and unjust. The best that could happen to many girls was that the penal authorities' sense of superiority and belief that reformation was futile would lead them to abandon their assimilative project and let the girls return to their homes, families, or reserves. However problematic or unhappy those home environments were, they usually offered more hope of a second chance than incarceration in a training school.

Seven

Conclusion

The public criticisms of Grandview voiced in the 1960s reflected broader dissatisfactions with the existing juvenile justice system. Although there were some depressing continuities over the twentieth century with regards to juvenile justice, there were also changes and disruptions, not only in children's actual law-breaking but also in the social and political responses to youth criminality. In the early 1960s a number of events came together to produce a re-evaluation of the federal Juvenile Delinquents Act and the wider juvenile justice system that had grown up around that Act. Although this reassessment was perhaps best symbolized by a federal inquiry into juvenile delinquency established in 1961, there were other indications that police, child welfare advocates, and court and penal personnel were questioning the JDA after more than five decades of its administration.

The political and social re-evaluation that transpired in the early 1960s thus provides a logical ending point for this historical study, because it not only offers an opportunity to reflect on the first five decades of juvenile justice under the JDA, but also suggests some of the problems that remained unsolved, even within the confines of the newly constructed Young Offenders Act.

By the 1960s clear voices of critique were heard – ranging from the legal community through politicians (sometimes encouraged by families who felt damaged by their contact with juvenile justice) to reform groups such as the Elizabeth Fry Society, recently established in Ontario in the 1950s. Older reform groups such as Big Sisters were also questioning their provision of services, sometimes reorienting their goals. These re-evaluations were often still couched in optimism, echoing the long-standing modernist hope that delinquency, like poverty, might be vanquished if only war was declared on it. U.S. examples, always influential in Canada, included new urban campaigns to address inner-city poverty and delinquency, though much of the optimism of local organizing and the political rhetoric of social regeneration were faltering by the 1970s as riots, race tensions, and economic restructuring were dealing a death blow to liberal "social work solutions" to delinquency.[1] By the late 1960s, key U.S. court decisions were revealing a shift from the long-standing paternalism of the juvenile court towards an emphasis on due process in law.[2] Moreover, by the time the federal YOA was passed, Canadian provincial regimes had already altered some of their laws and approaches towards juveniles – just as the 1908 law was presaged by precedents at the provincial level. In Ontario, critiques of the Training Schools Act led to new attention being placed on the need for due legal process, although a commitment to the "welfare" potential of the law remained strong across the political spectrum.

The federal government established the inquiry into juvenile delinquency in 1961 with an overhaul of the JDA in mind. The reigning Progressive Conservatives were influenced in part by a menacing demographic reality: because of the baby boom the country had an increasing number of young people, and statistics from the late 1950s and early 1960s also suggested a growth in youth arrests and incarcerations. At Grandview, for instance, admissions climbed from thirty-nine in 1958 to seventy-one in 1961. Federal statistics indicated rising adult incarcerations as well, leading to the government's desire to "forestall a massive increase in the penitentiaries" by tackling youth crime.[3] The inquiry, staffed by Department of Justice experts and headed by Allan Macleod, a lawyer and career civil servant, was instructed to examine the nature and extent of delinquency, the thorny issue of federal provincial co-operation in the area of youth justice, and parliament's role in revising the JDA.[4]

Coming to an accord on all these issues proved to be difficult, a fact clearly apparent in the testimony given across the country. Although agreement reigned on a few key issues, such as the desirability of standardizing the age limits of the JDA, many other areas of disagreement remained. Moreover, the number of those testifying – ranging from social workers to penal personnel, judges to police, psychiatrists to bureaucrats, and youth workers to professors – was overwhelming. The testimony seemed proof positive that the age of experts had arrived, at least when it came to trying to understand the puzzles of delinquency. If, as one expert stated, the country could really find no more imaginative solutions than it had in 1908, then it was a rather sad state of affairs. Nor were the expert recommendations entirely unpredictable. Professors insisted that more research should be done, sometimes involving trips to New York City. Social workers argued that more social and probation services were necessary. The police expressed suspicion of how the courts would provide adequate solutions.

The report was relatively silent on some issues, mainly because witnesses did not identify them as major problems. Those involved did not see gangs as the urban blight they were in U.S. cities, nor were drugs seen as a significant threat to the young – a view nonetheless challenged by Elizabeth Fry testimony, and certain to change within a decade. Participants did not consider "race" a major category of analysis in relation to criminalization, even though intermittent testimony clearly contradicted that view: racist observations indicated all too well that youth already *were* racialized. In Nova Scotia a chief of police noted that he had seen few problems with girls, save for the "negro section of society where the occasional girl goes astray."[5] Although the issue was not raised consistently in Ontario, and one Northern witness testified that Native youth were not a delinquency problem, in Winnipeg the superintendent of a Catholic girls' refuge countered that many of her problems were either girls of low intelligence or "many Indian and Métis who were of a very low class culture."[6]

A strong emphasis remained on sexual activity defining girls' delinquency, but there was also a very preliminary awareness that sentencing girls for this "crime" had led to arbitrary and unfair treatment. The inquiry was receptive to critics who argued that juveniles needed some of the same legal protections – the right to counsel, to appeal, to not be detained unnecessarily, to have a clear charge against them – that adults had. In its recommendations, the inquiry suggested that conduct labelled as "incorrigibility, unmanageability . . . or being in moral danger should not be included within the offence provisions of the federal Act, but should be dealt with under provincial legislation."[7] Presumably the province would somehow be better able to deal with child protection issues. Consternation about status offences such as sexual immorality, then, was part of broader concerns about civil rights, resulting in recommendations to narrow the jurisdiction of the JDA and eliminate some of its vague wording. Even court workers who had used these sections for years had to admit that no clear legal measuring sticks were in place to ascertain what comprised incorrigibility or sexual immorality. At its most liberal, the report even conceded that what was labelled sexual immorality might well be "acts of curiosity and immaturity" on the part of young people.[8]

More generally, witnesses did not challenge the linkage between sexual misconduct and girls' delinquency. The problem with girls was "mainly sexual misconduct," testified a Jewish Family Services agency. Calgary police agreed, noting that those who only had a few indiscretions to their names, and were not full-fledged "promiscuous" girls, were taken home to their parents rather than directly to the detention home. Repeating concerns heard as far back as 1908, one Ontario penal worker also stressed that the mentally retarded were more likely to succumb to immorality, because these girls were "easy prey."[9] Ontario debates concerning the TSA in 1965 saw the same linkages made; the cabinet minister presenting the legislation only referred to girls in relation to the "immorality" issue.[10]

Some of the traditionally dichotomized views of girls as either innocent victims or sexually voracious threats to society surfaced when the commissioners dealt with both the "contributing to delinquency" sections of the JDA and the issue of sexual assault charges. In the case of sexual assault charges, the commissioners worried that testifying against abusive adults might incur "personality damage" in the child, but they also warned that some experts believed that all female complainants should be medically examined to guard against false accusations resulting from "mental or moral delusion, frequently found especially in young girls."[11] Clearly the expert discourse on sexual abuse, in which girls might be relaying false fantasies, still held sway. In the case of contributing to delinquency, the report fretted that a distinction had to be made between the "exploited" and the "wanton" girl, because the latter may have actually sought out sex with men who then had to face contributing charges. The courts, the commissioners added, should not let such a girl go scot-free without making any attempt to change her behaviour; moreover, the courts had a larger responsibility to protect the "conventional mores" of society.[12]

The claim to be protecting conventional mores was an honest admission that this goal was precisely what the law was about, and that is why, in the early 1960s, there were few direct, frontal challenges to the emphasis on girls' sexual delinquency. Even those with more radical critiques of the system, such as the Elizabeth Fry Societies, worked within the boundaries of this definition. Noting that "very often female delinquency is sexual delinquency," Elizabeth Fry witnesses added that even matters such as petty theft might be indirectly linked to sex, because a "girl might steal the kind of things that she thinks girls of her age, interested in attracting boys, should have." Still, in contrast to other submissions, they opposed institutionalization as the answer: "By putting her in an institution at the very time when contacts with boys are important and need to be developed in a proper way, the result is to separate her unnaturally from male companionship," leaving her unable to deal "normally" with males when she was released.[13]

Also in accord with earlier definitions of delinquency, some overlap occurred in the analyses of the causes of boys' and girls' downfalls, though there is no doubt that the "norm" for the experts was still the delinquent male. Although the report made a strong effort to look at multiple causes of delinquency, including both "individual and environmental" problems, ranging from education to unemployment, it placed a strong emphasis on the inadequate or dysfunctional family as a key site of character maladjustment and therefore delinquency. There was some concern that "middle class crime" such as "auto theft in the suburbs" was increasing, but more witnesses saw people from marginal economic backgrounds to be most at risk, symbolized by one judge's reference to the "tarpaper shacks from which most delinquents come."[14]

There was agreement from many witnesses on a few issues, leading to clear recommendations concerning new legislation. Some provision for hiding the identity of young offenders was needed, and the ability to sentence to training school should be limited. Young offenders must be segregated by sentence and age. Parents should be at court hearings, and the term juvenile delinquent should be abandoned, not simply because it was stigmatizing, but also because some youth (presumably boys) supposedly embraced the label as a symbol of bravado and strength. Commissioners agreed that the social services supporting the system were far too meagre and that the "contributing" sections should be removed from the JDA, though, if need be, amendments on parental responsibility would be added to the Criminal Code. But the commissioners did come out firmly against the idea of "punish the parent" laws, seeing these as ineffectual and unproductive – an interesting admission considering the promotion of such laws in recent years by neo-conservative governments.[15] Many witnesses endorsed the need to provide clearer standards of legal protection to juveniles, some even advocating a treatment/welfare perspective: the "justice" or "civil rights" approach, then, did not stand in singular opposition to the "welfare" approach at the time. Given the cases in which detention had been abused by the authorities, it was not surprising that calls were made for more circumscribed use of detention and the need to bring children promptly before the court.

Despite some agreement, there were clearly areas that would remain problems. The relationship between law and psychiatric experts attached to the court, given their different interests, was one question that was unresolved. The issue of when a teenager should answer to his or her serious crimes as an adult – at sixteen or eighteen – had been a point of contention with the JDA since at least the 1920s and remains a concern today. Uneven "justice by geography" was another troubling issue in 1965. Although some witnesses were inclined to reiterate the problem as being one of untrained judges,[16] the real weakness was lack of diagnostic, foster, and probationary care in less affluent, rural, and Northern areas. Again, regional disparities in youth justice remains a current issue, though today it is also connected to the lack of culturally sensitive services for disadvantaged and racialized youth, and even to the desire of Quebec to protect its less punitive approach to juvenile justice from federal control.[17] There was also debate about the power and arbitrary discretion exercised by police as front-line contacts with delinquents, an anxiety that is also tied to issues of race and racism today. The police, worried some witnesses appearing before the 1965 inquiry, were "taking it upon themselves to exercise a social worker function." The final report recommendations urged that police not have so much informal power concerning diversion, and not be in the business of recreation.[18] The *Police Club for Boys* and the kindly Sergeant Clay in *Youth and the Law* were now seen as problematic: policing and social work had to know their boundaries. But witnesses were not of one mind on this issue, with some arguing that recreational work was simply the police doing preventative work; today, this task might be relabelled as police public relations work. The report also agonized over whether society should mandate or force treatment on young offenders, which again remains a troubling question today, and especially so for those debating whether we should force underage girls off the streets into "safe houses." Finally, the question of provincial versus federal jurisdiction remained thorny, not simply because of political boundaries, but also because changes at the federal level were likely to have a financial cost at the local level. Again, this question would become a major issue of contention in the following years.

The official inquiry of the early 1960s may not have produced a major paradigm shift in thinking about delinquency, but it did create a moment of re-evaluation, and at a federal level it set in motion a chain of political events that was eventually to culminate in the creation of the new Young Offenders Act.[19] That this legislation took twenty years to create was not simply a political accident; rather, it reflects a lack of clear agreement on how to fix the juvenile justice system. In the twenty years after the federal report was released in 1965, debates centred, in part, on the underlying aims of the juvenile justice system, often referred to as the welfare (treatment or rehabilitation), justice (due process and civil rights), and crime control (punishment and protection of society) approaches. Should new legislation stress methods of dealing with lawbreakers, clarifying legal process and accountability? Or should it attempt to save children from becoming criminals through guidance and treatment (the long-time rhetorical goal of the JDA)? The controversy that ensued in Ontario after the Training School Act changes of 1965 indicated that there was, as yet, no resolution to this debate, as the government and its advisors drawn from the "treatment" lobby traded arguments with the legal experts who argued that the new TSA still conflated delinquency, dependency, and neglect (as laws had done since the nineteenth century) and allowed children considered to be the "refuse" of society to be "dumped" into training schools without a proper legal consideration of the facts of the case.[20]

The attempts at a new federal act failed in 1967, 1970, and 1975, and by the time the next two efforts were made in 1979 and 1981 the political, economic, and social climate had changed. Political shifts towards more conservative governments, and the impact of victims' rights and law and order lobbies, along with the traumas of economic downturns and restructuring, all helped to create a context in which the crime control approach gained increased ideological authority. Ironically, academic research and writing in the 1960s and early 1970s had critiqued both the paternalism and arbitrariness of the welfare approach, and in the process questioned the modernist faith in "treatment" as a means of rehabilitation. Feminist critiques of the arbitrariness of labelling girls "delinquent" were part of this. As a result, those advocating welfare solutions philosophically associated with the old JDA found themselves increasingly on the defensive, and those prescribing a more legalistic civil rights approach found they were sometimes allied – unintentionally – with a growing law and order lobby.[21] By 1984 the crime control model had become extremely powerful, so much so that there were fewer strong voices able to offer spirited philosophical objections to the abandonment of prevention and treatment, often delivered through social services, as the main goal of the juvenile justice system. What is remarkable is how quickly – within a decade – the ideological raison d'être of the earlier juvenile justice system evaporated.

When the YOA was finally passed in 1982, and came into effect in 1984, it stressed both the accountability of youth for their crimes and due process. The emphasis on due process can lead to more legalism (thus enhancing the need for more lawyers), requiring funds for courtroom counsel and not for probation or other services. For girls, the new YOA appeared to usher in real progress with the removal of the old status offences such as sexual immorality. Both feminist research and the political critique of the unfair double standard embedded in many juvenile justice regimes apparently had a broader social effect.

But, as Marge Reitsma-Street argues, discrimination may have simply reinvented its form. Despite the gender-neutral law, "failure to comply with probation" charges for girls (matters such as breaking curfew) increased under the YOA, leading to more custodial care. In other words, a new "masked" status offence was emerging for girls, with gender inequities "surfacing in new forms." Contrary to public images, after the advent of the YOA the use of "minimal sanctions" for girls decreased and the "use of custody increased."[22] Other feminist criminologists argue that the definitions of femininity and sexuality have not been radically transformed, only altered slightly. As a result, old "status" offences of immorality can be relabelled as new Criminal Code sexual offences or as "medical problems" needing mandatory institutionalization and treatment – a form of "hidden incarceration" couched in the language of girls' need for a "structured environment."[23] While in the past girls were arrested for running away, they are now arrested for prostitution, which is often the end result of having to survive on the streets after running away. Girls' sexuality is still under "protective" surveillance, yet little is being done to address the more substantive reasons behind girls heading to the streets or engaging in law-breaking. The conclusion of one prominent criminologist – that "female delinquency has changed little over the last two decades," with girls still criminalized for behaviour overlooked in boys – is a sobering, and depressing, thought.[24]

As the history of the application of the JDA and TSA in Ontario makes clear, we should be wary of judging legislation only by its stated intent: rhetoric is not always reality. When the 1982 YOA was introduced into Parliament there was much talk about increased attention to rehabilitation, but the underlying rationale was greater youth accountability – making youth accountable for their misdeeds – though in practice this imbalance might have been altered had there been a political will to do so. The new YOA also appeared to place more control in the hands of the state, perhaps at the expense of the family, but this too is an oversimplification. Both the JDA and the YOA carried a strong emphasis on the family as the primary agent of youth control – an agent that the state should support, as long as it works in tandem with dominant social norms. Rather than suggesting a dichotomy between these so-called "public" and "private" spheres, I believe that it is more useful to look at their interaction, co-operation, and also conflict, in the same way that we have explored how and why families used the JDA to assert moral and economic control over delinquent daughters.

Then too, any idealization of a golden age of JDA paternalism is belied by a more complex historical reality. The financial cost of rehabilitation – even if we disagree with the treatment prescribed – often meant that the service was not forthcoming, as attested to by the constant calls by training schools like OTSG for even a modicum of psychological services for abused young girls, or for meagre funds for their education. Furthermore, protection and treatment may have been the JDA's dominant watchwords, but they were also accompanied, in many judges' sentences, by calls for the protection of society and youth accountability. Nor were treatment and protection necessarily the social outcome of the law. Along with claims about saving children came very real efforts to punish them by showing them the "majesty of the law." Both paternalism and punishment co-existed within the JDA, as they do still within the YOA.

What was crucial to the history of juvenile justice were the changing ideological suppositions that framed and gave the law meaning, the social context in which the law was enforced, and the way in which law then emerged as a complex set of symbols and social practices. After all, anti-delinquency legislation never specifically targeted Native youth, yet that is precisely what began to happen in practice; their criminalization was a product of the intensified stresses of colonialism and economic development, social and cultural alienation, and racism. Similarly, many clauses of the old JDA were posed as gender-neutral, but their application was not so.

To understand the process of girls' criminalization, then, we need to understand how systems of meaning constructing notions of femininity, sexuality, and family interacted with the material and social context framing children's lives. Class relations, economic marginality, gender norms, and racist ideology were all important variables shaping who was apprehended, why they were designated delinquent, and which children ended up in training school. Children's conflicts with the laws were undoubtedly also conditioned by violence, tensions, addictions, and illness within their families, leading many experts and reformers to suppose that, in the last instance, the inadequate family held the key to delinquency. But the inequalities and alienations of class, gender, and race relations also had a profound impact on even these seemingly "classless" or gender-neutral factors.

Setting up a historical debate about the JDA as a contest between humanist interpretations that vaunt the good motives of reformers trying to save children and neo-Marxist analyses that blame a class or corporate conspiracy for changes in delinquency regimes is far too simplistic, and most certainly misrepresents a historical materialist analysis. For one thing, both sides of this debate ignore the importance of the historical agency of those children and their families who were touched by the juvenile justice system. These children and families utilized the law to their own ends, sometimes endorsing its aims, at other times protesting its condemnation of children. The question is also not simply if those with authority, whether they were Big Sisters or judges, were well intentioned. Rather, we need to analyse the underlying rationales for their actions and, most importantly, the outcomes of their social, legal, and political agendas for children who did actually end up in conflict with the law.

After all, during these decades the juvenile justice system was designed and administered by those with the greatest authority, affluence, and cultural capital in order to preserve the "conventional mores" of social discipline, the work ethic, restrained female sexuality, and the patriarchal family. The conventional wisdom assumed that these values would provide protection for children and also prepare them for a law-abiding and therefore secure future as adult citizens. As that agenda worked itself out, it inevitably focused most stringently and coercively on those children who were already disadvantaged by violence, economic insecurity, and social and racial marginalization.

Some radical criminologists have suggested yet another approach to juvenile justice, this one labelled the "community or societal change model."[25] Starting with the premise that crime is produced not simply by individuals, but by the conditions of society, especially the inequalities and alienations of the social order, this line of thought suggests that crime must be understood as a "reaction to one's life conditions." Since youthful offenders are often outsiders to educational opportunities and the labour market, experiencing alienation simply by virtue of their age, and given that they may also feel powerless because of violence or sexual, class, or racial oppression, this argument has considerable resonance. Although it accepts short-term measures to aid offenders in the here-and-now, the community change model also advocates for a more dramatic social transformation of the very processes that sustain violence, inequality, alienation, and colonialism. Although it has rarely been tested in social practice, perhaps now is the time, given the dismal history of all the other approaches, to take up and embrace this more radical model.

Notes

One: Introduction

1 D. Owen Carrigan, *Juvenile Delinquency in Canada: A History* (Concord, Ont.: Irwin Publishing, 1998), pp.178-82.

2 Bernard Schissel, *Blaming Children: Youth Crime, Moral Panics and the Politics of Hate* (Halifax: Fernwood Publishing, 1997), p.44.

3 Anthony Doob, "Transforming the Punishment Environment: Understanding Public Views of What Should Be Accomplished at Sentencing," *Canadian Journal of Criminology*, 43,3 (July 2000), pp.323-40.

4 Alan Leschied et al., *Female Adolescent Aggression: A Review of the Literature and the Correlates of Aggression* (Ottawa: Solicitor General, 2000).

5 Patricia Pearson, "Teenage Mutant Ninja Canadians: Are We Raising a Generation of Monsters?" *Chatelaine* 66,5 (May 1993), p.75. See also Patricia Pearson, *When She Was Bad: Violent Women and the Myth of Innocence* (New York: Viking, 1997).

6 Yasmin Jawani, "Erasing Race: The Story of Reena Virk," *Canadian Woman Studies: les cahiers de la femme* 19,3 (Fall 1999), pp.178-84.

7 Elizabeth Comack, "New Possibilities for a Feminism 'in' Criminology? From Dualism to Diversity," *Canadian Journal of Criminology* 41,2 (April 1999), pp.161-70.

8 Marge Reitsma-Street, "Justice for Canadian Girls: A 1990s Update," *Canadian Journal of Criminology* 41,3 (July 1999), pp.335-59.

9 Alexandra Highcrest, "When Protection Is Punishment," *The Globe and Mail*, Aug. 14, 2000.

10 Reitsma-Street, "Justice for Canadian Girls," p.346.

11 Maureen Cain, "Towards Transgression: New Directions in Feminist Criminology," *International Journal of the Sociology of Law* 18 (1990), p.4.

12 Comack, "New Possibilities," p.165.

13 Christopher Webster et al., "Assessment and Treatment of Mentally Disordered Young Offenders," in *The Young Offenders Act: A Revolution in Canadian Juvenile Justice*, ed. Alan Leschied, Peer Jaffe, and Wayne Willis (Toronto: University of Toronto Press, 1991), p.198.

14 *Report of the Toronto Juvenile Court*, 1920, RG 47, City of Toronto Archives.

15 Judge Beaulieu, "A Comparison of Judicial Roles under the JDA and YOA," in *Young Offenders Act*, ed. Leschied, Jaffe, and Willis, p.139.

16 *The Globe and Mail*, Nov. 17, 1999, Nov. 8, 1997. One former guard was found guilty, while the former chief psychologist was not. In the case of the psychologist, two charges were withdrawn, he was acquitted on eight, and eleven were stayed by the judge due to problems with evidence.

17 Carrigan, *Juvenile Delinquency in Canada*, chap. 1.

18 Susan Houston, "The 'Waifs and Strays' of a Late Victorian City: Juvenile Delinquents in Toronto," in *Childhood and Family in Canadian History*, ed. Joy Parr (Toronto: McClelland and Stewart, 1982), pp.129-42; Paul Bennett, "Taming 'Bad Boys' of the 'Dangerous Classes': Child Rescue and Restraint at the Victoria Industrial School, 1887-1935," *Histoire Sociale/Social History* 21 (May 1988), pp.71-96; John Milloy, *A National Crime: The Canadian Government and the Residential School System, 1897-1986* (Winnipeg: University of Manitoba Press, 1999), p.33; Carolyn Strange, *Toronto's Girl Problem: The Perils and Pleasures of the City, 1880-1930* (Toronto: University of Toronto Press, 1995).

19 One example: The Youthful Offenders Act of 1894 allowed young offenders to be separated from older offenders during their arrests and trials, and it permitted the courts to place children with the Children's Aid Society or in homes for destitute children.

20 Cynthia Commachio, "Dancing to Perdition: Adolescence and Leisure in Inter-War English Canada," *Journal of Canadian Studies* 32,3 (Fall 1997), pp.5-35.

21 Jeffrey Keshen, "Wartime Jitters over Juveniles: Canada's Delinquency Scare and Its Consequences, 1939-45," in *Age of Contention: Readings in Canadian Social History, 1900-45*, ed. Jeffrey Keshen (Toronto: Harcourt Brace, 1997), pp.364-86.

22 Carrigan, in *Juvenile Delinquency in Canada*, p.96, says this was a cause of rising delinquency in the two world wars: "Many families were deprived of the guiding influence of fathers and older brothers." A more sophisticated version of this idea that the father-headed family provides a control on delinquency is found in some power/control theory. See Bill McCarthy and John Hagan, "Gender, Delinquency and the Great Depression: A Test of Power Control Theory," *Canadian Review of Sociology and Anthropology* 42,2 (1984), pp.153-77.

23 On the post-World War II period, see Mary Louise Adams, *The Trouble with Normal: Postwar Youth and the Making of Heterosexuality* (Toronto: University of Toronto Press, 1997); Ruth Roach Pierson, *They're Still Women after All: The Second World War and Canadian Womanhood* (Toronto: McClelland and Stewart, 1986); Susan Prentice, "Workers, Mothers, Reds: Toronto's Daycare Fight," *Studies in Political Economy* 30 (1989), pp.115-41. On the Cold War, see Elaine Tyler May, *Homeward Bound: American Families in the Cold War Era* (New York: Basic Books, 1988).

24 Eric Schneider, *Vampires, Dragons and Egyptian Kings: Youth Gangs in Postwar New York* (Princeton, N.J.: Princeton University Press, 1999), p.51.

25 Paul Havemann, "From Child Saving to Child Blaming: The Political Economy of the Young Offenders Act, 1908-84," in *The Social Basis of Law: Critical Readings in the Sociology of Law*, ed. Stephen Brickey and Elizabeth Comack (Toronto: Garamond Press, 1986), pp.225-41.

26 Jane Gadd, "Making Parents Pay Won't Work, Critics Say," *The Globe and Mail*, Aug. 16, 2000; Anthony Doob and Jennifer Jenkins, "Loaded Dice in the Parenting Game," *The Globe and Mail*, Aug. 16, 2000.

Two: Defining Delinquency

1 Paul Tappan, *Delinquent Girls in Court* (New York: Columbia University Press, 1947), p.70; Howard Becker, *Outsider: Studies in the Sociology of Deviance* (New York: Free Press of Glencoe, 1966).

2 Elliot Leyton, *The Myth of Delinquency: An Anatomy of Juvenile Nihilism* (Toronto: McClelland and Stewart, 1979).

3 For one such U.S. study, see Elizabeth Clapp, *Mothers of All Children: Women Reformers and the Rise of Juvenile Courts in Progressive Era America* (University Park: The Pennsylvania State University Press, 1998).

4 In Ontario the 1893 Children's Protection Act had already established Children's Aid Societies, and a federal act of 1894 allowed separation of young offenders and their alternative placements in industrial schools. The Ontario Act allowed the intervention of an existing CAS for those of age twelve or under, including placement of the child in a foster home or industrial school. Canadian Welfare Council, *The Juvenile Court in Law* (Ottawa, 1941), pp.5-6. On the original Juvenile Delinquents Act, see also Gloria Geller, "Young Women in Conflict with the Law," in *Too Few to Count: Canadian Women in Conflict with the Law*, ed. Ellen Adelberg and Claudia Currie (Vancouver: Press Gang, 1987), pp.113-26; and W.L. Scott, *The Genesis of the Juvenile Delinquents Act* (Ottawa: Canadian Welfare Council, 1966).

5 Although children in Ontario were processed under the JDA until they were sixteen, those sent to training school could remain under the care of the court afterwards, initially until they were twenty-one, later eighteen. For that reason, the following chapters necessarily look at teens beyond the "official" age of the JDA.

6 The definition regarding sexual immorality or vice was added in 1924 (see chap. 4 here).

7 Scott, *Genesis*, pp.9-10, 19. I have listed only some of the Act's important provisions. On juvenile and family courts, see Dorothy Chunn, *From Punishment to Doing Good: Family Courts and Socialized Justice in Ontario, 1880-1940* (Toronto: University of Toronto Press, 1992); Neil Sutherland, *Children in English Canadian Society: Framing the Twentieth Century Consensus* (Toronto: University of Toronto Press, 1978).

8 By 1942, of the nineteen juvenile courts in Ontario, twelve were simply presided over by reigning magistrates. Chunn, *From Punishment to Doing Good*, p.167.

9 Chunn, *From Punishment to Doing Good*, p.4.

10 Tappan, *Delinquent Girls in Court*, p.65.

11 J. Archambault, *Report of the Royal Commission to Investigate the Penal System* (Ottawa: Queen's Printer, 1938), p.188; Ontario, *Report of the Select Committee on the Problems of Delinquent Individuals* (Toronto, 1954).

12 John Hagan and Jeffrey Lyon, "Rediscovering Delinquency: Social History, Political Ideology and the Sociology of Law," *American Sociological Review* 42 (1977), p.594.

13 Judge H.C. Arrell, "Judicial and Welfare Aspects of the Family Court," *Canadian Journal of Corrections* 3,1 (January 1961).

14 Carrigan, *Juvenile Delinquency in Canada*, p.144. Carrigan draws on the theories of Hagan and Lyon, "Rediscovering Delinquency," and also asserts

that historians have adopted the views of Anthony Platt in a book published in 1977 – a somewhat dated view of the historiography.

15 Paul Havemann, "The Political Economy of the Young Offenders Act, 1908-84," in *Social Basis of Law*, ed. Brickey and Comack, pp.225-42.

16 Ibid., p.89.

17 Michel Foucault, *The History of Sexuality*, vol. 1 (New York: Vintage Books, 1980); and *Discipline and Punish: The Birth of the Prison* (New York: Pantheon Books, 1977).

18 Allan Hunt, "Foucault's Expulsion of Law: Toward a Retrieval," *Law and Social Inquiry*, 1992, pp.1-38.

19 Mona Gleason, *Normalizing the Ideal: Psychology, Schooling and the Family in Postwar Canada* (Toronto: University of Toronto Press, 1999), p.4.

20 Michael Hakeem, "A Critique of the Psychiatric Approach to the Prevention of Juvenile Delinquency," in *Juvenile Delinquency: A Book of Readings*, ed. Rose Giallombardo (New York: John Wiley and Sons, 1966), p.454.

21 Frederic James Farnell, "Boys and Girls, The Family and Delinquencies," *Medical Record*, Dec. 2, 1936, pp.504-5.

22 Welfare Council of Toronto, "A Plan for the Reduction of Juvenile Delinquency in Toronto," 1943, Department of Reform Institutions, RG 20-16-2, Container J, Archives of Ontario (AO).

23 City of Toronto, *Annual Report of the Chief Constable*, 1938, p.38, City of Toronto Archives.

24 Jennifer Stephen, "The Incorrigible, the Bad, the Immoral: Toronto's Factory Girls and the Work of the Toronto Psychiatric Clinic," in *Law, Society and the State: Essays in Modern Legal History*, ed. Louis Knafla and Susan Binnie (Toronto: University of Toronto Press, 1995), pp.405-42.

25 Theresa Richardson, *The Century of the Child: The Mental Hygiene Movement and Social Policy in the U.S. and Canada* (Albany, N.Y.: SUNY Press, 1989), p.169.

26 *Report of the Toronto Juvenile Court*, Judge Mott, 1920, RG 47, Box 135, City of Toronto Archives.

27 Ontario, *Annual Report of Training Schools*, 1948, 1959, AO.

28 Carolyn Strange, "Stories of Their Lives: The Historian and the Capital Case File," in *On the Case: Explorations in Social History*, ed. Franca Iacovetta and Wendy Mitchinson (Toronto: University of Toronto Press, 1998), pp.25-48.

29 On the 1920s, see Cynthia Commachio, "Dancing to Perdition: Adolescence and Leisure in Interwar English Canada," *Journal of Canadian Studies* 32,3 (1977), pp.5-35; and on the 1950s, Adams, *The Trouble with Normal*, especially pp.60-62.

30 "College Girl to Call Girl," *The Globe and Mail*, April 29, 2000. A full-page spread, with a tantalizing photo, the article misrepresents the mainstream of the sex trade.

31 Karen Tice, *Tales of Wayward Girls and Immoral Women: Case Records and the Professionalization of Social Work* (Urbana: University of Illinois Press, 1998), pp.79, 54, 184.

32 *Annual Report of the Family Court*, 1930, City of Toronto Archives.

33 Ibid., 1920.

34 Ibid., 1928.

35 Ibid., 1936.

36 D. Owen Carrigan, *Crime and Punishment in Canada: A History* (Toronto: McClelland and Stewart, 1991), pp.235-36. Carrigan's alarmist words – "The flood of immigrants has brought with it some violence-prone youth from Latin America and from Vietnam" – are reminiscent of earlier ethnocentric panics.

37 Toronto Big Sisters Association (TBSA), *Annual Report*, 1934, private records, Hamilton Big Sisters Association (HBSA), Hamilton, Ont. I found the Toronto annual reports within the Hamilton collection.

38 City of Toronto, Department of Public Welfare (DPW), "Report on the Investigation of the Recreational Opportunities for Teen Age Girls," Series 100, City of Toronto Archives.

39 TBSA, *Annual Report*, 1931, private records, HBSA.

40 H. Crawford, Executive Director, typescript, c. late 1940s, HBSA.

41 Emily Murphy, *The Black Candle* (Toronto: Coles Reprints, 1973 [1922]). On the origins of narcotic legislation, see Elizabeth Comack, "We Will Get Some Good out of This Riot Yet: The Canadian State, Drug Legislation and Class Conflict," in *Social Basis of Law*, ed. Comack and Brickey. On differential policing, see Clayton Mosher, *Discrimination and Denial: Racism in Ontario's Legal and Criminal Justice Systems, 1892-1961* (Toronto: University of Toronto Press, 1998).

42 Helen Gregory McGill, "The Oriental Delinquent in the Vancouver Juvenile Court," 1936, Japanese Canadian Citizens Association Collection, MG 28 V8, vol. 17, file 14, National Archives of Canada (NAC).

43 Although most writing characterizes these "first wave" feminists as racist, some variation existed within this group.

44 TBSA, *Annual Report*, 1933, HBSA.

45 Joanna Brenner, *Women and the Politics of Class* (New York: Monthly Review Press, 2001), p.157.

46 Archambault, *Report of the Royal Commission*, p.195.

47 Judges offered harsher dispositions based on social class, single-parent home, unmarried parents, family instability, overcrowded home, delinquency area, and other factors. Gloria Geller, "The Streaming of Males and Females in the Juvenile Justice System," Ph.D. thesis, University of Toronto, 1981, p.63.

48 *Child and Family Welfare* 7,3 (1936), p.42.

49 Albert Cohen, *Delinquent Boys* (New York: Free Press, 1955); Doreen Elliot, *Gender, Delinquency and Society* (Aldershot, U.K.: Avebury, 1988), p.5. On the evolution of criminology, see Narine Naffine, *Female Crime: The Construction of the Female in Criminology* (Sydney: Allen and Unwin Australia, 1987); Carol Smart, *Women, Crime and Criminology* (London: Routledge and Kegan Paul, 1976); and Colin Sumner, *The Sociology of Deviance: An Obituary* (London: Continuum, 1994). The sense of public fascination with working-class male gangs was prevalent in Canada as well as in the United States. See, for example, the study of Toronto boy gangs in the 1940s: Kenneth Rogers, *Street Gangs in Toronto: A Study of the Forgotten Boy* (Toronto: Ryerson Press, 1945).

50 Meda Chesney-Lind, quoted in Anne Campbell, "On the Invisibility of the Female Delinquent Peer Group," *Women and Criminal Justice* 2,1 (1990), p.43.

51 Naffine, *Female Crime*; Anne Campbell, *Girl Delinquents* (Oxford: Basil Blackwell, 1981).

52 The one Scottish Borstal they visited was co-ed. Borstals were separate "cottage-like" institutions where young male offenders from eighteen to twenty-one (later twenty-three) were housed. Canadians often extolled the need for Borstals here. The commissioners visited seven such institutions: five in Britain and two in Europe. Archambault, *Report of the Royal Commission*, chap. 17.

53 Geller, "Streaming of Males and Females," p.165.

54 Big Brothers, "Employment, 1917-18," Department of Labour Records, 7-12-0-9, RG 7, AO.

55 *Child and Family Welfare*, March 24, 1946.

56 Ontario, *Annual Report of Training Schools*, 1950.

57 Ontario Training School for Girls (OTSG), case file 820, 1940s, RG 60, AO.

58 Superintendent Charleson, quoted in Ontario, *Annual Report of Training Schools*, 1942.

59 W.I. Thomas, *The Unadjusted Girl: With Cases and Standpoint for Behaviour Analysis* (Boston: Little Brown and Co., 1923), p.98.

60 Moreover, girls' files may have been more likely to stress a broken home (often equated with single motherhood), assuming this would produce "moral" problems. See Elliot, *Gender, Delinquency and Society*, p.45.

61 B. Johnson, "Sex Delinquency among Girls," *Journal of Social Hygiene*, November 1943, pp.449-501. As Judge Hosking noted, juvenile courts were supposed to dispense "social," not "legal" wisdom. *Child and Family Welfare* 8,3 (September 1932), p.25.

62 "News Notes: The Toronto Family Court," *Child and Family Welfare* 7,9 (January 1933), pp.51-52.

63 Augusta Jameson, "Psychological Factors Contributing to the Delinquency of Girls," *Journal of Juvenile Research* 283 (1937), pp.25-32.

64 A key Freudian text was Kate Friedlander, *The Psychoanalytical Approach to Juvenile Delinquency* (London: Kegan Paul, 1947). These theories were also popularized in a "grab bag" way in the popular press of the 1940s and 1950s. Carole Groneman, *Nymphomania: A History* (New York: W.W. Norton, 2000), p.77.

65 Peter Blos, "Three Typical Constellations in Female Delinquency," in *Family Dynamics and Female Sexual Delinquency*, ed. Otto Pollak and A. Friedman (Palo Alto, Cal.: Science and Behavior Books, 1969), p.100.

66 Herbert Herskovitz, "A Psychodynamic View of Sexual Promiscuity," and Peter Blos, "Three Typical Constellations in Female Delinquency," in *Family Dynamics and Female Sexual Delinquency*, ed. Pollak and Friedman, pp.93, 103; Ames Roby, "The Runaway Girl," in *Family Dynamics and Female Sexual Delinquency*, ed. Pollak and Friedman, p.127.

67 Gleason, *Normalizing the Ideal*.

68 The 1950s, argues Diana Russell, was characterized by intense denial of incest as reality, in part due to the influence within this decade of Kinsey and Freud. Diana Russell, *The Secret Trauma: Incest in the Lives of Girls and Women* (New York: Basic Books, 1986), p.5.

69 Sidney Halleck, *Psychiatry and the Dilemmas of Crime* (New York: Harper and Row, 1967), p.141. Friedlander, in *Psychoanalytical Approach to Juve-*

nile Delinquency, pp.174-75, also suggests that "girls give in easily" due to Oedipal desires.

70 Moreover, the girl might not "feel guilt, just remorse." See Lora Tessman and Irving Kaufman, "Variations on a Theme of Incest," in *Family Dynamics and Female Sexual Delinquency*, ed. Pollak and Friedman, p.141.

71 Hilary Allen, *Justice Unbalanced: Gender, Psychiatry and Judicial Decisions* (Philadelphia: Milton Keynes, 1987).

72 Geller, "Streaming of Males and Females," p.107.

73 Tadeusz Grygier, quoted in J. Carn, "Social Adjustment, Personality and Behaviour in Training Schools in Ontario: An Analysis," M.A. thesis, Waterloo Lutheran University, Waterloo, Ont., 1970.

74 On the emergence of such ideas in the United States, see Ruth Alexander, *The 'Girl Problem': Female Sexual Delinquency in New York, 1900-1930* (Ithaca, N.Y.: Cornell University Press, 1995), pp.63-64. Importantly, she notes that liberal ideas were not always applied to working-class girls.

75 Groneman, *Nymphomania*, p.75.

76 Halleck, *Psychiatry and the Dilemmas of Crime*, p.139.

77 This was similar to the dichotomized, racist characterization of unwed mothers in the 1940s and 1950s: white girls were "neurotic," while Black girls were the products of "social pathology." Regina G. Kunzel, "White Neurosis, Black Pathology: Constructing Out-of-Wedlock Pregnancy in the Wartime and Postwar United States," in *Not June Cleaver: Women and Gender in Post-War America, 1945-60*, ed. Joanne Meyerowitz (Philadelphia: Temple University Press, 1994), pp.304-31.

78 Rica Farquharson, "Let's Do Something Now!" *Canadian Home Journal* 40 (September 1943), p.50; *Financial Post* (under the misleading headline "How to Punish Juvenile Hoodlums") 45 (June 9, 1951), pp.11-12.

79 For example, Sidney Katz, "It's a Tough Time to Be a Kid," *Maclean's* 63 (Dec. 15, 1950), pp.7-9; Roderick Haig-Brown, "Problems of Modern Life and Young Offenders," *Saturday Night* 70 (May 28, 1955), pp.9-11; and Ruth Hobberlin, "Why Blame Comics, Movies for the Young's Delinquency?" *Saturday Night* 62 (Nov. 16, 1946), p.28.

80 Adele Saunders, "Is Home Life Breaking Up?" *Chatelaine*, June 1943, p.8. For the same views on latchkey kids and negligent moms, see Nora Lea (Canadian Welfare Council spokesperson), "Children in a World at War," speech, May 1943, Canadian Welfare Council (later, Canadian Council on Social Development) Papers, MG 28 I10, vol. 87, f.1856, NAC. For an analysis of bad mother ideology, see Molly Ladd-Taylor and Lauri Umansky, eds., *'Bad Mothers': The Politics of Blame in Twentieth Century America* (New York: New York University Press, 1998).

81 Such fears were shared by professionals sympathetic to criminalized women. The director of one Elizabeth Fry Society office outlined the violence and abuse that drove girls to the streets, but her list of parental problems included the negligent working mother who "believed financial security is more important than her daughter." Phyllis Haslam, "The Damaged Girl in a Distorted Society," March 1961, Dorothy Flaherty Papers, MG 31 K25, vol. 15, NAC.

82 Gerald Zoffer, "Underworld Evils Breed Juvenile Delinquency," *Saturday Night* 61 (Jan. 12, 1946), pp.6-7.

83 *Atlantic Advocate* 49 (August 1959), pp.59-63.

84 Katz, "It's a Tough Time to Be a Kid," p.44.

85 Jane Becker, "A Harvard Man's Life among Toronto's Young 'Have-nots,'" and David Lewis Stein, "The 'Have' Delinquents: Why Do They Go Wrong?" *Maclean's*, Jan. 25, 1964, p.23.

86 By culture, I am referring again to the "culture of poverty" theories. In a more recent dissection of this problem in the United States, Brenner, in *Women and the Politics of Class*, pp.135-36, attributes the emphasis on "culture" both to the class position of the professionals and the dominant ideologies concerning the causes of poverty.

87 Herskovitz, "Psychodynamic View of Sexual Promiscuity," p.89.

88 Geller, "Streaming of Males and Females."

89 OTSG Superintendent to Deputy Minister, letter, Nov. 6, 1952, RG 20-16-2, Container J21, file 56.8, AO.

90 Susan Lees, *Ruling Passions: Sexual Violence, Reputation and the Law* (Buckingham, U.K.: Open University Press, 1997), p.17.

91 A vast literature exists on this issue. One of the best-known U.S. scholars is Meda Chesney-Lind, "Judicial Enforcement of the Female Sex Role, the Family Court and Female Delinquency," *Issues in Criminology* 8 (1977), pp.51-70; and her "Sexist Juvenile Justice: A Continuing International Problem," *Resources for Feminist Research* 13 (1985), pp.7-9. See also Smart, *Women, Crime and Criminology*.

92 Kerry Carrington, *Offending Girls: Sex, Youth and Justice* (Sydney: Allen and Unwin Australia, 1993), pp.27, 107.

Three: "An Ounce of Prevention": Managing Girls' Misdemeanours

1 Executive Director H. Crawford, typescript of speech, late 1940s, historical file, Hamilton Big Sisters Association (HBSA).

2 Cynthia Commachio, *Nations Are Built of Babies: Saving Ontario's Mothers and Children, 1900-1940* (Montreal and Kingston: McGill-Queen's University Press, 1993), p.4.

3 Patricia Rooke and R.T. Schnell, *Discarding the Asylum: From Child Rescue to the Welfare State in English-Canada, 1800-1950* (Lanham, Md.: University Press of America, 1983); James Struthers, "Lord Give Us Men, Women and Social Work in English Canada, 1918-1953," in *The Benevolent State: The Growth of Welfare in Canada*, ed. Allan Moscovitch and Jim Albert (Toronto: University of Toronto Press, 1987), pp.126-43.

4 Katharine Arnup, *Educating for Motherhood: Advice for Mothers in Twentieth Century Canada* (Toronto: University of Toronto Press, 1994).

5 Theresa Richardson, *The Century of the Child: The Mental Hygiene Movement and Social Policy in the United States and Canada* (Albany, N.Y.: SUNY Press, 1989).

6 Zachary's book was used extensively by a social worker's study of girls in Toronto. See City of Toronto, Department of Public Works (DPW), "Report on the Investigation of the Recreational Opportunities for Teen Age Girls" (see chap. 2, n.38).

7 Lea, "Children in a World of War" (see chap. 2, n.80).

8 Folder 1942-45, annual and other reports, HBSA.

9 Because of more plentiful records I concentrate primarily on the Hamilton Big Sisters Association, but I also draw, when noted, on the Toronto Big Sisters.

10 Annual reports folder, 1919-29, HBSA.

11 Estelle B. Freedman, *Maternal Justice: Miriam Van Waters and the Female Reform Tradition* (Chicago: University of Chicago Press, 1996), p.xiii.

12 Molly Ladd-Taylor refers to these as "sentimental" and "progressive" maternalists, while Elizabeth Clapp's later definition of "traditional" and "pragmatic" maternalists is similar. Ladd-Taylor's U.S. study, though, sees a decisive break between feminism and maternalism after the 1920s and a "depoliticization of motherhood" in the wake of debates on the Equal Rights Amendment. Canadian reform traditions took a different course. Molly Ladd-Taylor, *Mother-Work: Women, Child Welfare and the State, 1890-1930* (Urbana: University of Illinois Press, 1994), p.75; Clapp, *Mothers of All Children*, p.4 (see chap. 2, n.3).

13 Historical folder, HBSA.

14 Kelly Hannah-Moffat, *Punishment in Disguise: Penal Governance and Federal Imprisonment of Women in Canada* (Toronto: University of Toronto Press, 2001), pp.33, 45.

15 Tamara Myers, "Maternal Rule: Female Probation Officers," from a forthcoming book on the Montreal Juvenile Court. My thanks to Tamara Myers for sharing her unpublished work with me. The fear that bad mothering was often a key to female delinquency had a long history. See also Lucia Zedner, *Women, Crime and Custody in Victorian England* (Oxford: Clarendon Press, 1991).

16 Binders (excerpts from annual reports), 1919-20, HBSA. By "amorphrodite" they most likely meant "hermaphrodite."

17 Minute books, Oct. 11, 1926, Sept. 8, 1930, HBSA.

18 Minute books, Nov. 14, 1921, HBSA.

19 Binders, 1920s, HBSA.

20 *Annual Report*, 1941, HBSA.

21 Executive Director Crawford, radio address, 1954, HBSA.

22 Annual report file, 1936, HBSA.

23 Scholarship book, 1928, Toronto Big Sisters Association (TBSA).

24 *Annual Report*, 1937, HBSA.

25 Executive Director's speech to the CAS, typescript, c. 1940s, HBSA.

26 Binders, 1950-60; newspaper clipping, *Hamilton Spectator*, Aug. 29, 1952, HBSA.

27 Folder on annual and other reports, 1930s; report of Executive Secretary, 1934, HBSA.

28 The 1930s quote is from *Annual Report*, 1934; World War II quote from *Annual Report*, 1941; also, annual report file, 1941-45, HBSA.

29 Report of Executive Secretary, 1934; folders on annual and other reports, 1940s; unnamed newspaper clipping, March 10, 1948, HBSA.

30 Binders, 1924, HBSA.

31 Speech of board member, c. 1959, HBSA.

32 Helen C. Robinson, *Decades of Caring: The Big Sister Story* (Toronto: Dundurn Press, 1979), p.31.

33 Minutes, Dec. 5, 1919, HBSA.

34 TBSA, *Annual Report*, 1941, HBSA.

35 For the executive director's response, see Robinson, *Decades of Caring*, p.80; on the matter of drinking, see minute books, clipping from 1947 Annual General Meeting, address of General Secretary Robertson, TBSA.

36 Robinson, *Decades of Caring*, p.81.

37 Dr. Williams, Regional Director, Big Brothers and Big Sisters, "The Problem Child," annual report file, 1919-29, HBSA.

38 Folders of annual and other reports, 1919-29 file; annual report, 1921-22, HBSA.

39 Crawford, typescript, c. 1940s, folder of historical material, HBSA.

40 Folder of annual report material, 1942-46, HBSA.

41 Folder of annual report material, 1946, HBSA.

42 On the YWCA, see Diana Pedersen, "Keeping Our Girls Good: The YWCA and the 'Girl Problem,' 1870-1930," *Canadian Woman Studies: les cahiers de la femme* 7,4 (Winter, 1986), pp.20-24; Wendy Mitchinson, "The YWCA and Reform in the 19th Century," *Histoire Sociale/Social History* 12,24 (1979), pp.368-84; Adams, *The Trouble with Normal*, p.75.

43 Annual report file, 1937, HBSA.

44 Augustine Brannigan, "Mystification of the Innocents: Crime Comics and Delinquency in Canada, 1931-49," *Criminal Justice History* 7 (1986), pp.111-44. Even Canadian Communists later joined in the denunciation of this manifestation of "American cultural imperialism" and the "idealization" of violent crime through such comics.

45 G. Zoffer, "Psychological Factors in Juvenile Crime," *Saturday Night* 61 (Jan. 26, 1946), p.18.

46 Report of Superintendent C.C. Golding, March 27, 1944, Special Board Reports, Box 256, Toronto Board of Education Archives.

47 CBC Citizens' Forum, "Prisons or Playgrounds," recording no. 99076 (1949), NAC.

48 CBC Citizens' Forum, "Meet the Gang," recording no. 29095 (1940s), NAC.

49 "Your Town," draft, Canadian Council on Social Development (CCSD) Papers, MG 28, vol. 88, 1856b, NAC.

50 William Turnbull to Commissioner of Public Welfare, letter, March 30, 1949, Series 100, 467004-4, DPW, file 1351, City of Toronto Archives.

51 "Your Town."

52 "Report of the Mayor's Conference re Juvenile Delinquency and Associated Problems," February 1950, Series 100, file 1355, City of Toronto Archives. Persuading citizens to pressure their neighbours to attend church, or making a general call to attend to youths' spiritual needs, was less easily accomplished, in no small part because church leaders faced declining interest from working-class youth and their families.

53 City of Toronto, DPW, "Report of the Investigation of the Recreational Opportunities for Teen Age Girls," p.11.

54 Ibid.

55 Charles Hendry (School of Social Work, University of Toronto), June 4, 1964, Series 100, DPW, file 1353, City of Toronto Archives.

56 Schneider, *Vampires, Dragons and Egyptian Kings* (see chap. 1, n.24), points out that such programs provided a temporary cure only.

57 Adams, *The Trouble with Normal*, p.53.
58 National Film Board (NFB), *Police Club for Boys*, 1954, NFB Archives (Robocinematique), Montreal.
59 *Youth and the Law*, video no. 7505-0548, 1961, Audio Visual Collection, NAC. The film, though made in the United States, was used for educational purposes in Canada.
60 *Comes a Time*, video no. 9103-0451, 1961, NAC. Although listed as 1961, I am convinced that this film is a later production given the fashions shown within it – perhaps 1971?
61 NFB, *Who Is Sylvia?*, 1957. Even the scenery of this film – shot almost entirely in a school and in the domestic confines of the subject's home – stands in contrast to films about boys, which take place far more in public spaces.
62 NFB, *Borderline*, 1956. As Adams points out in *The Trouble with Normal*, these films had a double educational value, because they were directed not only at teens but also at parents who needed to be educated as well.
63 Peggy Pascoe, *Relations of Rescue: The Search for Female Moral Authority in the American West, 1874-1939* (New York: Oxford University Press, 1990). Pascoe uses the term "female moral authority" primarily to describe nineteenth-century women reformers' attempts to "rescue" Chinese, Indian, and Mormon women, but it does have resonance with some twentieth-century efforts.
64 By the 1950s Big Sisters were more likely to be commenting on the need to make significant changes to the youth justice system. They were also advocating minor changes. For example, along with groups like the Toronto Women's Law Association, they urged a higher age limit for the JDA, believing that this change would aid seventeen- to eighteen-year-old girls who were being sent to inappropriate adult facilities.
65 Pat Carlen, "Out of Care, Into Custody: Dimensions and Deconstructions of the State's Regulation of Twenty-two Young Working-class Women," in *Gender, Crime and Justice*, ed. Pat Carlen and Anne Worrall (Philadelphia: Open University Press, 1987), pp.126-60.

Four: Judging Girls in Court

1 Anonymous (Anon.) file, 1940s, York County Family Court Records (YFC Records), Box 1602, Archives of Ontario (AO).
2 Tamara Myers, "Criminal Women and Bad Girls: Regulation and Punishment in Montreal, 1890-1930." Ph.D. thesis, McGill University, Montreal, 1996.
3 Ibid., p.155.
4 Initially passed in 1918, this statute was the product of fears during World War I that (lower-class) women and men on the home front were abandoning marital decency for immoral liaisons, thus also endangering child morality. The statute was often seen as a companion statute to the JDA, with legal decisions about 220a impacting on the JDA. Attempts were made to tighten it up in the 1930s after appeals indicated that judges would not find parents immoral simply because they were living common law.

5 Bruno Theorêt, "Régulation juridque pénale des mineures et discrimination à l'égard des filles: la clause de 1924 amendment La Loi sur les jeunes delinquents," *Canadian Journal of Women and the Law/Revue Femmes et Droit* 4 (1990-91), pp.539-55. On the lack of controversy, see W. Scott to Deputy Minister, Feb. 20, 1924, Department of Justice, RG 13, vol. 2180, file 361/1924, NAC.

6 Helen Gregory McGill, *The Juvenile Court in Canada* (Ottawa: Canadian Council on Child Welfare, 1925), p.34; and Elsie McGill, *My Mother the Judge* (Toronto: The Ryerson Press, 1955), pp.166-68. Later some provinces began to pay for court necessities such as probation officers.

7 Canadian Welfare Council, *Report of the Committee on the Revision of the Juvenile Delinquent Act* (Ottawa, 1956), p.4.

8 Interviews at Edmonton Home for Girls, March 1962, Committee on Juvenile Delinquency Records, vol. 1, RG 36/33, NAC.

9 Helen Kinnear was first appointed to the County Court of Haldimand in 1943 and later, in 1947, was also made a juvenile court judge.

10 Amanda Glasbeek, "Maternalism Meets the Criminal Law: The Case of the Toronto Women's Court," *Canadian Journal of Women and the Law* 10,2 (1998), p.480. The Women's Court was established in 1913 as a maternal feminist reform project; it offered women separate hearings, shielded from public scrutiny and overseen by a female judge.

11 City of Toronto, *Annual Report of the Juvenile and Family Court*, 1920, City of Toronto Archives.

12 Canadian Welfare Council, *Juvenile Courts in Canada* (Ottawa, 1942), p.18.

13 Bernard Green, "The Determination of Delinquency in the Juvenile Court of Metro Toronto," S.J.D. thesis, University of Toronto, 1968.

14 Bernard Green, "Trumpets, Justice and Federalism: An Analysis of the Ontario Training Schools Act of 1965," *Canadian Journal of Corrections* 8,3 (1966), p.254.

15 Ontario Training School for Girls (OTSG), file 480, 1940s, AO.

16 OTSG, file 1651, 1950s, AO. The judge also asked, "Why are you so angry with the world?" Her anger, of course, may have directly resulted from her experiences of incest.

17 YFC Records, Box 1519, 1950s, AO.

18 City of Toronto Archives, *Annual Report of the Juvenile and Family Court*, 1920, 1935, 1950. Charges do vary over time: for instance, in 1940, 68 per cent of the girls were charged with truancy; in 1950 it was less than 1 per cent.

19 Dorothy Chunn, "Boys Will Be Boys: Girls Will Be Mothers: The Legal Regulation of Childhood in Toronto and Vancouver," *Sociological Studies in Child Development* 3 (1990), p.99.

20 For example, Ontario statistics on the occupation of fathers of juveniles before the court showed a very high percentage of "labourers," those in "manufacturing and mechanical," as well as "not given," which could be those who were underemployed or unemployed. Also, the statistics on the native-born and "foreign"-born are revealing. In the years when reformers were using narratives of immigrant children (as described in chap. 2), from 1937 to 1945 the majority of delinquents were clearly native-born, with the majority of their parents also native-born. Only a small percentage of immi-

grant parents came from non-Anglo "foreign" countries, precisely the kind of immigrants who were sometimes used as "examples" of children needing saving. See Canada, Dominion Bureau of Statistics, *Annual Report on Juvenile Delinquents*, 1945.

21 An amendment of 1921 permitted the juvenile court to postpone or adjourn the hearing for an advisable period, or *sine die*; in other words, this could be an indefinite adjournment prior to finding the child delinquent. How this ruling was recorded seemed to vary in different courts.

22 "Juvenile Courts – Ontario," 1938-41, Canadian Council on Social Development Papers (CCSD), MG 28 I 10, vol. 85, NAC.

23 Anon. file, 1940s, YFC Records, RG 22, Box 1600, AO. The court worker noted critically that the mother "wears slacks all the time."

24 OTSG, case file 769, 1940s, RG 60, AO.

25 Girls in the Vancouver juvenile court frequently appeared on morals charges; from 1915-35, 85 per cent of girls sent to the Industrial Home went there for incorrigibility and morals offences. Alison Hatch and Curt Griffiths, "Child Saving Postponed: The Impact of the Juvenile Delinquents Act on the Processing of Young Offenders in Vancouver," in *Dimensions of Childhood: Essays on the History of Children and Youth in Canada*, ed. Russell Smandych, G. Doods, and A. Esau (Winnipeg: Legal Research Institute, 1991), pp.205-32. For further discussion of this concern with sexuality, see Indiana Matters, "Sinners or Sinned Against? Historical Aspects of Female Delinquency in British Columbia," in *Not Just Pin Money: Selected Essays on the History of Women's Work in British Columbia*, ed. Barbara Latham and Roberta Pazdro (Victoria: Camosun College, 1984), pp.265-78; Tamara Myers, "Qui t'a debauchée? Female Adolescent Sexuality and the Juvenile Delinquents' Court in Early Twentieth-Century Montreal," in *Family Matters: Papers in Post-Confederation Canadian Family History*, ed. Lori Chambers and Edgar-André Montigny (Toronto: Canadian Scholars' Press, 1998), pp.377-94; Mary Odem, *Delinquent Daughters: Protecting and Policing Adolescent Female Sexuality in the United States, 1885-1920* (Chapel Hill: University of North Carolina Press, 1995); and Alexander, *'Girl Problem'*.

26 Anon. file, 1940s, YFC Records, RG 22, Box 1607, AO.

27 Anon. file, YFC Records, Box 1602, AO.

28 OTSG, file 1455, 1950s, AO.

29 Anon. file, 1940s, YFC Records, Box 1607, AO.

30 OTSG, file 2230, 1950s, AO.

31 Anon. file, YFC Records, Box 1598, AO.

32 OTSG, file 853, 1940s, AO.

33 YFC Records, Box 1512, 1950s, AO.

34 OTSG, file 850, 1940s, AO.

35 YFC Records, Box 1598 and 1600, 1940s, AO.

36 OTSG, file 155, 1930s, AO.

37 OTSG, file 173, 1930s, AO.

38 OTSG, file 755, 1940s; see also file 450, AO.

39 OTSG, file 2300, 1950s, AO.

40 OTSG, file 2212, 1950s, AO.

41 Galt Inmates, 1952-53, Department of Reform Institutions Records, RG 22, 16-2, Container J-21, file 56.8, AO.

42 Reitsma-Street, "Justice for Canadian Girls," p.346 (see chap. 1, n.8).

43 OTSG, file 280, 1930s, AO.

44 OTSG, file G925, 1940s, AO.

45 Ward file 220, 1930s, RG 60, AO.

46 OTSG, file 285, 1930s, AO.

47 OTSG, file 2326, 1950s, file 290, 1930s, AO.

48 For more detailed discussions of how sexual abuse was viewed, see Joan Sangster, "Masking and Unmasking the Sexual Abuse of Children: Perceptions of Violence against Children in the 'Badlands' of Ontario, 1916-1930," *Journal of Family History* 25,4 (2000), pp.504-26; Anne-Marie Cliche, "Un Secret Bien Gardé: L'Inceste dans la Société Traditionnelle Québécoise, 1858-1938," *Revue d'Historie de l'Amérique Française* 50,2 (1996), pp.201-26; Linda Gordon, *Heroes of Their Own Lives: The Politics and History of Family Violence* (Boston: Viking, 1988), chap. 7; Elizabeth Pleck, *Domestic Tyranny: The Making of American Social Policy against Family Violence from Colonial Times to the Present* (New York: Oxford University Press, 1987), pp.95-97, 156-57; and Diana Russell, *The Secret Trauma: Incest in the Lives of Girls and Women* (New York: Basic Books, 1999).

49 Anon. File, YFC Records, Box 1516, AO. Yvette said she was returning home; the records give no indication as to if she did, and if so how long she stayed there.

50 OTSG, file 1565, 1950s, AO; and June Callwood, "The Most Heartbreaking Job in Canada," *Maclean's* 66 (December 1953), pp.12-13, 90-92.

51 OTSG, file 275, 1930s, AO.

52 OTSG, file 835, 1940s, AO.

53 Anon. file, YFC Records, Box 1518, AO.

54 City of Toronto Archives, *Annual Report of the Chief of Police*, 1930 (robbery) and 1925 (babynapping).

55 OTGS, file 193, 1930s, AO.

56 OTSG, file 2011, 1950s, AO.

57 OTSG, file 785, 1940s, AO.

58 OTGS Superintendent to Deputy Minister, letter, Nov. 6, 1952, RG 20, Series 16-2, Container J21, AO.

59 The inspiration was Clifford Shaw and Henry McKay, *Juvenile Delinquency and Urban Areas* (Chicago: University of Chicago Press, 1942). For a Canadian study, see Barbara Nease, "Measuring Juvenile Delinquency in Hamilton," *Canadian Journal of Corrections* 8 (1966), pp.133-45.

60 Nease, "Measuring Juvenile Delinquency in Hamilton." My conclusions here differ from those of Nease, who maintained that the "bad neighbourhood" issue was less likely to influence the police vis-à-vis girls.

61 Green, "Determination of Delinquency," p.46.

62 NAC, "Youth and the Law" (see chap. 3, n.59).

63 OTSG, file G6, 1930s, AO. Some children were sent out to beg on the streets, though that was less common after the 1930s.

64 Gerald Markowitz and David Rosner, *Children, Race, and Power: Kenneth and Mamie Clark's Northside Center* (Charlottesville: University Press of Virginia, 1996), p.84. For a similar pronouncement see Tadeusz Grygier, "Social Adjustment, Personality and Behaviour in Ontario's Training

Schools," 1966, p.52, RG 20-148, Container 11, AO: "Psychotherapy was not favoured for subjects of low economic status."

65 OTSG, file 420, 1940s, AO.

66 OTSG, file 2080, 1950s, AO.

67 In the 1950s more girls were sent out to work as mother's helpers rather than as maids. The training school often selected the girls seen as less capable at other jobs, which is an interesting comment on how child care was perceived in a period supposedly idealizing motherhood.

68 OTSG, file 830, 1940s, AO.

69 OTSG, file 470, 1940s, AO. She said her varicose-veined leg was the result of his abuse.

70 OTSG, file 700, 1940s, AO.

71 OTSG, file 1480, 1940s, AO.

72 Anon. file, 1950s, YFC Records, Box 1514, AO.

73 OTSG, file 150, 1930s, AO.

74 OTSG, file 1555, 1940s, AO.

75 OTSG, file 330, 1940s, AO. The mother said they were married, although the PO did not believe her.

76 Anon. file, 1940s, YFC Records, Box 1594, AO.

77 Anon. file, 1940s, YFC Records, Box 1524, AO.

78 "Juvenile Courts," file, judgment of case, Jan. 26, 1938, CCSD, vol. 86, NAC.

79 OTSG, file 71, 1930s; and anon. file, 1940s, YFC Records, Box 1513, AO.

80 OTSG, file 60, 1930s, AO.

81 OTSG, file G87, 1930s, AO.

82 OTSG, file 2000, file 1610, 1950s, AO.

83 OTSG, file 1455, 1950s, AO.

84 OTSG, file 1495, 1950s, AO.

85 Chunn, "Boys Will Be Men," p.105.

86 Chunn, *From Punishment to Doing Good*, p.182 (see chap. 2, n.7).

Five: Treating the Intractable: Training Schools for Girls

1 Foucault, *Discipline and Punish*, pp.170-94 (see chap. 2, n.17).

2 Hannah-Moffat, *Punishment in Disguise*, pp.23,91 (see chap. 3, n.14).

3 Ontario, Statutes of Ontario, *An Act Respecting Industrial Schools*, 1874, c.29, s.4.

4 Industrial Schools Association of Toronto (ISAT), "History of the ISA," ISAT Records, MU 1412, Series D, Archives of Ontario (AO). See also Paul Bennett, "Taming the Bad Boys of the Dangerous Classes: Child Rescue and Restraint at the Victoria Industrial School, 1887-1935," *Histoire Sociale/ Social History* 21 (1988), pp.71-96.

5 The girls were to be "lifted out of the low sphere in which they lived, changing culture, speech, modesty, dress, manners, deportment cleanliness and feminine virtues in general." ISAT, "History of the ISA."

6 Susan Houston, "Victorian Origins of Juvenile Delinquency: A Canadian Experience," *History of Education Quarterly* 12 (Fall 1971), pp.254-80.

7 Strange, *Toronto's Girl Problem*, pp.133-39 (see chap. 1, n.18).

8 Strange, *Toronto's Girl Problem*; Iliana Arapis, "'Sugar and Spice and

Everything Nice': The Idealization of Girlhood at the Alexandra Industrial School for Girls, 1891-1936," M.A. thesis, Queen's University, Kingston, 1994, p.51. On the B.C. case, see Matters, "Sinners or Sinned Against?" (see chap. 4, n.25).

9 The phrase "taming rebel souls" appears in ISAT, *Annual Report*, 1917, AO.

10 Arapis, "Sugar and Spice," p.35. The quotes "preferred to loaf and gossip" and "honour citizens" are from ISAT, *Annual Report*, 1917, 1933, AO. Girls might sew as many as 10,000 dresses, 20,000 towels, and 7,000 pillow cases, among other things, for the government (ISAT, *Annual Report*, 1915).

11 ISAT, *Annual Report*, p.16, AO. The picture, which appeared in the reports in 1915, 1918, and again in 1929, was obviously a popular symbol of success for the Alexandra.

12 Letter to Ministry, Feb. 9, 1934, ISAT Records, MU 1412, Series B, correspondence, p.1408, AO.

13 Ontario, *Statutes of Ontario*, 1931, c.60 s.3(1).

14 See Mary McDonald, "Opening the 'Door of Opportunity': Claims-Making and the Establishment of the First Ontario Training School for Girls," paper presented to the Canadian Historical Association, 1998.

15 OTSG, file G6, 1930s (originally an Alexandra committal), and OTSG, file 197, 1930s, AO. The girl was assured that OTSG was not a "bad" industrial school, but a new, fine training school for girls who "lacked advantages." Later judges were clearer about the correctional nature of the school.

16 "Past slowly erased" is a common term used in both the ISAT and OTSG files. See, for instance, ISAT, *Annual Report*, 1927, AO.

17 Unnamed clipping, Sept. 6, 1933, Grandview clipping file (GCF), A 988.1007.198, Cambridge City Archives (CCA).

18 Barbara Brenzel, *Daughters of the State: A Social Portrait of the First Reform School for Girls in North America* (Cambridge, Mass.: MIT Press, 1983), p.66.

19 Tamara Myers and Joan Sangster, "Retorts, Runaways and Riots: Patterns of Resistance in Canadian Reform Schools for Girls, 1930-60," *Journal of Social History*, 2001, pp.669-97.

20 John Foote, "History of School," 1951, GCF, CCA.

21 John Okeefe, "Last Chance School for Girls," *Canadian Weekly*, 1967, GCF, CCA.

22 The official age of release was twenty-one until 1949, when it was lowered to eighteen. A young woman might escape the system before age twenty-one if she was married or a model parolee.

23 OTSG, file 320, 1930s, AO.

24 OTSG, file 250, 1930s, AO.

25 OTSG, file 165, 1930s, AO. "Ill-used" sometimes meant sexual abuse.

26 OTSG, file 915, 1940s, file 245, file 131, 1930s, AO.

27 The whole story could be reinterpreted. Girls, for example, didn't count their calories; they were put on diets. Ontario, *Annual Report of Training Schools*, 1940.

28 Galt file, 1956, Department of Reform Institutions Records, RG 20-16, Container 43, AO.

29 Callwood, "Most Heartbreaking Job in Canada," p.91 (see chap. 4, n.50).

30 OTSG, file 250, 1930s, AO.

31 OTSG, file 60, 1930s, AO. C.J. Neelands was in charge of the Public Institutions Branch (including training schools) before the Department of Reform Institutions was established in 1946.

32 Galt file, 1954, RG 20-16, Container J32, AO.

33 OTSG Superintendent to Deputy Minister, Nov. 18, 1953, Galt file, RG 20-16, Container J15, AO.

34 Galt file, 1953-54, RG 20-16, Container J15, AO.

35 OTSG, file G54, AO. The medical examiner, stating that she thought her fantasy characters were in the room with her, saw this as a sign of unbalance, but is this condition so entirely unusual for younger children who are lonely and imaginative?

36 Ontario, _Annual Report of Training Schools_, 1946.

37 Galt file, 1951-52, RG 20, Container J9, AO. The superintendent discouraged a fundamentalist preacher with an "emotional" brand of religion. Entries in the girls' files applaud regular churchgoing, but social workers were wary of dogmatic fundamentalist parents.

38 OTSG, file 820, 1940s, AO. The main reason for committal was disobedience and conflict within her mother's and father's homes.

39 OTSG, file 1079, 1940s, AO.

40 Galt file, 1951-52, RG 20-16, Container J15, AO.

41 Clipping, Oct. 20, 1955, Galt file, RG 20-6, Container J37, AO.

42 Ontario, _Annual Report of Training Schools_, 1952.

43 Ontario, _Annual Report of Training Schools_, 1947.

44 Galt file, 1957, RG 20-16, Container J47, AO.

45 OTSG, file 2328, 1950s, AO.

46 Excerpt from _If I Were Young Again_, GCF, CCA.

47 One example of the strict rules: a girl received another twenty-four hours in detention just for talking to another girl held in a nearby detention room. OTSG, file 171, 1930s, AO.

48 Unnamed clipping, Nov. 7, 1944, Juvenile Delinquency file, RG 20-16, Container J1, AO.

49 Clippings, Committee on Reform Institutions file, RG 20-16, Container J36, AO.

50 Isobel MacNeil to Deputy Minister, Nov. 18, 1953, Galt file, 1953-54, RG 20-16, Container J15, AO.

51 OTSG, file 235, 1930s, AO.

52 OTSG, file 340, 1940s, AO.

53 OTSG, file 801, 1940s, AO.

54 OTSG, file 604, 1940s, file T5, 1950s, AO. The second letter came from one of the girls sent to the OTSG wing in the Mercer Reformatory.

55 MacNeil to Deputy Minister, Nov. 18, 1953, Galt file, 1953-54, RG 20-16, Container J15, AO.

56 OTSG, file 1651, 1950s, AO. Superintendents were always begging for more medical and psychiatric services.

57 OTSG, file 1560, 1950s, AO.

58 OTSG, file 1470, 1950s, AO.

59 Ruth Bentley to Department of Reform Institutions, Galt file, 1958, RG 20-16, Container J54, AO. This action is supported by the case files.

60 Callwood, "Most Heartbreaking Job in Canada," pp.12-13, 90-92; and Galt file, 1958-59, RG 20-16, Container J54, AO.

61 OTSG, file 2261, 1950s, AO.

62 OTSG, file 775, 1940s, AO. This situation was complicated, because it appears that a Toronto Judge first told the woman about the case (so much for confidentiality), and then that woman became involved as an advocate, reminding the provincial secretary that she had met his "charming wife" socially.

63 OTSG, file 775, 1940s, AO.

64 OTSG, file 85, 1930s, AO.

65 See James Scott, *Weapons of the Weak: Everyday Forms of Peasant Resistance* (New Haven, Conn.: Yale University Press, 1985), p.xvi.

66 OTSG, file 2034, 1950s, AO. The psychiatrist believed the girl's claims that she did not have intercourse with her eighteen-year-old boyfriend. Even when doctors disagreed with parts of the committal, they did not push for release.

67 T.M. Foster, "Make-Believe Families: A Response of Women and Girls to the Deprivation of Imprisonment," *International Journal of Criminology and Penology* 3 (1975), pp.71-78. For a discussion of girls' culture in training school in the 1960s, see Gisela Konopka, *The Adolescent Girl in Conflict* (Englewood Cliffs, N.J.: Prentice-Hall, 1966). Although Konopka is disapproving of homosexuality, she has useful insights on other aspects of girls' lives.

68 OTSG, file 1685, file 2020, 1950s, AO. A study on Galt noted, "Girls who go awl score well on psychology tests for initiative, leadership and self reliance." See Grygier, "Social Adjustment, Personality and Behaviour in Ontario Training Schools," p.41 (see chap. 4, n.64).

69 Mercer Reformatory file 7733, RG 20, D13, AO.

70 OTSG, file 1572, 1950s, AO.

71 Superintendent to Deputy Minister, July 4, 1956, Galt file, 1956, RG 20-16, Container J43, AO.

72 Estelle Freedman, "The Prison Lesbian: Race, Class and the Construction of the Aggressive Female Homosexual, 1915-65," *Feminist Studies* 22,2 (1996), pp.397-424; Robin Brownlie, "Crimes of Passion: Lesbians and Lesbianism in Canadian Prisons, 1960-94," paper presented to the Canadian Historical Association, 1998.

73 OTSG, file 97, file 197, 1930s, AO.

74 OTSG, file 1010, 1940s; and Superintendent to Deputy Minister, Nov. 9, 1953, Galt file, RG 20-16, Container J15, AO.

75 OTSG, file 95, 1930s, AO.

76 OTSG, file 989, 1940s, AO.

77 Minutes of Committee on Juvenile Delinquency, Oct. 26, 1962, RG 36/33, NAC.

78 Ontario, *Annual Report of Training Schools*, shows that awls were reduced to 1 per cent in the 1950s and were 0 per cent at St. Mary's Training School for Girls. Having read the files for the 1950s, I find the figure of 1 per cent hard to believe, as I do the idea that absolutely no one ever ran away from the Catholic training school.

79 Galt file, 1958, RG 20-16, Container J47, AO. The famous Gluecks, for

instance, continued to be influential in 1950s criminology; in one research project they noted that some qualities of male delinquency, such as "resisting authority, periods of aggression," were part of "normal" development. June Callwood, "Will Your Teenager Turn to Crime?" _Maclean's_ 67 (Sept. 15, 1954), pp.101-2.

80 Galt file, 1957-58, RG 20-16, Container J47, AO. The superintendent wanted no books to be available. They even quibbled over the provision of a half sandwich (Bentley) or a whole one (the ministry) at night.

81 In 1948 the province had set up a separate section of the Mercer Reformatory, with its own register, as a "Training School" for difficult inmates. Girls could be transferred under sections 26 and 27 of the federal Prisons and Reformatories Act, though it was often difficult to do so if they had been convicted under section 7 of the TSA, because they had not been convicted of a crime. Once they were seventeen or eighteen, teenagers could be put in the Mercer to begin with, as Ontario – unlike some other provinces – designated juveniles as those sixteen and under.

82 Elizabeth Fry astutely tried to enlist Women's Institutes and other groups in protest. Its officials noted there was "no time for communal games or worship" and that the physical design was "punitive." But the minister got support from other community groups that were persuaded the girls were "sadistic trouble makers who broke windows and cut themselves and others with glass and some had VD." Galt file, 1957, RG 20-16, Container J47, AO.

83 Ontario, _Hansard: Debates of the Legislative Assembly of Ontario_, March 2, 1965.

84 OTSG, file 8480, 1940s, AO. Corporal punishment had supposedly been abolished when Isobel MacNeil took over in 1949.

85 Lydia Jackson, "A Study of Sado-Masochistic Attitudes in a Group of Delinquent Girls by Means of a Specially Designed Projection Test," _British Journal of Medical Psychology_ 22 (1949), p.53.

86 Phyllis Haslam, quoted in J.A. Edmison, "The Problem of the Female Criminal," _Saturday Night_ 75 (June 1960), pp.25-26.

87 A study done in the 1970s found that 86 per cent of the girls had carved at least once. Robert Robertson Ross and Hugh Bryan McKay, _Self-Mutilation_ (Lexington, Mass.: Lexington Books, 1979), p.3. Ross was among those later charged with sexual abuse by some OTSG girls (see n.113).

88 Ross and McKay, _Self-Mutilation_, pp.114, 134.

89 Jiwani, "Erasing Race," p.180 (see chap. 1, n.6).

90 Callwood, "Most Heartbreaking Job in Canada," p.66: "Troublemakers in the school make the best adjustment to normal living."

91 Sibylle Artz, _Sex, Power and the Violent Schoolgirl_ (Toronto: Trifolium Books, 1998), p.183.

92 OTSG, file T3, 1950s, AO.

93 OTSG, file T75, 1950s, AO.

94 OTSG, file G820, 1940s, AO. Some of the older girls supposedly used violence to gain a transfer to the Mercer.

95 Pearson, _When She Was Bad_ (see chap. 1, n.5).

96 OTSG, file 830, 1940s, AO.

97 OTSG, file 2289, 1950s, AO. She somehow feels she is "worthless," lamented the female psychologist.

98 OTSG, file 345, 1940s, AO.

99 OTSG, file 785, 1940s, AO.

100 OTSG, file 2295, 1950s, file 982, 1940s, AO.

101 OTSG, file 1088, 1940s, AO.

102 OTSG, file G11, file 71, 1930s, AO.

103 Ontario, *Annual Reports of the Minister of Public Welfare, Annual Reports of Training Schools*, AO: I analysed these from 1933 to 1964, looking at returns from placement as a percentage of the total placements for the year. Girls were usually more likely to be returned, though in the years 1945-49 this was not the case (with numbers so high for Bowmanville in 1947 – 97 per cent – that it looked like a major prison break had occurred), and in 1949-51 the numbers evened out for boys and girls. In some years (1940, 1944, 1954, 1962) girls' rate of return stood at about 50 per cent.

104 OTSG, file 2095, 1950s, AO.

105 OTSG, file 830, 1940s, AO.

106 OTSG, file G150, 1930s, AO.

107 Isobel MacNeil memo to Deputy Minister, Dec. 14, 1952, Galt file, RG 20-16, Container J21; Ruth Bentley speech, clipping, Jan. 1, 1959, Galt file, Container J53; and OTSG, file 230, 1930s, AO.

108 Memo of Ruth Bentley to Ministry, Feb. 20, 1956, RG 20-16, Container J37, AO.

109 Ontario, *Hansard*, A. Grossman, March 2, 1965, pp.869, 871.

110 Green, "Trumpets, Justice and Federalism," p.249 (see chap. 4, n.14). See also the reply by Tadeusz Grygier, "A Minor Note on the Trumpet," *Canadian Journal of Corrections* 8,3 (1966).

111 Ontario, *Hansard*, S. Lewis, March 2, 1965, pp.878-79.

112 The same psychologists (see chap. 5, n.87) later claimed that it was their intervention that resulted in improvements because they persuaded the authorities to allow clothes, makeup, room decorating, and other minor improvements.

113 One psychologist, Robert Robertson Ross, was later charged with sexual abuse but acquitted after his first trial, and a second trial did not take place. For this discussion I do not rely on institutional documents because I was not given access to OTSG records after 1960. Many survivors feel that some perpetrators of abuse were never punished; their views have been dramatically rendered in a play, *The Girls of Grandview*, performed by Toronto's Friendly Spike Theater Band.

114 Ontario, *Debates*, A. Grossman, March 2, 1965, p.871; S. Lewis, p.880.

Six: Race, Gender, and Delinquency: The Criminalization of First Nations Girls

1 On the United States, see Mike Davis, *City of Quartz* (New York: Vintage Books, 1992), chap. 5. On Canada, see Schissel, *Blaming Children*, pp.58-65 (see chap. 1, n.2). For overviews of Aboriginal youth and crime, see Linda Fisher and Hannele Janetti, "Aboriginal Youth in the Criminal Justice System," in *Issues and Perspectives on Young Offenders in Canada*, ed. John Winterdyk (Toronto: Harcourt Brace, 1996), pp.237-56; Carol LaPrairie,

"Native Juveniles in Court: Some Preliminary Observations," in *Deviant Designations: Crime, Law and Deviance in Canada*, ed. Thomas Fleming and Livy Visano (Toronto: Butterworths, 1983), pp.337-50; and Bernard Schissel, "Cultural Perception and Mainstream Law," in *Juvenile Crime and Delinquency: A Turn of the Century Reader*, ed. Ruth Mann (Toronto: Canadian Scholars' Press, 2000), pp.321-34.

2 Carrigan, *Juvenile Delinquency in Canada*, p.195 (see chap. 1, n.1).

3 Michael Young, "The History of Vancouver Youth Gangs, 1900-85," M.A. thesis, Department of Criminology, Simon Fraser University, Burnaby, B.C., 1993; Rogers, *Street Gangs in Toronto* (see chap. 2, n.49); Marcus Klee, "Between the Scylla and the Charybdis of Anarchy and Despotism: The State, Capital and the Working Class in Great Depression Toronto, 1929-40," Ph.D. thesis, Queen's University, Kingston, 1998.

4 Enakshi Dua, "Canadian Anti-Racist Feminist Thought: Scratching the Surface of Racism," in *Scratching the Surface: Canadian Anti-Racist Feminist Thought*, ed. E. Dua and A. Robertson (Toronto: Women's Press, 1999), p.19.

5 Vic Satzewich and Li Zong, "Social Control and the Historical Construction of 'Race,'" in *Social Control in Canada: A Reader on the Social Construction of Deviance*, ed. Bernard Schissel and Linda Mahood (Toronto: Oxford University Press, 1996), p.264.

6 The literature on this is vast, encompassing labour, immigration, and criminal justice history, to name some areas. See, for example, Walter Tarnopolsky, *Discrimination and the Law in Canada* (Toronto: Richard De Boo, 1982); James W. St. G. Walker, *"Race," Rights and the Law in the Supreme Court of Canada* (Waterloo: Wilfrid Laurier University Press, 1998), pp.12-50; Constance Backhouse, *Colour Coded: A Legal History of Racism in Canada, 1900-1950* (Toronto: University of Toronto Press, 1999). For a more general discussion of race and feminist theory, see Adrien K. Wing, ed., *Critical Race Feminism: A Reader* (New York: New York University, 1997); and Marlee Kline, "Race, Racism and Feminist Legal Theory," *Harvard Women's Law Journal* 12 (1989), pp.115-50.

7 Sherene H. Razack, *Looking White People in the Eye: Gender, Race and Culture in Courtrooms and Classrooms* (Toronto: University of Toronto Press, 1998), pp.8-10.

8 Floya Anthias and Nira Yuval-Davis, eds., *Racialized Boundaries: Race, Nation, Gender, Colour and Class and the Anti-Racist Struggle* (London: Routledge, 1992); Anne Stoler, "Making Empire Respectable: The Politics of Race and Sexual Morality in 20th-Century Colonial Cultures," *American Ethnologist* 16,4 (1989), pp.634-59.

9 See, for example, Patricia Hill Collins, "It's All in the Family: Intersections of Gender, Race and Nation," *Hypatia* 13,3 (Summer 1998), pp.62-81; Kimberlé Crenshaw, "Mapping the Margins: Intersectionality, Identity, Politics and Violence against Women of Colour," *Stanford Law Review* 43 (July 1991), pp.1241-99; and her "Demarginalizing the Intersection of Race and Class," *Chicago Legal Forum*, 1989, pp.139-68.

10 John Milloy, *A National Crime: The Canadian Government and the Residential School System* (Winnipeg: University of Manitoba Press, 1999), p.33.

11 Statistics on the "race" of training school inmates were published in

Ontario, *Annual Report of the Minister of Public Welfare* and, after 1938, *Annual Report of Industrial Schools and Training Schools*. Once the federal government agreed to pay for Indians with federal status, this was noted in the OTSG register, allowing me to locate some files. However, not all First Nations girls (even those from reserves) had official Indian status. Some girls were Métis, and some may have lived off reserves and been paid for by the municipality even if they did have status.

12 The average number of Native admissions yearly for the period 1950-59 was 7 per cent. *Census of Canada*, 1941, vol. 1, table 11, lists Indians as .8 per cent of the Ontario population; *Census of Canada*, 1951, vol. 2, table 32, lists Indians as .8 per cent of the Ontario population. The highest number of Native admissions to St. Mary's Training School for Girls was 9.3 per cent of admissions in 1958; on average they were 5.8 per cent of St. Mary admissions in the 1950s. Ontario, *Annual Report of Training Schools*, 1950-59.

13 OTSG, file 2197, 1950s, RG 60, AO.

14 OTSG, file 840, 1940s, AO.

15 *Annual Report of Training Schools*, Report of Training School Advisory Board, 1940, 1943, 1944 (for Whitton's recommendation that both "defectives" and "Indians" be placed in different institutions), and 1955.

16 OTSG, case file, 1929, 1950s, AO. On the patriarchal Indian Act, see Kathleen Jamieson, *Indian Women and the Law in Canada: Citizens Minus* (Hull, Que.: Ministry of Supply and Services, 1978); and Winona Stevenson, "Colonialism and First Nations Women in Canada," in *Scratching the Surface*, ed. Dua and Robertson.

17 Patricia Monture, "A Vicious Circle: Child Welfare and the First Nations," *Canadian Journal of Women and the Law* 3,1 (1989), pp.1-17; Emily Carasco, "Canadian Native Children: Have Child Welfare Laws Broken the Circle?" *Canadian Journal of Family Law* 5,1 (1986); Marlee Kline, "Complicating the Ideology of Motherhood: Child Welfare Law and First Nations Women," in *Mothers in Law: Feminist Theory and the Legal Regulation of Motherhood*, ed. Martha Albertson Fineman and Isabel Karpin (New York: Columbia University Press, 1995), pp.118-41. Custody battles persist; see Kirk Makin, "Native Loses Custody Fight with White Couple," *The Globe and Mail*, May 4, 1999.

18 Maysie Rogers, "Indian Affairs," *Canadian Welfare*, March 1, 1951, p.18.

19 Joint Committee of the Senate and House of Commons, 1946-48, quoted in Harry B. Hawthorne, *A Survey of the Contemporary Indians of Canada*, Part 1 (Ottawa, 1967), p.326.

20 Some Children's Aid Societies did cover Native communities, but this was not uniform. Hawthorne, *Survey of the Contemporary Indians*, p.327.

21 Hawthorne, *Survey of the Contemporary Indians*, p.329.

22 Mary Woodward, "Juvenile Delinquency among Indian Girls," M.A. thesis, University of British Columbia, Vancouver, 1949, pp.3, 12.

23 Rogers, "Indian Affairs"; and Woodward, "Juvenile Delinquency."

24 Woodward, "Juvenile Delinquency," pp.12, 18; John Honigmann, "Social Disintegration in Five Northern Communities," *Canadian Review of Sociology and Anthropology* 2 (1965), pp.199-214; Philip Bock, "Patterns of Illegitimacy on a Canadian Indian Reserve: 1860-1960," *Journal of Marriage and the Family* 126 (May 1964), pp.143-48.

25 Stella Hostbjor, "Social Services to the Indian Unmarried Mother," *Child Welfare*, May 1961, pp.7-9.

26 "Social Workers Report, Nov. 1954, B.C." Department of Indian Affairs (DIA), RG 10, vol. 8464, file 901/23-21, part 2, NAC. My thanks to Jessa Chapuk-Hall for showing me this reference. See also Indian Agent for Nipissing to DIA, c. 1948, RG 10, vol. 100680, file 43, 18-16, NAC.

27 Woodward, "Juvenile Delinquency."

28 Chapleau Agency to Mercer Superintendent, letter, Aug. 22, 1966, DIA, RG 10, vol. 10721, file 484, 18-28, NAC.

29 Clare Brant, "Native Ethics and Rules of Behaviour," *Canadian Journal of Psychiatry* 35 (August 1990), pp.534-39.

30 Rogers, "Indian Affairs," p.23. By the mid-1960s social work writing is starting to stress community development and the need to involve Native peoples in the delivery of social services. See "Indian and Métis Conference," *Canadian Welfare*, March-April 1963, p.124.

31 Indian Agent Swartman to Cannon Sanderson, Red Lake, Ont., letter, 1950s, DIA, RG 10, vol. 11437, file 494, 18-4, NAC.

32 Director of Psychology and Neurology to the Minister, Feb. 11, 1958, RG 20, Container 46, AO.

33 Dorothy Chunn, "Secrets and Lies: The Criminalization of Incest and the (Re)formation of the 'Private' in British Columbia, 1890-1940," paper presented at Canadian Law and Society Association, St. John's, Nfld., June 1997; and Sangster, "Masking and Unmasking the Sexual Abuse of Children," pp.504-26 (see chap. 4, n.48).

34 OTSG, file 2353, 1950s, AO.

35 OTSG, file 1666, 1950s, AO.

36 OTSG, file 265, 1930s, AO.

37 OTSG, file 2105, 1950s, AO.

38 OTSG, file 1647, 1950s, AO.

39 Memo of Director of Psychology and Neurology for the Minister, Feb. 11, 1958, RG 20, Container 47, AO. The stereotype of Native peoples as alcoholics still has an effect on court cases involving women. See Teressa Nahanee, "Sexual Assault of Inuit Females: A Comment on 'Cultural Bias,' " in *Confronting Sexual Assault: A Decade of Legal and Social Change*, ed. Julian Roberts and Renate M. Mohr (Toronto: University of Toronto Press, 1994), pp.192-204.

40 OTSG, file 525, file 840, 1940s, AO.

41 OTSG, file 2115, 1950s, AO.

42 OTSG, file 1595, 1950s, file 265, 1930s, AO.

43 Tina Loo, "Tonto's Due: Law, Culture and Colonization in British Columbia," in *Essays in the History of Canadian Law: British Columbia and the Yukon*, ed. H. Forster and J. McLaren (Toronto: University of Toronto Press, 1995); Robin Brownlie, "A Fatherly Eye: Two Indian Agents on Georgian Bay, 1918-39," Ph.D. thesis, University of Toronto, 1996; E.J. Dickson-Gilmore, "Finding the Ways of the Ancestors: Cultural Change and the Invention of Tradition in the Development of Separate Legal Systems," *Canadian Journal of Criminology*, July-October 1992, pp.479-502; Jo-Anne Fiske, "From Customary Law to Oral Traditions," *B.C. Studies* 115-116 (1997-98), pp.267-88; Joan Ryan, *Doing Things the Right Way: Dene*

Traditional Justice in Lac La Martre, NWT (Calgary: University of Calgary Press, 1995); Vic Satzewich, "Where's the Beef? Cattle Killing, Rations Policy and First Nations 'Criminality' in Southern Alberta, 1892-95," *Journal of Historical Sociology* 9,2 (1996), pp.188-212; and R.C. Macleod and Heather Rollason, "Restrain the Lawless 'Savage': Native Defendants in Criminal Courts of the North West Territories," *Journal of Historical Sociology* 10,2 (1997), pp.157-83.

44 OTSG, file 1694, 1950s, AO. It is difficult to know how important the issue of religion was, since there was only a passing reference to it: "The grandmother is with the Church of Jesus Christ. . . . P is interested in another mission and also wanted to attend a Longhouse wake."

45 Patricia Monture-Angus, *Thunder in My Soul: A Mohawk Woman Speaks* (Halifax: Fernwood Publishing, 1995); Rupert Ross, *Dancing with a Ghost: Exploring Indian Reality* (Markham, Ont.: Octopus Publishing, 1992); and Kjikeptin Alex Denny, "Beyond the Marshall Inquiry: An Alternative Mi'kmaq Worldview and Justice System," in *Elusive Justice: Beyond the Marshall Inquiry*, ed. Joy Mannett (Halifax: Fernwood Publishing, 1992), p.10.

46 The average age of entry was fourteen for Native girls and fifteen for non-Native. At least 60 per cent of the OTSG First Nations girls had reserve origins or connections.

47 OTSG, file 1886, 1950s, AO.

48 OTSG, file 2076, 1950s, AO.

49 OTSG, file 1666, file 1555, 1950s, AO.

50 OTSG, file 2115, 1950s, AO. Indian Affairs was not even given an adequate chance to find alternative care for her before she was committed.

51 Although this period saw growing urbanization of Native peoples, the majority of Native peoples still lived on reserves. Likewise, over half of the OTSG Native girls were from reserves; about one-third of those were Ojibwa/Cree from the "Far North," while many others came from Southwestern Ontario or from close to Lake Huron, where reserves had been established in the nineteenth century. Few came from Toronto or Hamilton. In 1966, 69 per cent of Ontario Native peoples still lived on reserves. Some 30 per cent of Indian bands were in "remote" areas, with 45 per cent in rural areas. James Frideres, *Native Peoples in Canada: Contemporary Conflicts* (Scarborough, Ont.: Prentice-Hall, 1993), pp.148-52.

52 OTSG, file 875, 1940s, AO.

53 OTSG, file 1647, file 2170, 1950s, AO.

54 Given the high numbers of cases originating in the Far North, the claim that girls were "lonesome for [their own] people" was common. See Probation Officer in Toronto to Superintendent of Sioux Lookout Agency, letter, 1962, RG 10, vol. 11438, file 494, 18-28, part 2, NAC.

55 OTSG, file 2085, file 2085, 1950s, AO.

56 Clare Brant and P.G.R. Patterson, "Native Child Rearing Practices: Their Role in Mental Health," unpublished paper, pp.108, 112, in Clare Brant, "A Collection," Trent University Archives (TUA), Peterborough, Ont. Brant's training was in mainstream psychiatry, but he also developed new theories based on his reading of anthropological works and his own medical practice and work for Native rights and welfare. His writing, and some of the articles he used, were deposited in the Trent University Archives after his death in

1995. The writing was collected in an unpublished manuscript: Clare Brant, "A Collection of Chapters, Lectures, Workshops and Thoughts," TUA. Brant also influenced the writing of Rupert Ross, *Dancing with a Ghost* and *Returning to the Teaching: Exploring Aboriginal Justice* (Toronto: Penguin Books, 1996).

57 Brant, "Native Ethics and Rules of Behaviour," pp.120, 130.

58 OTSG, file 1521, file 1666, file 2050, file 1519, 1950s, AO.

59 Clare Brant, "Communication Patterns in Indians," p.31, in Brant, "A Collection," TUA; OTSG, file 1694, 1950s, AO.

60 OTSG, file 2115, 1950s, AO.

61 Marlene Brant Castellano, "Native Social Work Education in Canada: Issues and Adaptions," unpublished typescript, Trent University Library, Peterborough, Ont.

62 OTSG, file 1820, 1950s, AO.

63 OTSG, file 1428, 1950s, AO.

64 Mary-Ellen Kelm, *Colonizing Bodies: Aboriginal Health and Healing in British Columbia, 1900-50* (Vancouver: UBC Press, 1998), p.175.

65 On earlier testing, see Jennifer Stephen, "'Factory Girls' and the Toronto Psychiatric Clinic," in *Law, Society and the State: Essays in Modern Legal History*, ed. Susan Binne and Louis Knafla (Toronto: University of Toronto Press, 1995), pp.405-37.

66 OTSG, file 1595, file 1647, 1950s, AO.

67 OTSG, file 1771, 1950s, AO.

68 OTSG, file 1172, 1950s, AO.

69 "Juvenile Delinquency," c. 1960, DIA, RG 10, vol. 10721, file 484, 18-28, NAC.

70 OTSG, file 2353, 1950s, AO.

71 OTSG, file 1666, 1950s, AO.

72 OTSG, file 1666, file 1555, file 1694, 1950s, AO.

73 OTSG, file 2170, 1950s, AO. As one doctor wrote, "Like other Indian girls, if placed early in the institution the main problem is continued awls." In this case, she was far from home in the North. Although statistics were kept on awls, they were not broken down by race, so that it is difficult to test out his claim.

74 Brant and Patterson, "Native Child Rearing Practices," p.112. Like non-Native inmates, Native girls were almost never sentenced to OTSG for violent behaviour, but they could become violent once there.

75 Himani Bannerji, *Thinking Through: Essays on Feminism, Marxism and Anti-Racism* (Toronto: Women's Press, 1995), p.37.

76 OTSG, file 875, 1940s, AO.

77 OTSG, file 1353, 1950s, AO.

78 Although none of the Native girls documented in these files attempted suicide while in OTSG, we have limited information on them after their release. Along with Ellen, there is evidence that another inmate of Galt attempted suicide after her release. Mercer Reformatory for Females, file 10395, 1950s, RG 20, D-13, AO.

79 Clare Brant, "Suicide in the North American Indian: Causes and Prevention," 1986, pp.170-181; and "Inquiry – Suicides at the Prison for Women," 1991, p.205, in Brant, "A Collection," TUA.

80 OTSG, file 1572, 1950s, AO.
81 OTSG, file 1555, 1950s, AO.
82 Ibid.
83 OTSG, file 1929, 1950s, file 525, 1940s, AO.
84 OTSG, file 1666, 1950s, AO.
85 Razack discusses the problems of "talking culture" in *Looking White People in the Eye*, p.61: "Power should not be subsumed under culture."

Seven: Conclusion

1 Schneider, *Vampires, Dragons and Egyptian Kings*, chap. 8 (see chap. 1, n.24).
2 Ira M. Schwartz, "The Death of the Parens Patriae Model," in *Young Offenders Act*, ed. Leschied, Jaffe, and Willis, pp.136-57 (see chap. 1, no.13).
3 Department of Justice, *Juvenile Delinquency in Canada: The Report of the Department of Justice* (Ottawa, 1965), p.2. Grandview statistics are from OTSG, file 1962, RG 20, Container J76, AO. The federal justice minister who initiated the report was E. Davie Fulton, who had once been the originator of anti-crime comics legislation.
4 The commissioners came from the Criminal Law section, the RCMP, penitentiaries, and the parole service; none worked in the field of juvenile justice. They admitted that this meant they had an immense learning curve. Department of Justice, *Juvenile Delinquency in Canada*, p.4.
5 Committee on Juvenile Delinquency (CJD) Minutes, vol. 1, April 5, 1962, RG 36/33, NAC.
6 CJD Minutes, vol. 1, March 8, 1962, NAC.
7 Department of Justice, *Juvenile Delinquency in Canada*, p.285.
8 Ibid., p.65.
9 CJD Minutes, March 8, 1962, March 1, 1962, Dec. 11, 1962, NAC.
10 Ontario, *Hansard: Debates of the Ontario Legislative Assembly*, March 2, 1965.
11 Department of Justice, *Juvenile Delinquency in Canada*, p.121.
12 Ibid., p.209.
13 CJD Minutes, Feb. 5, 1962, NAC.
14 CJD Minutes, April 6, 1962, NAC.
15 Department of Justice, *Juvenile Delinquency in Canada*, pp.200-1. The laws were referred to then as "punish the parent," today as "make the parent pay."
16 Some urban judges noted that the problem was untrained rural judges. However, this question of juvenile courts hiring non-legal judges and experts had long been an issue of contention within child welfare and juvenile justice circles.
17 Anthony Doob and J.B. Sprott, "Interprovincial Variation in the Use of the Youth Courts," *Canadian Journal of Criminology* 38,4 (1996), pp.75-84.
18 CJD Minutes, Feb. 6, 1962, NAC; and Department of Justice, *Juvenile Delinquency in Canada*, p.288.
19 This process is covered in more detail in the writing of criminologists. See, for example, Raymond Corrado and Alan Markwart, "The Evolution and

Implementation of a New Era of Juvenile Justice in Canada," in *Juvenile Justice in Canada: A Theoretical and Analytical Assessment*, ed. R. Corrado et al. (Toronto: Butterworths, 1992), pp.137-228.

20 The legal experts noted that this happened largely because there were no other treatment facilities. For this debate (which also transpired in the newspapers), see Green, "Trumpets, Justice and Federalism" (see chap. 4, n.14); and the reply from Grygier, "Minor Note on Trumpet," pp.246-67 (see chap. 5, n.109).

21 Havemann, "From Child Saving to Child Blaming," pp.225-41 (see chap. 1, n.25).

22 Reitsma-Street, "Justice for Canadian Girls," p.348 (see chap. 1, n.8).

23 Meda Chesney-Lind and Randall G. Sheldon, *Girls' Delinquency and Juvenile Justice* (Pacific Grove, Cal.: Brooks/Cole Publishing, 1992), pp.163-64. See also Marge Reitsma-Street, "A Review of Female Delinquency," in *Young Offenders Act*, ed. Leschied, Jaffe, and Willis, p.273.

24 Chesney-Lind and Sheldon, *Girls' Delinquency*, p.209.

25 Susan Reid-MacNevin, "A Theoretical Understanding of Current Canadian Juvenile-Justice Policy," in *Young Offenders Act*, ed. Lescheid, Jaffe, and Willis, p.21. See also S. Reid and M. Reitsma-Street, "Assumptions and Implications of New Canadian Legislation for Young Offenders," *Canadian Criminology Forum* 7 (1984), pp.1-19.

Index

abuse
  physical 53, 54, 95
  sexual 35-36, 53, 54, 87-89, 95,
    99, 125, 174
accommodation 122-26, 163-68
adolescence 43-44, 57, 75
advanced colonialism 146-51
Alberta 3
anti-delinquency reform 8
Arapis, Iliana 107
"awls" (AWOLs) 120, 129-30, 164,
  165
baby boom 43
Becker, Howard 13
behaviourism 23
Bentley, Ruth 119, 158
Big Brothers 16, 32-33
Big Sisters Association (BSA) 8, 16,
  27, 29-30, 71, 72, 83, 99, 104,
  109, 142, 151, 171, 180
  delinquency prevention 41,
    42-43, 44-62, 66-68
  Hamilton 27, 29-30, 41, 44-57,
    58, 68
  Toronto 44, 47, 49, 53, 55, 57,
    58
Blackboard Jungle 63
Blatz, William 23, 57
Borderline 65
Borstals 32
Bowmanville boys' school 110, 131,
  138
boys
  delinquency and 25-26, 31-33,
    38-39, 61, 63-64, 69, 75-79,
    105, 175
  sexuality and 34-35
Brant, Clare 150, 158-60, 164-65,
  166
"broken home" 32-34
Burbidge, Henry 50

Cain, Maureen 4
Callwood, June 88
Campbell, Anne 32
Canadian Association of Child Protection Officers 71
Canadian Association of Social
  Workers 148
Canadian Girls in Training (CGIT)
  61
Canadian Welfare Council 14, 31,
  44, 60, 71, 148
Carlen, Pat 67
Carrigan, D. Owen 8, 101, 144
carving 132-33, 164, 166
CBC Radio 59-60
censorship 59, 63
character-building 53
child, theories of 42-44
child-blaming 1, 11
child prostitution 3
child psychology 22, 43
child welfare 42, 56, 70, 72, 73, 74,
  94-95, 141
Children's Aid Society (CAS) 14, 16,
  20-21, 56, 72, 84-85, 86, 92,
  100, 105, 107, 123, 147, 149,
  182n.19, 183n.4
Children's Protection Act (1893)
  107, 183n.4
Citizens' Forum (CBC) 59-60
citizenship-building 58
Clapp, Elizabeth 189n.12
Clarke, C.L. 23
class 55, 66, 73, 109, 121, 179
  delinquency and 6, 8, 24, 37, 39,
    40, 41, 61, 62, 91-97, 106, 112
  race, criminalization and 91-97,
    168-70
Cold War 10-11
colonialism 146-51, 166, 168-70,
  179

Comack, Elizabeth 5
Comes a Time 64
Commachio, Cynthia 42
community model 180
conflicts with law 75-91
conservation-withdrawal 163-64
conventional mores 180
corporal punishment 17
cottage system 106, 109-43
countercultures 128-29, 164
court supervision, responding to
    98-100
court system
    judging girls in 69-102
    Native girls in 151-57
crime addiction 62
crime comics 58-59
Criminal Code 14, 169, 175
criminalization
    class and 91-97
    gender and 168-70
    race and 91-97, 144-70
criminology 4, 20, 24, 180, 185n.49
critical legal studies 4
culture clashes 157-63
culture of poverty theories 188n.86
dance of power 65-68
dancing 61, 62
Davis, Fred 63
de Beauvoir, Simone 22
delinquency
    class and 6, 8, 24, 37, 39, 40, 41,
        61, 62, 91-97, 106, 112
    definition of 5-6, 13-40
    as disease 23
    ethnicity and 24, 26-27
    films and 63-65
    gender and 6, 8, 31-39, 144-70
    gendering 31-39
    as labelling 13
    law and 13-19, 75-91, 98-102
    major vs. minor 75-76
    narratives of 24-31
    Native girls and 144-70
    neighbourhoods and 92, 94
    prevention of 41-68
    race and 6, 8, 28-29, 40, 91-97,
        144-70, 173
Department of Indian Affairs 148-49

Depression 10, 21, 22, 31, 32, 52
detention homes 57, 72
detention in training schools 121-22,
    130-31
discipline 54, 57, 65, 104, 126-35,
    150
doli incapax 14-15
domesticity 67, 107
Draper, Denis 22
drinking 22, 153, 156
drop-out rates 62
dysfunctional families 93
Elizabeth Fry Society 131, 140, 142,
    150-51, 171, 173, 174, 187n.81
employment 56, 62
ethnicity, delinquency and 24, 26-27
eugenics 22-23, 36, 43
examination 104
expert discourses 19-24, 37-38
extraversion, sexual 55
family, role of 17-18, 20-22, 24, 32,
    39, 53, 54, 56, 67, 71, 81-82,
    86-88, 95-96, 106, 151-52,
    154-56, 167-68
feeble-mindedness 23, 66
femininity 33, 55, 62, 67, 119, 121,
    179
feminism 2, 24, 40, 102, 135,
    176-77, 185n.43
feminist critical race theory 146
feminist historians 65-68
films 59, 61, 62, 63-65
First Nations 3, 6, 7, 9, 28, 92, 94,
    135, 143, 144-70, 179
foster care 105, 123, 152
Foucault, Michel 20, 24, 47, 66,
    104, 133
Freud, Sigmund 23, 35, 36-37, 64
functionalism 23
Galt Training School, *see* Ontario
    Training School for Girls
gangs 22, 31-32, 60, 62, 144
Geller, Gloria 32
gender
    colonialism and 168-70
    criminalization and 168-70
    delinquency and 6, 8, 31-39,
        144-70
gender roles 58

gendering delinquency 31-39, 60
Girl Guides 61, 62, 75
Gleason, Mona 21
Glueck, Eleanor 33
Glueck, Sheldon 33
Grandview training school, *see*
    Ontario Training School for Girls
Green, Bernard 141
Grygier, Tadeusz 141
Guest, Edna 83
Hall, George Stanley 57
Halleck, Sidney 36, 37
Hamilton Mental Health Clinic 125
Hannah-Moffat, Kelly 47, 104
Havemann, Paul 11
heterosexual relationships 43, 58, 62
hierarchical observation 104
Houston, Susan 106
Hunt, Allan 20
immorality 15, 38, 39, 55-57, 71,
    72, 79-91, 93, 97, 98, 106, 111,
    142-43, 150, 152, 173-74
incarceration, *see* training schools
incest 35-36, 88, 97, 151
incorrigibility 25
Indian Act 169
industrial schools, *see* training
    schools
Industrial Schools Act (1874) 105,
    107
Industrial Schools Association Board
    107
institution-building 9
intelligence tests 161-62
introversion, sexual 55
juvenile courts 10, 14-19, 21, 24,
    41, 42, 48, 48, 56, 60, 69-102
    in law and practice 70-75
Juvenile Delinquents Act (JDA) 2-4,
    5, 7, 9-10, 11-12, 14-15, 17-19,
    26, 30, 31, 42, 64, 70-71,
    101-02, 107, 147, 171, 172,
    175-76, 178-79, 191n.64
Kinnear, Helen 72-73
Ladd-Taylor, Molly 189n.12
Laframboise, Donna 8
law
    conflicts with 75-91
    delinquency and 13-19

and practice, juvenile courts in
    70-75
Laycock, Samuel 23
Lea, Nora 44
learning problems 22
legal regime 14-19
leisure activities, *see also* recreation
    immoral 55, 56
lesbianism 55, 128-30
Leyton, Elliot 13
Li Zong 145
linguistic issues 161-62
Little Sisters, *see* Big Sisters Associa-
    tions
Local Council of Women 44, 109
"love lights" 128-30
Macdonald Institute 120
MacLachlan, Ethel 71, 72-73
Macleod, Allan 172
MacMurchy, Helen 23
MacNeil, Isobel 122
marginalization 69
Marxism 13, 66
masochism 132
maternal justice 44-57, 67
maternalism 44-57, 73, 104
Mayoralty Task Force on Delin-
    quency (Toronto) 60-61
McGill, Judge Helen Gregory 10,
    28, 71, 72-73, 78
media 58-60
    representation of delinquency in
    37-39
mediation 54
mental hygiene 22-23, 43, 61
mentoring 58
Mercer Reformatory 128, 131, 134
Montreal Juvenile Court 48
moral authority 66
moral mothers 41
moral regulation 66
moral surveillance, *see* surveillance
morality 32-33, 38, 44, 47, 55-57,
    102; *see also* immorality
Mott, Hawley S. 71
movies, *see* films
Murphy, Judge Emily 28-29
Myers, Tamara 48, 70
narratives of delinquency 24-31

Native girls 144-70; *see also* First
 Nations
  accommodation and 163-68
  colonialism and 146-51, 166,
   168-70
  in court system 151-57
  culture clashes and 157-63
  family and 151-52, 154-56,
   167-68
  gender, criminalization and
   168-70
  intelligence tests and 161-62
  linguistic issues and 161-62
  in OTSG 147, 152, 157, 158,
   160-63, 164, 166-68
  racism and 144-46, 149, 156-57,
   158, 161-62, 165, 167, 168-70
  residential schools and 146, 148,
   149, 152, 154
  resistance of 163-68
  welfare state and 146-51
  withdrawal of 158-60, 163-64
Neelands, C.J. 116
neighbourhoods 92, 94
normalization 20, 21, 70, 74, 101
normalizing judgements 104
nymphomania 36
observation home 57
offence, types of 75-78
Ojibwa 161
"On the Spot" newsreel 63
Ontario 11, 16, 23, 72, 75-78, 89,
 105-09, 147, 149
Ontario Censor Board 63
Ontario Training School for Girls
 (OTSG) 8, 57, 109-43, 147, 152,
 157, 158, 160-63, 164, 166-68;
 see also training schools
Orde decision 31
parens patriae 14
parent-blaming 56
Parent-Teacher Association (PTA) 60
parents, *see* family
parole 135-40
passive resistance 128-35
pastoral power 47
paternalism 7, 70, 74, 102, 162,
 178-79
patriarchy 5, 21, 24, 35, 40

Patterson, Margaret 73
Pearson, Patricia 2, 5, 135
peer pressure 22
petty theft 90-91, 95, 106, 111, 153
philanthropy 50, 53, 110
physical abuse 53, 54, 95
placements 116-17, 135-40, 165
Police Club for Boys 63, 176
police 63-64, 75, 92-93, 176
popular culture 58
post-structuralism 13
poverty 22, 30, 52, 54, 94-96, 97,
 111-12
power, dance of 65-68
pre-delinquent boys 64
pre-delinquent girls 50-51, 55, 57
pregnancy 34, 38, 62, 80, 138-39,
 165, 167
prisons vs. playgrounds 57-62
prisons, women's 104
probation 42, 49, 55, 61, 71, 78-79,
 82, 88, 93-94, 101, 157, 165
probation officers 20, 21, 25-26, 89,
 92, 94, 97, 100, 167
procedural paternalism 70
Progressive Conservative Party
 (Ontario) 140-41
promiscuity 3, 34, 40, 80-85, 88, 97,
 138-39, 152-53, 161, 165, 166,
 173-74
prostitution 34, 71, 84, 86
Protestant Women's Federation 122
psychiatrists/psychiatry 20-22, 23,
 36, 43, 100, 125-26, 158-59
psychoanalysis 23, 35-36, 65
psychologists/psychology 21-22, 23,
 35-36, 43, 83, 100, 108, 112,
 125-26, 131, 158-59
Pugh, Clifford 60
Quebec 70, 111, 176
race
 class, criminalization and 91-97,
  173
 delinquency and 6, 8, 28-29, 40,
  91-97, 144-70, 173
racialization 145
racism 124, 135, 144-46, 149, 156-57,
 158, 161-62, 165, 167, 168-70,
 173, 179, 185n.43, 187n.77

Rebel Without a Cause 63
recreation, community-based 53, 57-62, 66
reform, anti-delinquency 8, 41-68
reform schools, *see* training schools
Reitsma-Street, Marge 177-78
religion 47, 61, 70, 108, 119
residential home 56
residential schools 146, 148, 149, 152, 154
resistance 126-35, 163-68
respectability 56
role models, recreation and 60, 63
Ross, Robert Robertson 200n.113
runaways 96, 130, 164
Russell, Diana 186n.68
safe room 54
same-sex relationships 128-30, 164
Satzewich, Vic 145
Schissel, Bernard 1
Schneider, Eric 11
scholarship work 50-51
Scott, James 128
Scott, W.I. 14
Select Committee on Reform Institutions 122
sexual abuse 35-36, 53, 54, 87-89, 95, 99, 125, 174
sexual behaviour 23, 31, 33-36, 38, 39-40, 43, 55, 57, 62, 65, 78, 80-91, 93, 98, 101-02, 111, 119, 128-29, 138-40, 142-43, 150, 153, 173-74
sexual double standard 55, 71, 102
sexual purity examinations 82-83
sine die 78
slashing 132-33
slum clearance 61
social pathology 23
social regulation 9
social reproduction 9
social responsibility 44-45
social work 22, 25, 42-43, 45, 53, 67-68, 108, 148-51
socialized justice 16-17
societal change model 180
Stephen, Jennifer 23
suffrage 41, 66
suicide 165-66

Supreme Court 17
surveillance 16-17, 56, 69-70, 177
Tappan, Paul 13
theft, *see* petty theft
Theorêt, Bruno 71
theories of the child 42-44
Thomas, W.I. 33
Tice, Karen 25
Toronto Board of Education 59
Toronto Family Court 17, 78
Toronto Juvenile Court 22
Toronto Welfare Council 22
Toronto Women's Law Association 191n.64
Training School Act (Ontario) (TSA) 16, 105-06, 107-08, 140-41, 143, 147-48, 172, 178
Training School Advisory Board 23, 33
training schools 7-8, 9, 15, 33, 37, 57, 67, 77, 79, 80, 86, 87, 88, 98, 103-43, 147-48
  academic training in 114-16
  adaption and accommodation to 122-26
  countercultures in 128-29, 164
  critiques of 140-43
  evolution of 105-09
  girls' reactions to 112-14, 127
  Native girls and 157-63
  placement of students from 116-17, 135-40
  public reactions to 121-22
  race and 158-63
  recreational activities at 119-21
  rules and resistance in 126-35
  same-sex relationships in 128-30, 164
  solitary confinement in 121-22, 130-31
  therapy in 122-26
  violence in 133-35
  vocational training in 114-19
Trelawney training school 111
Trent University archives 204n.56
truancy 55, 111
United States 14, 28, 33, 43, 45, 54, 55, 62, 70, 158, 171-73, 187n.74
venereal disease 62, 80

Virk, Reena 2
welfare dependency 30
welfare state 146-51
Whitton, Charlotte 108, 148
Who Is Sylvia? 64-65
withdrawal, Native girls and 158-60,
    163-64
Women's Institutes 109-10
Young Offenders Act (YOA) 1, 2, 3,
    6, 7, 12, 104, 171, 172, 176-79
Youth and the Law 63-64, 92, 176
Youthful Offenders Act (1894)
    182n.19
YWCA 50, 53, 56, 57-58, 119, 120
Zachary, Caroline 43

AGMV Marquis

MEMBER OF SCABRINI MEDIA

Quebec, Canada
2002